Praise for *The Mayor of MacDougal Street*

"A genial and picaresque ramble." —*New York Times Book Review*

"Van Ronk's wonderful memoir . . . is mandatory reading for anybody interested in what Utah Phillips called the 'Great Folk Scare' of the 1960s. Van Ronk is a fine raconteur, writing the compelling story of his slow rise to cult folksinger status and near superstardom without an iota of pretension. His anecdotes of rumrunners, mountebanks, and beatniks are often hilarious. . . . The great virtue of this memoir . . . is the capsule prose snapshots of about a dozen blues-folk greats including Ramblin' Jack Elliot, Brownie McGhee, Sonny Terry, and Leadbelly. . . . There are many lively vignettes in this memoir. . . . But the charm of *The Mayor of MacDougal Street* lies in its unvarnished simplicity—just like that of its author." —Douglas Brinkley in the *Boston Globe*

"****. Gravel-voiced, folk singing giant Dave Van Ronk was an early Dylan mentor, and his (sadly posthumous) memoir lives and breathes the Village underground from the early 1950s through the late '60s taking in the walk-up apartments, political infighting, Washington Square hootenannies, sleazy club owners, and primitive drug copping with a scraping wit that's not afraid to deflate sacred cows on the Left, Right, and Centre." —*MOJO*

"*The Mayor of MacDougal Street* will, at some point, make you want to pull out a Van Ronk record, even if it's just his familiar growling blues like 'Cocaine.' But the book is also a gem by itself, because Van Ronk was an urban griot, one of those tribal elders who passes on the history of the village interwoven with his personal asides, many of them hilarious." —*New York Daily News*

"As a chief conspirator, guitarist Dave Van Ronk observed much, and—in the posthumously completed *The Mayor of MacDougal Street*—captures the glory with wry wit. . . . Van Ronk is an erudite wiseacre." —*Relix*

The Mayor of
MacDougal Street

Also by Elijah Wald

Escaping the Delta:
Robert Johnson and the Invention of the Blues

Narcocorrido:
A Journey into the
Music of Drugs, Guns, and Guerrillas

Josh White: Society Blues

The Mayor of MacDougal Street

a memoir

Dave Van Ronk

with Elijah Wald

with a foreword by Lawrence Block

DA CAPO PRESS

A Member of the Perseus Books Group

"Gaslight Rag," "Zen Koans Gonna Rise Again," and "Last Call" words and music by Dave Van Ronk, copyright © Folklore Music (ASCAP).

Estate of Dave Van Ronk is represented by Folklore Productions, Santa Monica CA, www.folkloreproductions.com.

Designed by Jeff Williams
Set in 11-point Granjon by the Perseus Books Group

The Library of Congress has cataloged the hardcover edition as follows:

Van Ronk, Dave.
   The mayor of MacDougal Street : a memoir / Dave Van Ronk with Elijah Wald.—1st Da Capo Press ed.
       p. cm.
   Includes index.
   ISBN 0-306-81407-2 (hardcover : alk. paper)
   1. Van Ronk, Dave. 2. Folk singers—United States—Biography. I. Wald, Elijah. II. Title.

ML420.V246A3 2005
782.42164'092—dc22

                                                                                          2004027556

First Da Capo Press paperback edition 2006

ISBN-13: 978-0-306-81479-2
ISBN-10: 0-306-81479-X

Published by Da Capo Press
A Member of the Perseus Books Group
http://www.dacapopress.com

Da Capo Press books are available at special discounts for bulk purchases in the U.S. by corporations, institutions, and other organizations. For more information, please contact the Special Markets Department at the Perseus Books Group, 11 Cambridge Center, Cambridge, MA 02142, or call (800) 255-1514 or (617) 252-5298, or email special.markets@perseusbooks.com.

 *For Andrea*

Contents

Contents

Acknowledgments

$\mathcal{D}$ave died before this book could be completed, and it would have been impossible to finish it without all of the people who made their interviews with him available. Whenever possible, I contacted interviewers and got their permission, and I am grateful and pleased that not one of them refused the request. However, I was not able to reach everyone whose interviews I found, and hope that if I have used anyone's material without permission, they will understand the special circumstances.

In the course of this project the material was worked and reworked so many times that I am not sure what ended up being used, and therefore I give equal thanks to all the people who did interviews that were consulted: Jim Allen, Scott Barretta, Ronald Cohen, Art D'Lugoff, Aiyanna Elliott, Bob Fass, Beth C. Fishkind, Pete Fornatale, Emily Friedman, Cary Ginell, Cynthia Gooding, Mark Greenberg, Stefan Grossman, Bill Hahn, David Hajdu, Mike Joyce, Roy Kasten, Peter Keane, Jeff Kenney, Marty Kohn, Jody Kolodzey, Joe LaMay, Christine Lavin, Doreen Lorenzo and Michael Scully, Kip Lornell, Rod MacDonald, Sonny Ochs, John Platt, Bruce Pollock, Mike Regenstreif, Ralph Rush, Anthony Scaduto, Vin Scelsa, Michael Schumacher, Richard Skelly, Michael Stock, David Walsh, and Robbie

Wolliver. (And if I've missed anyone, please forgive me . . .) I also must thank George Auerbach, Suze Rotolo, and David Massengill, who among other things steered me to material I otherwise would have missed.

Both Dave and I conducted some further interviews to fill out missing details. For their time and insight, many thanks to Roy Berkeley, Oscar Brand, Lenni Brenner, Tom Condit, Gina Glaser, Al Graham, Lee Hoffman, Sam Hood, Barry Kornfeld, Tom and Midge Paxton, Aaron Rennert, Irwin Silber, Patrick Sky, Terri Thal, Wavy Gravy, and Izzy Young.

For various and sundry sorts of assistance along the way, thanks first of all to Andrea Vuocolo Van Ronk, without whom none of this would have been possible, and further to Mary Katherine Aldin, John Cohen, Ron Cohen, Charles Freudenthal, Mitch Greenhill, Martin Jukovsky, Don Paulsen, Eve Silber, Happy Traum, Richard Weissman, Stefan Wirz, and undoubtedly a number of other people whose names would be here if I were better organized.

A thousand thanks to Lawrence Block for his introduction. For editorial comments, thanks to Jeff McLaughlin. Thanks to my agent, Richard P. McDonough, for finding this book a home, and to Ben Schafer at Da Capo, who has been itching to be its editor for more years than any of us cares to remember.

Acknowledgments

Foreword: Back in the Day

Early in August 1956 I boarded a train in Buffalo and got off seven or eight hours later at Grand Central Terminal. I found the clock under which I was supposed to meet Paul Grillo, and remarkably, he was there. I'd recently completed my freshman year at Antioch College, in Yellow Springs, Ohio, where Paul had been one of my hall advisers. (In this capacity he and his roommate had mentored me and the other fifteen or twenty residents of my freshman dormitory.) Now, during a three-month work period, Paul and I were going to room together, along with a third fellow, Fred Anliot.

Paul had already found a place for us to live, and furnished me with the address—147 West 14th Street. He pointed me toward the subway and sent me on my way. I took the shuttle to Times Square, the IRT to 14th Street. I got a key from the landlady—Mrs. Moderno, if memory serves—and climbed three flights of stairs to a very large room with bright yellow walls.

We lived there for two or three weeks. Then we decided the place was too expensive—it was $24 a week, split three ways—and someone, probably

Paul, found us a cheaper place at 108 West 12th Street. The rent there was $12 a week, but that didn't make it a bargain, and we were just about bright enough to realize we couldn't live like that. Within two weeks we were out of there and installed in a one-bedroom apartment on the first floor at 54 Barrow Street, where the rent was $90 a month. It must be a co-op by now, and it's probably worth half a million dollars. Back then it was a terrific place to live, and I was there until the end of October, when it was time to go back to school.

So I was in the Village for only three months that year, and that's awfully difficult to believe. Because I met so many people and did so many things. I was working five days a week from nine to five in the mailroom at Pines Publications, on East 40th Street. I spent nights and weekends hanging out, and where I mostly hung out was MacDougal Street.

That very first night in New York, I had two addresses to check out, and managed to get to both of them. One was a jazz club called Café Bohemia, at 15 Barrow Street, where I nursed a drink at the bar and listened to Al Cohn and Zoot Sims. The other was the Caricature, a coffeehouse on Mac-Dougal Street, where a fellow I'd met a year earlier at Camp Lakeland— we were both counselors there that summer—was a regular player in Liz's nightly bridge game.

I could have met Dave Van Ronk there that first night—at Liz's, not at the Bohemia—because, as he mentions, it was a regular place of his. But I met him instead at one of the Sunday sessions in Washington Square Park, which is where I quickly learned to spend my Sunday afternoons. The circle was always overflowing with people playing instruments and singing folk songs, and there was something very special about the energy there. This was, you should understand, *before* the folk music renaissance, and before the curious synthesis of drugs and politics made college kids a breed apart. The great majority of collegians were still gray-flannel members of the Silent Generation, ready to sign on for a corporate job with a good pension plan. Those of us who didn't fit that mold, those of us who'd always sort of figured there was something wrong with us, sat around the fountain in Washington Square singing "Michael Row the Boat Ashore" and feeling very proud of ourselves for being there.

The only thing wrong with Sunday afternoons was that they ended at six o'clock and some of us figured that there ought to be a way to keep the party going. For a while, 54 Barrow Street was our after-hours. Our apartment—living room, bedroom, kitchen—filled up with people with guitars and banjos and voices, and the party went on for four or five hours. I'm not sure how long we hosted it. We passed 54 Barrow to other Antiochians when we had to go back to Ohio, and they may have kept the party going for a while, but eventually it moved to larger quarters on Spring Street.

By then I was a lifer. I'd visited New York twice with my parents—my father had grown up in Manhattan and the Bronx—and I'd always assumed somehow that I'd wind up living there, but it was during those three months that I became a New Yorker and, more to the point, a Villager. I've lived in other places—Wisconsin, Florida—and in other parts of New York City, but Greenwich Village has always drawn me home, and has indeed been my residence for most of the past thirty years. I started out, you'll recall, on 14th Street a few doors from 7th Avenue. Since then I've lived on 12th Street, on Barrow Street, on Bleecker and Greenwich and Jane, on Charles, on Horatio, on West 13th. Now, for about a dozen years, I've been on West 12th a few doors from 8th Avenue.

"Why should I go anywhere?" Dave said of the Village. "I'm already here."

♬   ♬   ♬

Whenever you got here, it was better ten years earlier.

That's what people say now, complaining about gentrification. It's what they said twenty years ago, complaining about tourists. It's what they said forty years ago, complaining about hippie kids.

I suspect they've always said it. I suspect they said it to Edna St. Vincent Millay and Floyd Dell.

It seems to me—because I was around then, because I remember it fondly, because it was gone alas like my youth, too soon—that Greenwich Village was a very special place during my first years in it. And the people who just moved here yesterday will probably think the same themselves, when their youth is as remote and as inaccurately recalled as is mine.

Once, back in the early sixties, I decided to leave New York. I told Dave I was going to return to Buffalo. He was incredulous and asked why, a question I was somehow unable to answer. "Well," I managed, "that's my hometown. That's where I'm from."

He thought about it, then looked off into the middle distance. "I know a woman," he said, "who was born in Buchenwald."

♫   ♫   ♫

Dave Van Ronk and I became friends during my first three-month stint in New York. The friendship lasted for forty-five years.

I couldn't begin to guess how many times I heard him sing. I caught him at no end of venues in New York, but I also managed to catch up with him in Los Angeles and Chicago and Albuquerque and New Hope, Pennsylvania, and somewhere in Westchester County. There was never a time when I didn't want to listen to that voice.

One night he and I and Lee Hoffman sat drinking in her apartment— she was then married to Larry Shaw—and cowrote a batch of songs that wound up in *The Bosses' Songbook*. (*Songs to Stifle the Flames of Discontent* was the subtitle, and nobody got author credit for any of the songs; a note in the introduction explained that most of the authors were on enough lists already.) Another song of mine, "Georgie and the IRT," wound up on his second album. Some years later, I provided the liner notes for another album, *Songs for Aging Children.*

When Dave died, I spent a couple of weeks playing his records. The music lasts. The song's there, and so's the singer, present in every note.

What fades, what's hard to recapture, is the off-stage presence. The nights—and there weren't enough of them, just handfuls scattered over the years—spent sitting around and talking. Dave was self-taught, and never did a better teacher meet a more receptive pupil; he knew more about more subjects than anyone I've ever met.

I wish to God he hadn't left us so soon. And I wish this wonderful book he's given us could be a little longer. But then I wished that of every set I ever heard him sing. And Dave had a long-standing policy of never doing more than a single encore. You should always leave them wanting more, he said. And he always did.

♫   ♫   ♫

I was pleased and honored when Elijah Wald asked me to write an introduction to *The Mayor of MacDougal Street*. The task has turned out to be far more difficult than I'd expected, and I can't say I'm happy with the result.

Dave doesn't really need someone to open for him. I've taken up enough of your time. I'll get off the stage now, knowing at least that I'm leaving you in very good hands.

Lawrence Block
Greenwich Village
July 2004

The Mayor of
MacDougal Street

1

Prehistory:
Youth in the Outer Boroughs

Back at Our Lady of Perpetual Bingo, where I went to school, along with the rack, thumbscrew, and bastinado, they had the curious custom of announcing grades in the final exams and then making everybody hang around for an extra week before turning us loose for summer vacation. Presumably they did this to reinforce our belief in Purgatory.

Needless to say, to a bunch of twelve-year-olds this was all of a piece with the spanking machine rumored to be kept somewhere in the basement. The nuns who taught us probably shared our views in this matter, for it fell to them to keep a facsimile of order among a seething, fidgeting mass of twenty-five or so preadolescents. In retrospect, I almost sympathize with them.

Our seventh-grade teacher, whose name I recall as Sister Attila Marie, tried desperately to keep us amused. Since her usual boffo shtick—twisting a miscreant's ear until the audience howled with glee—seemed inappropriate to the circumstances, she resorted to subtler forms of torment. She led sing-alongs: as I recall, her big number was "When Irish Eyes Are Smiling." She read us stories: I'll never forget her reading of "The Lady or The Tiger"; her voice, in both timbre and accent, bore an uncanny resemblance to that of Jimmy Durante. And once, in a dazzling display of creativity, she hit on a program guaranteed to keep the class stupefied for an entire day: she required each pupil to give a fifteen-minute talk on "What I Want to Be When I Grow Up." We had a day to prepare.

Me, I was ready. I had given the matter careful consideration, but to be on the safe side I jotted down a few notes, and I showed up filled with the anticipatory delight of the born ham. Seating myself at my desk, I resigned myself to listening to a sorry series of future postmen, priests, abbesses, lawyers, and nurses squirmingly tout their dismal aspirations.

Fortunately, I hadn't long to wait. I was the first kid in the second row. When my turn came, I confidently strode to the front of the class: "What I want to be when I grow up," I began, "is a migratory worker—which isn't just one thing. I want to travel from town to town doing odd jobs to make enough money to move on . . . " I was just coming to the part about the box-cars, but I got no further. Sister Attila Marie was charging at me from the back of the room, her face an all-too-familiar beet red. She was screaming, "A *bum!* You want to be a *bum!*"

Needless to say, the moratorium on ear twisting was lifted there and then.

♫   ♫   ♫

I was born in a Swedish hospital in Brooklyn, on June 30, 1936. When I started to swell up to a rather enormous size at an early age, my grandmother used to swear I'd been switched. Whenever I'd trip over something—which was frequently—she'd say, "Oh God, it's the Swede again."

My father and mother separated very shortly after I was born. I never met the man, and I have never felt a pang or so much as a twitch of curiosity about him. What you don't know, you don't miss. Until I was nine or ten years old, I was sometimes with my mother and sometimes with one or another of a succession of "aunts." Some were better than others, and one of the better ones was Emma "Mom" Hogan. She had been a rumrunner for Legs Diamond back in Prohibition and had even managed a speakeasy, so naturally I thought she was the greatest thing since canned clams. She loved jazz, and in that house the radio was always playing: Duke Ellington, Louis Armstrong, Benny Goodman, Count Basie—I heard them all, sometimes on live broadcasts. Fats Waller had a regular show on Sunday afternoons, of which I was a devoted fan. Boy, I loved that guy! Years later I got to know Herman Autrey, Fats's trumpet player, and when I told him how much I had loved his playing on that show, he laughed and said, "I don't know how you ever heard me. They wouldn't let me face the mike, just stood me in a corner and made me play into the wall." I remember Eddie Condon, too, and the Chamber Society of Lower Basin Street. The small combos were my favorites, because they sounded like they were having fun.

Around 1945 my mother and I moved to Richmond Hill, in Queens. At first we stayed with my grandparents and my Uncle Bill, but the place was too small for all of us, so my mother took a furnished room a few blocks away. I hated Richmond Hill. There were trees, detached houses, backyards—and paralyzing boredom. It was a neighborhood of working stiffs, all trying to be oh, so respectable. Sundays were especially excruciating. Of course everybody had to go to church, and afterward the kids weren't allowed to change out of their Sunday best. No rough games, because you might tear something or get dirty. Mostly we would stand around on the corner, glaring down at our insistently shiny shoes. Everybody was perfectly miserable, even the grown-ups.

The move had a few compensations, though. My grandfather had been a semiprofessional pianist, playing in Catskill resorts around the turn of the century until my grandmother snagged him and put him to work. He knew all the pop songs of that time: Harry von Tilzer, Harrigan and Hart, Ben Harney, and of course Scott Joplin. "That was music," he used to say. "This jazz stuff sounds like the tune the old cow died with" or, for variation, "like a nanny-goat pissing in a dishpan." He was a country boy, and had a delicate way with the language.

I have only vague memories of hearing him play: I recall "The Maple Leaf Rag" and a rip-snorting version of "The Stars and Stripes Forever," guaranteed to send any six-year-old into transports of martial ecstasy. Unfortunately, by the time we moved to Richmond Hill, there was no longer a piano in the house; my uncle had chopped it up and thrown it out, saying, "What do we need this for? We've got the radio." He was a thoroughly modern American, with no interest in such archaic devices. He also threw out the autographed copy of Buffalo Bill's autobiography.*

---

*Don't get me wrong, I loved my uncle. For one thing, he taught me how to play harmonica . . . Strike three, come to think of it.

My grandmother was Brooklyn Irish, and time had stopped for her somewhere around 1910. She was a great storyteller, with an incredible memory for detail, and an indefatigable singer. She never stopped singing except to talk or eat—something was always either coming out or going in. And she didn't have a great voice, but boy was she loud; she drove the neighbors nuts. Most of her repertoire had been learned from her mother in Ireland, and I picked up all sorts of songs from her: Irish music hall numbers, rebel songs, ballads, minstrel songs, tearjerkers—I can still sing "The Gypsy's Warning" from beginning to end. I learned versions of Irish tunes with Gaelic choruses, though no one in my family had spoken Gaelic for hundreds of years; to us, they were just a succession of nonsense syllables: "Shonegga hanegga thamegga thu, baleshlecoghelee aushmedatheen." Many years later, Bob Dylan heard me fooling around with one of my grandmother's favorites, "The Chimes of Trinity," a sentimental ballad about Trinity Church, that went something like:

Tolling for the outcast, tolling for the gay,
Tolling for the [something something], long passed away,
As we whiled away the hours, down on old Broadway,
And we listened to the chimes of Trinity.

He made me sing it for him a few times until he had the gist of it, then reworked it into "Chimes of Freedom." Her version was better.

If you had asked anybody in my family, they would have stridently proclaimed themselves to be middle-class, but that was more a matter of aspiration than reality. My mother was a stenographer and typist. My uncle and my grandfather both worked in the Brooklyn Navy Yard. My grandfather was an electrician and subsequently became something of an aristocrat of labor. He was a great admirer of Eugene V. Debs. My grandmother hated Debs because she thought he was leading my grandfather off the straight and narrow and getting him drunk. She was probably right. In any event, the family was mostly Irish and thoroughly working class.

I went to Catholic school, and did pretty well for the first few years, but by high school I was thoroughly sick of it. It was not particularly interesting, and by that time I had decided I was going to be a musician or, barring that, some other sort of colorful ne'er-do-well. I was a voracious reader, though, with extremely catholic tastes, of the small "c" variety. My family was not particularly literary, so they left me pretty much alone and I just picked up whatever looked interesting. I remember reading Grant's memoirs, the Buffalo Bill autobiography, lots of Mark Twain, and a massive book called *Land and Sea*, which was some sort of anthropological study. I read Hemingway at thirteen, *The Sun Also Rises*, which bored me. My brain was like the attic of the Smithsonian.

My formal schooling ended when I was about fifteen. A truant officer picked me up in a pool hall—though he was actually there for the guy I was playing with—and I was hauled before the principal. That was an unprecedented occurrence: you never saw the principal, it was like being brought before Stalin. The principal looked down upon me from his authoritative height and called me "a filthy ineducable little beast"—that's a direct quote; you don't forget something like that. The upshot was that I was essentially told that if I didn't show up for school, it would be all right with them, that they wouldn't send the truant officer after me. That was fine with me.* The next year, I enrolled in something called "continuing education," and for a while I would go out to Jamaica, Queens, once a month, but I didn't take it seriously and that was the end of that.

My formal musical training was even less propitious. My mother had decided that I should learn to play the piano, so I used to have to go to the local Sisters of St. Joseph convent for my lessons, and then every afternoon I had to go to the same convent and practice for an hour after school. I leave it to the reader to imagine how much I hated that. It was the first time I learned how to read music, and I detested the whole experience with such a purple passion that until I was in my thirties, I had no desire to read standard notation or play the piano. At that point I began to notice how much better the piano would have suited my musical tastes, but by then I had been playing guitar for twenty years and had managed to make it into a serviceable substitute.

---

*It was like the old joke about this guy in the army who keeps walking around picking up pieces of paper, turning them over, and saying, "That's not it." He does this for weeks and weeks, and no one can figure it out, and finally they send him off to the shrink's office. He walks in, picks a piece of paper off the shrink's desk, and says, "That's not it." Then he picks up another piece, and says, "That's not it." Finally the shrink says, "Clearly you are not suited for the military life," and he writes out a psycho discharge. The guy picks it up, and says, "That's it!" That was exactly how I felt.

I always wanted to be a musician and performer. Looking back, the die was cast before I even realized I was in a crap game. When I was in first grade, one of the nuns discovered that I knew all three verses of the "Star Spangled Banner," and she was so enraptured by this phenomenon that she paraded me from class to class singing, "Oh, thus be it ever when free men shall stand . . ." Needless to say, this made me one of the most unpopular kids in the damn school—I was like that kid in *Tom Sawyer* who had memorized the most verses of scripture. But I loved the attention; I ate it up.

My first instrument, aside from those damn piano lessons, was a ukulele. This was the late 1940s, and Arthur Godfrey had tripped off a huge uke and Hawaiian music revival. There were still plenty of flappers and sheiks around, people who had grown up in the twenties and could chord a uke, so picking it up was pretty easy. I think the first thing I learned to play was "Cool Water." I must have played that thing a hundred times a day just for the pleasure of hearing it come out right. (I suspect the pleasure was all mine.) Pretty soon, I had a whole repertoire of ukulele numbers: "Back in Nagasaki Where the Men Chew Tobacky and the Women Wicky Wacky Woo," "I Want to Go Back to My Little Grass Shack in Kealakakua, Hawaii," and all that jive. I never got to be very good at it, because I could not develop a decent roll: you're supposed to get a very tight series of up and down strokes with your right hand, so it comes out like a roll on the drum, and I could never do that.* Still, by assiduous application I managed to acquire a reputation as the second-hottest twelve-year-old ukulele player in Richmond Hill.

That summer I also learned my first blues song. A friend of my mother's whom I called Aunt Esther had moved to Shaker Heights, Ohio, and I was packed off to spend the summer vacation there. It was, without a doubt, the most agonizingly boring summer I have ever spent in my life. Shaker Heights was even worse than Richmond Hill, and I was going totally bonkers. Then one afternoon I was sitting around the living room doing what twelve-year-old boys do best: sulking. In a desultory way, I

---

*I actually studied drums for a while, but that went nowhere. It was all discipline and no kicks. On uke or guitar, there was discipline but also kicks: once you learn how to finger a C chord, you strum the strings and, by god, it sounds like a C chord. On drums, if you're working on a nine-stroke roll, it takes days, weeks, months before it sounds like anything other than six men chopping wood in an echo chamber. There's no immediate gratification, and I've always insisted on immediate gratification.

was thumbing through a book that my aunt's upwardly mobile family kept by the piano, *The Fireside Book of Folk Songs*, and my eyes lit on this song that just totally blew me away. It was called "St. James Infirmary." I had to learn that song. Since my music-reading skills were minimal at best, I put the arm on my upwardly mobile cousin, who was studying piano at the time, and made him plunk his way through the piece, over and over, until I had learned the chords and the melody. That became my project for the summer, and it really saved my bacon. By the time I got back to Queens, I was playing the funkiest ukulele version of "St. James Infirmary" you ever heard.

Shortly, I got together with some of the local kids and we started a quartet. We called ourselves the Harmonotes, and on school-day mornings we would walk together as far as the "el" station, singing all the way. My mother had already taught me to sing harmony, starting me out on "Now Is the Hour," which had been a hit for Gracie Fields somewhere back in the twelfth century. It was simple harmony, a pretty tune, and a good place to start. Anyway, Tommy McNiff, John Banninger, Bob Linder, and I would get together for rehearsals a few times a week. We had no lack of models: the Four Aces, the Sons of the Pioneers, the Mills Brothers, and of course the Weavers, who were a big phenom right then. I did not think of the Weavers as folk singers especially—they were just another pop group with interesting harmonies. (Incidentally, I do not understand why the Weavers have received so little attention for their abilities as musicians and arrangers. The harmony in "Kisses Sweeter Than Wine" is a perfect combination of simplicity and inventiveness, not to mention the part singing in "Tzena, Tzena" and Pete Seeger's marvelous Zulu yodeling in "Wimoweh.") Tommy McNiff didn't like the Weavers, and I didn't like the Four Aces, so we compromised and sang both, along with the hits of the big radio stars, people like Eddie Fisher and Patti Paige: "'Twas just a garden in the rain . . . "

We also loved barbershop quartet stuff, and for that we had the Mariners and the Chordettes, both from the Arthur Godfrey radio show. We were singing all kinds of chords and intervals—diminisheds, augmenteds, ninths, thirteenths—without having the foggiest idea what they were, and I picked up a lot of seat-of-the-pants knowledge from that kind of material. For the rest of my life I continued to use those big fat barbershop chords, especially when I was working out voicings for guitar arrangements.

We only had one gig, a Christmas party at a German fraternal hall in Ridgewood, Brooklyn. Our pay was all the beer we could drink—I suppose they figured, How much beer can a fourteen-year-old kid drink? I do not recall the answer to that, but I am told that they carried me home like a Yule log.

It was around this time that I expanded my instrumental skills to include a guitar. I acquired my first in a schoolyard swap, one of those perfect deals where both parties emerge feeling like successful thieves: in exchange for a pile of *Captain Marvel* comics, Conrad Fehling traded me a battered blond Kay orchestral arch-top. I forthwith removed two strings so I could play it like a ukulele, but the two unused tuning pegs rattled and clanked like Marley's ghost, so over the next few months I added a fifth and finally the sixth string. Then, with the help of a Mel Bay instruction book, I set out to prove Segovia's dictum that the guitar is the easiest instrument in the world to play badly.

By then my mother and I had our own apartment, and she would go to work every morning, leaving me to play hookey. I took the instruction book—it was called something like *Five Million Chords for the Guitar*—and made huge copies of the chord charts and tacked them to the ceiling above my bed. Then I would lie in bed all day and practice the changes. Of course, I didn't know what to *do* with them—there you are, you can barely use three chords, and suddenly you're playing an F sharp demented thirteenth, and you don't have the faintest idea where to put it—but it sounded kind of weird and nice. I would lie there and practice going from one chord to another at random, when I was supposed to be in school, and that experience helped kick off a personal philosophy: "If it can't be done in bed, it's not worth doing."

That was coming along fine, though one day a fellow truant came over to hang out and he didn't notice the guitar lying on the bed, and he flopped down on it, splitting the top from guzzle to zatch. I went calmly insane, picked the guitar up by the neck, and broke the bottom over his head—one of the most satisfying things I have ever done. Then I went out and cadged a beat-up old Harmony from someone. I was a bad kid.

I was also a klutzy kid. I was big for my age and always tripping over my own feet, and to exacerbate the problem, I had been born left-handed, and somewhere along the line a well-meaning "aunt" had decided I should be changed to a rightie. To effect this change, she enforced a form of home-made conditioned reflex therapy, based on the Pavlovian system of rewards and punishments. The punishment consisted of a whack upside the head. The reward was the absence of a whack upside the head.

This was very effective, and as a result manual skills have never come easily to me, which proved to be something of a problem when I decided to be a guitar player. My left hand could handle the chords just fine, but getting my right hand to do what I wanted it to do always required a lot of effort. Years later, my wife Terri was talking to Barry Kornfeld, who is one of the best guitarists I've ever known, and she said, "Barry, Dave is such a klutz that he can barely tie his shoes. How is it that he can play the guitar?" Barry made a wise face, stroked his beard, and said, "It is one of the mysteries of the industry." And indeed it is. I think quickly, musically. When I click into a piece—not when I'm just potchkeying around with it, but when I really get into it and find the groove—I know where everything should be, I understand what the structure should be, measure by measure. But getting my goddamn hands to do it is really a brute, and I had to accept the fact pretty early on that I was never going to be a superchops guitarist.

Even while I was fooling around with barbershop and pop songs, I had never stopped listening to and loving jazz. I wanted to play it, but there was nobody around that I could pick it up from, the way I had the other music. Finally, I realized I would have to bite the bullet and take some guitar lessons. There were not a lot of jazz guitarists teaching in Richmond Hill, so at first I wasted some time studying with a local hamfat who tried to teach me stuff like "Oh Mein Papa" and "Flight of the Bumblebee." Then I got lucky, and somehow found out about Jack Norton.

Jack, or "the Old Man," as we used to call him, had played in the Jean Goldkette band and known Bix Beiderbeck and Eddie Lang. He taught most of the band instruments, including some he didn't even play, but he played guitar, drums, and all the reeds. He even played flute—he would say, "Well, it's just a question of embouchure; the fingering is the same as saxophone or clarinet." And he also taught trumpet and trombone quite effectively. In fact, I wanted to study trumpet with him, but he took one look at my teeth and said that too much air would escape and I would never be able to get a commanding tone.

Jack's apartment was in Briarwood, Queens, and he used to hold court and teach on Saturday mornings and afternoons. A bunch of us kids would spend every Saturday there. We would sit in the living room playing records, arguing, trading licks, and generally horsing around while we waited for our turn in the studio with the Old Man. We were all jazz nuts, and very opinionated, a sort of Austin High Gang manqué. After the last lesson was given, there would be a big mess of spaghetti and meatballs cooked up by Norton's friend Arlene. She was a big, blowzy redhead, very hip, and we were all sure she had "a past."

Jack showed me some of the fingerings I would continue to use for the rest of my life. He was of the old orchestral jazz school, the musicians who played nonamplified rhythm guitar in the big bands: "Six notes to a chord, four chords to the bar, no cheating," as Freddie Green used to say. And he also would sometimes use wraparound thumb bar chords and things like that, which had dropped out of the jazz world when more classical guitar techniques came in.

Along with the basic instrumental skills, Jack taught us something far more important: how to listen. He saw musical phrases as sentences, with pauses, parentheses, asides, and raised or lowered dynamics for emphasis, and he heard the silences as much as the notes. He would sit his students down, put on a Duke Ellington or a Joe Venuti–Eddie Lang record, and analyze it with us. Or we would play "Name That Musician." He would play a record without saying who it was and then ask, "Who was that on tenor?" This was not just some kind of parlor game. Though he never put it in those terms, it was ear training. He was making us listen, and after a while, if you really paid attention, you got so you could at least make a pretty good guess as to who was playing every instrument. There are people you can't fool, people who can tell you, "No, that's not Ben Webster, that's Coleman Hawkins," or "That's not Pres, that's Paul Quinichette," and be right every time, and to do that, you can't just groove with the music. You have to listen with a focus and an intensity that normal people never use. But we weren't normal people, we were musicians. To be a musician requires a qualitatively different kind of listening, and that is what he was teaching us.

He used to play tricks on us. I remember one time he put on a Count Basie record, and it was one of those arrangements with a recurring theme, a riff going on and it builds and builds and builds. By about the third chorus it was raising the roof, and Jack said, "Watch what the rhythm section's doing during that chorus."

Two or three of us said, "Well, they've sped up a little, haven't they?"

He said, "Let's set a metronome and see."

So we backed up a couple of choruses, set the metronome so that it was keeping the same time as the band, and listened to what happened. It turned out that we were right in a way, because the tempo did change. By that chorus the rhythm section had slowed down slightly—just a little, but you could tell from the metronome. So it was just the opposite of what we had thought: the tempo had slowed, and that was creating this fantastic tension.

That was a real education, and I have spent the rest of my life working with what I learned on those Saturday afternoons at Jack's place. These days, I probably couldn't tell you which one is Ben Webster and which one is Coleman Hawkins, but I used to could, and it would just take a few months of careful listening before I could do it again. I moved on to other things and did not need that particular skill anymore, so it was no longer important to me. But what has remained important, and what I use all the time, is that I learned how to listen.

Another thing I learned from Jack was that I needed to think like an arranger. I got in the habit of listening to the whole arrangement, not just what the guitarist was playing or what the singer was doing. Without that training and what I learned hanging out with other jazz musicians and would-be jazz musicians, all my other musical experiences would not really mean much. For the rest of my life, I continued to use things I learned from Jelly Roll Morton, from Duke Ellington, and from some of the stride piano players: James P. Johnson, Fats Waller, Willie "the Lion" Smith. That was my foundation, and it prepared me for all the music I would learn later from people like Leadbelly, Josh White, Scrapper Blackwell, and Furry Lewis, all of whom were marvelous arrangers. Jack taught me that less is more. Like Jimmy Yancey. Never use two notes when one will do. Never use one note when silence will do. The essence of music is punctuated silence.

Around this same time, I made another life-changing discovery: I found that just a subway ride away, there was a bigger world than Queens, or even Brooklyn.

Through my musical interests, I had acquired a sort-of girlfriend named Cindy, and she had a friend named Rochelle. Rochelle Weissman was hip. She was cool. She was an older woman (sixteen), and she knew all about something called folk music. Every Sunday afternoon she would haul her beloved Favilla—a flat-top, nylon-string guitar, the farthest thing possible from my big band arch-top—down to Washington Square Park in Greenwich Village, where the folk foregathered to raise their voices in song. "So," she asked me one afternoon, "would you like to come over with me some Sunday?"

Would I ever! Folk music! Washington Square! Greenwich Village! I coolly said, "It might be amusing," and we agreed to meet on the IND platform at Continental Avenue in Forest Hills.

When I arrived on Sunday, I barely recognized her. She was decked out in a leotard, a dirndl skirt, a Mexican peasant blouse, and silver hoop earrings. Her hair was ironed straight and tied back in a pony tail. I don't recall what she had on her feet, but I like to think it was sandals. She eyed my Robert Hall slacks and sports shirt with undisguised contempt. "You look like a tourist," she said. I noted the inflection she used when she said "tourist." I was learning. Rochelle explained that these were her Village togs, which she wore on these occasions to "blend in."

"With what?" I wondered, but I kept my mouth shut.

By this time I had heard and read a good deal about Greenwich Village. The phrase "quaint, old-world charm" kept cropping up, and I had a vivid mental picture of a village of half-timbered Tudor cottages with mullioned windows and thatched roofs, inhabited by bearded, bomb-throwing anarchists, poets, painters, and nymphomaniacs whose ideology was slightly to the left of "whoopee!"

Emerging from the subway at the West 4th Street station, I looked around in a state of shock.

"Jesus Christ," I muttered. "It looks just like fucking Brooklyn."

2

Jazz Days

Inauspicious as it may have been, that first trip to Greenwich Village was the starting point for a desultory migration across the East River and into the life of a professional musician. There is no way I can sort out an exact chronology for this hegira, but it started around 1951 and continued in stages over the course of the next few years. I never officially left home, but I would go over to Manhattan and end up crashing on somebody's floor overnight, and then it got to be two nights, then three, until eventually I was spending most of my time in Manhattan—though every few days I would make the trek back to Queens to change my underwear and see if I could mooch some money. Gradually these visits grew less frequent, and by the time I was about seventeen, I was living in Manhattan full-time.

Originally, my plan was to make a living playing jazz, and to that purpose I added yet another instrument to my musical armory: a tenor banjo. This probably requires some explanation, since it has been a good many years since anyone switched from guitar to banjo in order to be a jazz musician.

In the 1940s the jazz world had been rocked by what came to be known as the "mouldy fig wars." During that period, a revival of interest in early jazz coincided with the beginnings of what is now called bebop. A duel to the death was proclaimed, and critics solemnly lined up: you were either a "progressive," hailing the innovations of the boppers, or a warrior in the defense of the traditional New Orleans style—a "mouldy fig." In hindsight, both sides had their merits and both took their positions to ridiculous extremes. The modernists were aesthetic Darwinists, arguing that jazz had to progress and that later forms must necessarily be superior to earlier ones. The traditionalists were Platonists, insisting that early jazz was "pure" and that all subsequent developments were dilutions and degenerations. This comic donnybrook dominated jazz criticism for ten or fifteen years, with neither side capable of seeing the strengths of the other, until it finally subsided and died, probably from sheer boredom. Before that point, though, a lot of otherwise sensible people had made asses of themselves.* I remember a friend during this period telling me that he had been on his way to some big jazz festival but had discovered that Charlie Parker was playing, and was so disgusted that he turned around and drove home. This made perfect sense to me.

Being an adolescent, I was naturally an absolutist, so as soon as I became aware that this titanic tempest in a teapot was going down, I had to jump one way or the other. As a result, I turned my back on a lot of good music. When I was twelve or thirteen, Charlie Christian was my favorite guitarist, I had amassed a huge collection of the Benny Goodman sextet, and I listened to bebop and modern jazz. By the time I was fifteen or sixteen, I had come to regard all of that music as a sorry devolution from the pure New Orleans style. I was convinced, intellectually and ideologically, that the traditionalists had the better of it, and that led me to a lot of good music, but it also led me away from a lot of good music and toward a lot of truly terrible music. It was an ideological judgment rather than a musical one, and it was stupid. It turned me on to Jelly Roll Morton, Sidney Bechet, and Louis Armstrong, but also led me to support any aggregation of toothless incompetents over Dizzy Gillespie or Charlie Parker. I gave away all my Gillespie records and acquired recordings of old New Orleans relics, many of whom had probably never been very good even in their youth and prime.

I also switched from guitar to tenor banjo, since according to the canons of those times, guitar was not a proper instrument for a traditional jazz

---

*Albeit sometimes wittily. Eddie Condon on bebop: "In my day we didn't flat our fifths, we drank 'em." Or Miles Davis on hearing a Bunk Johnson record: "They sound like a prison band, and they should be kept there until they stop playing like that."

band. (I have since seen pictures of the most canonical New Orleans jazz bands, such as Buddy Bolden's, and they show guitars to have been at least as common as banjos back at the dawn of jazz, but I did not know that in 1953.) I did not like the banjo much—it clanged like some kind of wind-up toy, and I had trouble fitting my fingers on the neck—but there was a lot of pressure on me. So I switched over and quickly became one of the worst tenor banjo players on the trad scene. And to be the worst at tenor banjo, you're really competing, because that's a fast track. I couldn't keep time in a bucket, I kept blowing the chord changes, and no sane jazz musician would ever have hired me, except for one thing: I had a loud voice and I didn't mind taking vocals. A lot of people who played jazz at that point—and some even today—thought that taking vocals was *infra dignitatem:* a real jazz musician didn't sing. (Just as a real jazz musician didn't dance.) Exceptions were made for a few of the older guys, like Jack Teagarden or Louis Armstrong, but a lot of people stopped taking Mose Allison seriously as a pianist the minute he opened his mouth.

In addition, working in clubs that had no sound systems of any kind, anyone who wanted to be a singer had to be able to make do without a mike. I had a very loud voice—as some wit remarked at the time, "When Van Ronk takes a vocal, the hogs are restless for miles around"—and if the key was right, I could cut through a seven-piece band. (That was the standard trad outfit: trumpet, trombone, clarinet, piano, bass, drums, and of course a banjo. If there was a little extra money, they would sometimes add a second trumpet, because a lot of those guys liked the Yerba Buena's two-trumpet sound.) So I took the vocals, and in return they would let me hold my banjo.

Thus, with my Vega in hand, I set out to be a professional jazzman. By that time I was already six foot two and weighed about 220 pounds. Six or seven months later, thanks to my devotion to jazz, I weighed 170. I didn't have the sense God gave a duck. I had never starved before, and I had no idea of the great range of possibilities out there in the world—one of them being starvation. At first I was just sitting in occasionally with pick-up bands, and for a while a bunch of kids my own age also put together our own group. Since we thought we were a pretty clever bunch, we came up with a real thigh-slapper of a name: the Brute Force Jazz Band. We thought that was very witty; audiences thought it was very accurate. We played where we could, at rare intervals and to no great acclaim, and then I ended up with a relatively steady organization called the Jazz Cardinals—though I was still doing pick-up work whenever I could get it. The Cardinals were led by a Dutchman named Eric Huystedt who sounded very much like Sidney Bechet, and we had a regular gig at a place called the Amber Lantern in New Jersey. Boy, did we get screwed! I remember one time we divvied up all the money we had made that evening, and it came to forty-seven cents each.

Those were the waning days of the trad-Dixieland revival. I was "just in time to be too late," as the song says, and the trad scene was by then dominated by a bunch of cornballs in funny hats, moonlighting insurance execs, and a smattering of dedicated musicians eking out a meager existence by gumping meals at the Automat. (Gumping is when you race the busboy to an unfinished plate of food, finish it, and repeat the procedure until you are no longer hungry or you get thrown out, whichever comes first.) It was really slim pickings. Often you would play for union scale and then have to slip the owner something back under the table. You were lucky to get two gigs in a week; more often you would get one gig in two weeks. Trying to live on that, even in the golden fifties, wasn't easy.

Still, I learned a lot by working with those bands. We were playing all the old chestnuts, things like "At the Jazz Band Ball" and "Fidgety Feet," and I was picking up some relatively sophisticated chord changes, which gave me an enormous leg up a few years later when I got involved in the folk scene. The joke in the early 1960s was that I was the only folksinger in New York who knew how to play a diminished chord, and while that was not quite true, it does indicate what set me apart from a lot of the other people.

Most of the jobs I played were outside New York City, especially over in Jersey. There was a country club in West Orange, a place in Fort Lee. One of the nice things was that I got to meet some of the old-timers. One time, I did a benefit concert out at Welfare Island with a pick-up group, and Eubie Blake showed up; I vividly remember him playing "Baltimore Rag." I also sat in on sessions at clubs like the Stuyvesant Casino and Child's Paramount; I recall one night when the line-up included Miff Mole, Jimmy McPartland, Coleman Hawkins, Johnny Hodges, and Ben

Webster, and there I was backing them.* I played with Joe Sullivan a couple of times, and once with Jimmy Rushing. I could never have worked officially in those places because I was not a member of the AF of M, the musicians' union, but they managed to squeeze me in. If the union delegate came by, Rushing or whoever was the titular leader would take over and I would get offstage. Of course, my instrument was still up there and the delegate knew perfectly well what was going on, but he wouldn't do anything about it.

There is an apprenticeship system in jazz, so even if the older musicians were not personally all that accessible or friendly, they felt an obligation to help the younger musicians. That is generally true of people who are serious about music. When the first Cro-Magnon started to bang on a bone, he was probably ready to show the second Cro-Magnon how to do it. Musicians are sweet people, and if you really care about music and want to learn, they will rally to you and do what they can to help you, even if you don't know shit from Shinola.

Of all the older musicians, the one I remember most fondly was Clarence Williams. Clarence was originally a piano player out of New Orleans, and he had come up to New York around the time of World War I. By the early 1920s he had established himself as just about the key figure in jazz in New York, and he was well qualified for the role. He was a damn good piano player, but more than that, he was a composer and songwriter, a publisher, and what they called a "record contractor." In those days, when a record company wanted to record some tunes, it would get hold of someone like Clarence and he would be given a budget to cut a certain number of sides. The rest was up to him: he would pick the tunes or write them himself, arrange them, pick the musicians, choose the recording studio, pay all the expenses, and whatever money was left over was his pay. Clarence arranged a lot of sessions for other people, and also plenty for himself under various names, the most famous of which was Clarence Williams and His Blue Five, a shifting group that at times included people like Louis Armstrong.

---

*Of course, Hawkins was a bit modern for my taste at that point—my idea of a really good saxophone player was one of the guys who played with King Oliver—but I was willing to put up with Coleman Hawkins. As for what he thought of me, all I can say is, he was always very polite . . .

Where Clarence really earned his place in history, though, was when the blues boom took off. Around 1920, there was a fluke hit, a thing called "Crazy Blues," recorded by a black singer named Mamie Smith. It came out of left field and sold close to a million copies, and all the commercial record companies immediately went into feeding-frenzy mode. One of them, Okeh records, called Clarence and said, "We want one of those." So Clarence went down south on a talent hunt and came back to New York with this hot young blues singer, and her name was Bessie Smith. Following the old rule of "finders, keepers," Clarence became the contractor for Bessie's early records. That meant that he not only played piano on a lot of them but got to write—and more importantly, publish—the songs, which was where the money was.

When I knew Clarence, he was retired and had a little place on 125th Street called the Harlem Thrift Shop. It was his office and hangout—as far as I could see, he never actually sold anything out of there. All that he had in that shop was his own self and two pianos. It was a tiny place, but he squeezed the second piano in there because what he was running was a kind of clearinghouse for piano players. If some out-of-town pianist was passing through New York, he would stop by to say hello to Clarence, and of course a lot of piano players lived in the city as well. So there I was, at sixteen and seventeen years old, sitting in a corner and listening to Clarence Williams play piano duets with James P. Johnson or Willie "The Lion" Smith or Joe Sullivan, people like that. I would sit in a corner, with my eyes like saucers. I mean, I was a schmucky little kid in some ways, but I was not so dumb that I didn't know how lucky I was.

Clarence liked to play a game that seems to be a favorite with most composers. As far as I can figure out, its name must be "And then I wrote . . ." because it always starts with the composer playing an arpeggio, smiling at whoever is listening, and saying, "And then I wrote . . ." and going into a tune. A lot of them were pretty familiar tunes, but some were real rarities, and there were a couple that I kept in my repertoire from then on. I also heard a lot of stories, gossip, and musician talk. At the time, I found some of it pretty shocking, because these musicians were the creators and inventors of the music I loved, and it turned out that quite often they were cantankerous old curmudgeons who hated each other's guts. For example, if you got Clarence Williams onto the subject of Jelly Roll Morton, his reaction would be something like "That plagiarist!? That thief!?" He would become apoplectic. So you learned not to mention Jelly Roll Morton around Clarence Williams. I am told that Duke Ellington felt the same way about Morton. I do not know what Morton had to say about Clarence—to my eternal regret, Morton died before I could get my hands on him—but I do know what he had to say about W. C. Handy, the man who wrote "St. Louis Blues," "Memphis Blues," and a bunch of other hits. What he said was "Well, yes, there was a lot of unprotected material around in those days . . . "

Back then, I found this pretty disenchanting. I thought, "How could this band of brothers, these great pioneers, talk of one another so irreverently?" It was terrible. Now, looking back, I find it pretty damn funny. I suppose that as I get older, I get more curmudgeonly myself, and I can identify with that kind of thing.

All in all, I was learning more than I could possibly assimilate—it took me years to even begin to get a handle on everything I was seeing and hearing. Admittedly, my failures in this respect may to some extent be traceable to other aspects of the jazz life: Eddie Condon once remarked that when you are a musician, a dozen people might offer to buy you a drink in the course of an evening but nobody ever walks up and says, "Hey, let me stand you to a ham sandwich." Between starvation and inebriation, it's a miracle that any of us survived, much less actually learned anything.

Of course, as a dedicated apprentice hipster, my experiences in this field were not limited to alcohol. My acquaintance with the demon weed dates to around 1954, a halcyon year for vipers.* I was working at yet another country club, somewhere on the prairies of New Jersey, with yet another pick-up trad jazz band. As we were shuffling off the stage to take our first break, the bass player, a little guy named Arnie, whispered conspiratorially, "Hey kid, you wanna try a new kind of cigarette?"

I was no square; I had read Mezz Mezzrow's *Really the Blues*, and knew all about marijuana. To let him know how hip I was, I said, "That's cool, Daddy"—I'm sure he was impressed—and we betook ourselves to the parking lot, where he produced a little, ratty-looking, tapered cylinder of grayish paper, stuffed, he said, with "dyno doojie."

---

*The term "viper" for marijuana smoker, which has sadly fallen into disuse, was derived from the sound made while inhaling.

"Take a deep drag, and hold it in your lungs as long as you can," he said. It was like inhaling a forest fire, but I did as I was told. "As long as I could" turned out to be about three-tenths of a second. I immediately hacked the smoke back up with a series of coughs that must have rattled every window in Monmouth County. Arnie was delighted. He laughed so hard, he almost fell down—so much for Big Dave the hipster.

After a few more tokes, I sort of got the hang of it, but where was the euphoria? Except for a slightly sore throat, I felt nothing. We smoked the joint down to a tiny butt, burning our lips in the process. The butt, he explained, was called a "roach" and could be disposed of in several ways. His preferred method was to knead some tobacco out of the end of a Chesterfield, push the roach into the vacated space, and twist the loose paper shut. "Shooting the bullet," he called it. So we finished the whole joint, and I still didn't feel a damn thing. I was baffled. Was the dope no good? Was Arnie putting me on? Had Mezz Mezzrow *lied*?

We could hear the horns warming up, so we hurried back inside, and I took my place on the stand, just in front of the bass and drums. I picked up my banjo. It looked silly, so I giggled. The drummer called the first tune, "Royal Garden Blues" in B flat, counted it down, and we were off and running. My hands were fascinating: they just kept moving without any conscious direction, making all kinds of wonderful patterns. Then the tune was over, and everybody stopped. But not me, I was really into it. Arnie kicked me and I chugged slowly to a stop. Wow, those fingers! The next piece featured me on the vocal.

Bob, the leader, called "Frankie and Johnny," an overdone ballad with about two hundred verses. This had never been one of my favorites, and by the time Frankie got around to shooting Johnny I was totally bored and wishing that I was singing "Cake Walking Babies from Home" instead. So I promptly switched songs, changing keys as I went along. Some of the guys tried to follow me, while the rest doggedly plodded on with "Frankie." The result was the musical equivalent of a three-way midair collision. I was ecstatic, still grinning from ear to ear as I was led from the stand. I had never had so much fun onstage in my life, but those killjoys made me sit out the rest of the set.

The audience, of course, never noticed a thing.

♫   ♫   ♫

As I was rapidly discovering, it is hard work surviving without a steady job. I could usually come up with a floor or a couch to crash on, but food was always a problem. We would have boosting expeditions—I never actually did this myself, but I was certainly party to the proceeds—where a group would go into a supermarket and secrete some small, high-value items such as caviar and potted shrimp about their persons. Then we would go out and shop these things off to our more affluent friends for bags of rice and bulk items that were too big to shoplift.

We would head out in the early morning on what we used to call the "dawn patrol." We would hit people's stoops at about four-thirty or five and get milk, eggs, sometimes even bread, and one copy each of the *New York Times*. A bunch of us were crashing more or less regularly in a loft on the Bowery, so we got a lot of tips from the local winos. There was a bird-seed factory right down the block, and if you got there for shape-up, those fortunate enough to be chosen would have the opportunity of unloading fifty-pound sacks of birdseed. I did that sometimes, and as it happened, the birdseed was marijuana, and in those days they didn't irradiate the stuff, so among other things we had a little farm going by the stove. Very nice, until one day the cat got at it. Somehow, though, heaving around fifty-pound sacks of marijuana took a lot of the romance out of dope for me.

I did all kinds of things. I was a bank messenger for a while—an insane business that is perfectly captured in Henry Miller's *Tropic of Capricorn*—and I did a little factory work. (I used to say that I had an assembly-line job dotting the eyes on Mickey Mouse dolls, which is not quite true, but close enough.) I knew a guy who had a catering service, and sometimes he would hire me when he had a big party, which paid a few bucks and also had some side benefits: there was often food left over, and once the customers got a bit tipsy, we would ferret away a bottle of champagne for every couple we served.

If worst came to worst, there were always day jobs busing tables in an Automat. However, by the mid-1950s I was getting involved with radical politics, and being a lefty could be an occupational hazard in even the most minor occupations. My friend Lenny was working a restaurant job, and the FBI came around and started asking his boss questions about a suspicious, dangerous character who was waiting tables, and of course the guy fired him.

There was also the problem of keeping clean. We had to do things like mooch showers. Haircuts were to be had only at the barber college down on the Bowery—either that or we'd cut each other's hair. We couldn't afford to get our clothes cleaned. We would gradually get grungier and grungier, and eventually you would be so grungy that they wouldn't even hire you to bus tables.

There were compensations, though. Our loft was at 15 Cooper Square, which was right across the street from the original Five Spot, and in those days Thelonious Monk was playing there as sort of a steady thing. We would go over and sit at the bar in the afternoon, and Monk would be there with his musicians, rehearsing and working out new tunes. Beer was ten or fifteen cents in the afternoon, and you could sit and listen to Monk and Coltrane and that band. As icing on the cake, off to the side there was an old-time telephone booth with accordion doors, and every now and again the band would take a break and somebody would go in there and roll a joint. Around five or six o'clock, when the prices changed, the band went home to get ready for the evening's show, and we would go into the telephone booth, and in the cracks of the door would be roaches. Those guys did not smoke lemonade; they had really good dope, so we would collect all these roaches and make new joints out of them, and get bombed out of our birds, basically on the house.

There was actually a lot of good music around that you could hear for free. I remember hearing Alexander Schneider conducting *Eine Kleine Nachtmusik* in Washington Square Park. And then, of course, there were the folksingers. Thanks to my Virgil, Rochelle, I had been introduced to the Sunday afternoon hootenannies in Washington Square at the outset of my descent into the Village. However, any interest I might have had in folk music had gone by the boards as soon as I cast my lot with the jazz fraternity, because if there was one thing that all jazz musicians could agree on, it was that folk music was irredeemably square. We thought of it as "hillbilly shit," a bunch of guys who didn't even know how to play their instruments and just got by with "cowboy chords." The little I heard while passing through the Square on Sundays confirmed my newfound snobbishness. It was essentially summer camp music, songs these kids had learned at progressive camps that I came to think of generically as Camp Gulag on the Hudson. The sight and sound of all those happily howling petit bourgeois Stalinists offended my assiduously nurtured self-image as a hipster, not to mention my political sensibilities, which had become vehemently IWW-anarchist. They were childish, and nothing bothers a serious-minded eighteen-year-old as much as childishness. So for a couple of years I avoided the place like the plague, for fear of contamination. If I had to pass anywhere in the vicinity, I would walk through as quickly as possible, obviating any possibility that I might get sucked in by something like "Blue Tail Fly" and shortly find myself doing the hora around the fountain and singing "Hey Lolly, Lolly Lo."

Eventually, though, I came to realize that there were some very good musicians operating on the fringes of the radical Rotarian sing-alongs. People like Tom Paley, Dick Rosmini, and Fred Gerlach were playing music cognate with early jazz, and doing it with a subtlety and directness that blew me away. I had heard that kind of playing before, but only on old 78s that I had picked up by chance while searching for jazz discs. At that time you couldn't just go out and buy an LP reissue of people like Mississippi John Hurt or Robert Johnson. In fact, the LP format had been introduced only a few years earlier. (I still have RL 101, the very first Riverside ten-inch record, a thing called *Louis Armstrong Plays the Blues*. At first I was very annoyed to find that instead of Louis solo, it was him backing blues singers like Chippie Hill and Ma Rainey. Then I started to listen and liked it very much.) If I wanted to find a lot of the older jazz stuff, I had to go out and look for used 78s. There was a place on 47th Street, the Jazz Record Center, which we called "Engine Joe's," and it was a treasure trove of jazz and jazz-related music of all sorts; it had writing on the stairs as you went up, saying, "Everything from Bunk to Monk," which the mouldy figs misquoted as "from Bunk to junk." There would be these stacks of records that you could look through, and some cost as much as ten bucks, but there were also some for twenty-five cents. They would have Jelly Roll Morton, Louis Armstrong, King Oliver, Sidney Bechet, Bessie Smith, and also all kinds of people that I had never heard of before, like Bumble Bee Slim and Furry Lewis. So what the hell, for two bits you could afford to indulge your curiosity.

I was never really a collector, because I was sleeping on floors and that sort of thing, and for record collecting you need a stable place to live. Still, I picked up a few 78s, and a lot of people I knew were accumulating collections—for a while there, you did not factor into the scene at all unless you could discuss cactus needles intelligently—so I had access to a fair amount of material. Also, the reissue series were beginning, and I shortly picked up a ten-inch record called *Listen to Our Story*, which Alan Lomax had put together for Decca.•It was a collection of ballads that had originally been issued on 78s, most of them by white hillbilly singers, but it included "Stackolee" by Furry Lewis and a thing called "True Religion" by Reverend Edward Clayborn, both with fingerpicked guitar.

When I heard "Stackolee," I assumed it was two guitars, one playing the bass line and the other playing the melody. I had no idea that there was such a thing as fingerpicking. My idea of playing guitar was either chopping fours—playing rhythm chords—or something like what Charlie Christian did. Then, sometime around 1954 or 1955, I happened to be walking across Washington Square Park of a Sunday afternoon, and I noticed this guy playing an old New York Martin, a very small, very sweet guitar, and he was doing something that sounded an awful lot like "Stackolee." It immediately grabbed my attention, because he was doing the whole thing by himself: his thumb was picking out the bass notes while he was playing the melody with his fingers. I had never seen anything like that, so I stood there and listened, and when he stopped playing, I immediately buttonholed him and asked him to show me what he was doing. That was Tom Paley, who later became a founding member of the New Lost City Ramblers. He was very nice, and graciously answered all my dumb questions, slowed the whole thing down, and gave me the general gist of how it worked.*

The advantages of fingerpicking were immediately obvious to me, because what I really wanted to do was sing and that style of playing was ideal for accompanying yourself. I rushed home to my guitar and went to work. I have never applied myself to any project with such intensity before or since. Paley had provided the key, but mastering the technique took time. I did not take any lessons—there was nobody around then, as far as I knew, who was giving any—but Sunday after Sunday I hit Washington Square, watching other fingerstyle guitar players, meeting them, and picking their

---

*I ran into Tom at the Vancouver Folk Festival about forty years later, and went out of my way to thank him for that afternoon, but he did not remember a bit of it. Some people don't have any sense of history.

brains. A few of them lived in the Village, but most were still living with their parents in the burbs. I made friends like Barry Kornfeld and Dick Rosmini, who were already picking like sonofabitches. Gradually, I improved—we all did, actually. When one of us figured something out, the knowledge would be shared, and our general level of skill rose. It was a combined process of experimentation and theft: you would come up with an idea, and the next thing you knew, all your friends would be playing it, but that was fine because when they came up with an idea, you would be playing it. As Machiavelli used to say, "Things proceed in a circle, and thus the empire is maintained."

Thus began my shift from jazz to folk music, a change that defied the general rule that things evolve from the simple to the more complex. In this case I made a move that was technically retrogressive, but it was about the only thing I could do to survive. I was a high school dropout, so there was no chance that I was going to become a professor of comparative philology or a nuclear physicist who played the guitar on the side. And much as I loved traditional jazz, I was sick to death of performing the music of King Oliver and Jelly Roll Morton for drunken undergraduates who wanted us to put on funny hats and sing "Yes Sir, That's My Baby." Even if I had been able to stomach it, that scene was all but dead, and there was no GI bill for veterans of the mouldy fig wars. It was clear that my career plans were due for an agonizing reappraisal, and unless I wanted to get out of music entirely, folk music was the only way I could jump. So I cast off my carefully cultivated jazz snobbery and set out to reinvent myself as a fingerpicking guitarist and singer. Like the man said, "Sometimes you have to forget your principles and do what's right."

3

Folk Roots and Libertarian Anarchy

Before embarking on the saga of the Greenwich Village scene in the formative years of the Great Folk Scare, I should probably provide a little background. First of all, the whole concept of what is meant by the word "folksinger" has changed dramatically since I came on the set. With the success of the singer-songwriters of the sixties (Dylan and Paxton and Ochs, oh my!), the scene became dominated by music that we would not even have considered part of the genre.

In the 1950s, as for at least the previous two hundred years, we used the word "folk" to describe a process rather than a style. By this definition—to which I still subscribe—folk songs are the musical expression of preliterate or illiterate communities and necessarily pass directly from singer to singer. Flamenco is folk music; Bulgarian vocal ensembles are folk music; African drumming is folk music; and "Barbara Allen" is folk music. Clearly, there is little stylistic similarity here, but all these musics developed through a process of oral repetition that is akin to the game we used to call "whisper." In whisper, one person writes down a sentence, then whispers it to another, who whispers it to a third, and so on around the room until the last person hears it and again writes it down; and then the two messages are compared, and often turn out to be wildly disparate. In the same way, if one follows songs that have been passed down through the oral folk tradition, one finds that lines like "Savory, sage, rosemary, and thyme" become "Miss Mary says come marry in time," and "Jordan is a hard road to travel" becomes "Yearning in your heart for trouble." The cumulative effect is a sort of Darwinian evolution that first produces different versions of the same song, and eventually leads to entirely new songs. It follows that the original authors of folk songs are usually unknown, and even when we do know something about them, the information is not necessarily relevant.

To an overwhelming extent, this folk process has been short-circuited in the developed world over the last hundred years or so, first by widespread literacy and later by the phonograph, radio, and TV. As a result, with the exception of a few holdouts—some rap and street poetry, kids' game rhymes, bawdy songs, and so forth—there is very little folk music in modern-day America. (Please don't hit me with that banjo.) It follows that the concept of a "folk revival" is oxymoronic. And yet, self-announced folk revivals keep surfacing, just as they have at least since the days of Sir Walter Scott. The impulse behind them is generally romantic and anti-industrial—and, a bit surprisingly, among Anglophones in recent times it has almost always come from politically left of center. (Elsewhere, interest in folkloric traditions has often been found in combination with extreme nationalism of the most right-wing and fascist variety.)

One of the first things that must be understood about these revivals is that the folk have very little to do with them. Always, there is a middle-class constituency, and its idea of the folk—whoever that might be—is the operative thing. The particular risorgimento in which I took part had begun some fifteen years prior to my arrival and grew out of the leftist movements of the Depression era. Desperate strikes, unemployment, and vast hordes of dispossessed small farmers engaged the sympathy and support of the middle class, which was pretty hard-hit itself. Enter the Communist Party. Communist organizers assisted tenant farmers in setting up unions in the South and Southwest, and supported rent strikes and anti-eviction campaigns in black ghettos in the Northeast, which, along with an anti-lynching campaign, established links with the black community. In spite of their small numbers, the Communists seemed to be everywhere, and they were damned good organizers.

In the course of their work among coal miners and textile workers in Appalachia, and with rural and ghetto blacks, some of the Communist field workers became aware of the music of the southern mountains and black singing traditions (especially gospel music). They saw these folk songs as social documents—I have heard people go to great lengths to prove that the most apolitical ditty was in fact a coded assault on the oppression of the workers—and also as potential organizing tools. At first, their enthusiasm met with little support among their urban counterparts. While they were celebrating eccentric hill-country balladeers like Aunt Molly Jackson, the cultural commissars were off on a crazed search for Communist art, encouraging sympathetic composers to write workers' oratorios. Before long, though, these progressive masterpieces fell into well-deserved oblivion, and picket lines and rallies began to feature that now-familiar fixture, the "folksinger."

The urban intelligentsia had always been susceptible to nostalgic longings for "simpler" times and lifestyles, but it had tended to present its rural gleanings as an adjunct to the "art song." Classical composers had produced settings of peasant airs and dances, which would be tossed in to lighten up programs of "serious music." Medieval lyrics were presented as educational artifacts, and dreaded accordingly. The new wave of politically progressive folksingers was something different. The tuxedos and evening gowns of the concert hall were replaced by work clothes, in a spirit of proletarian unity.

There was something else going on as well: a lot of both the middle-class left-wingers and the workers back in the 1930s were first- or second-generation immigrants, and the folk revival served as a way for them to establish American roots. This was especially true for the Jews. The folk revivalists were at least 50 percent Jewish, and they adopted the music as part of a process of assimilation to the Anglo-American tradition—which itself was largely an artificial construct but nonetheless provided some common ground. (Of course, that rush to assimilate was not limited to Jews, but I think they were more conscious of what they were doing than a lot of other people were.) The more nativist "folk" were often embarrassingly aware of this fact. When Roger Sprung, one of the original Washington Square bluegrassers, showed up with a couple of his buddies at the Asheville Folk Festival in the early 1950s, Bascom Lamar Lunsford, the festival organizer and a hard-shell North Carolinian, grilled them thoroughly before letting them perform.

"You boys from New York?" he asked, with obvious suspicion.

Roger said yes.

"You Jews?"

Roger said, "Uh, yeah."

"You know Pete Seeger?"

"Well, we've met him . . . "

"You Communists?"

No, they were not.

Lunsford himself was a racist, anti-Semitic white supremacist who in later years would steadfastly refuse to come to the Newport Folk Festivals because of Seeger's involvement. Nonetheless, he finally decided that Sprung and his cohorts were not Communists, and allowed them to appear. However, he was master of ceremonies, and when they were due to come on, he got up and announced, "Now, Ladies and Gentlemen, I would like to present the three Jews from New York."

The New York branch of the folk revival was strongly influenced by the Communist outlook, and one of the effects of this was that, along with performing traditional material, a lot of singers began composing topical songs based on folk models. Such urban, folk-styled creations were essentially a new music, consciously and often carefully crafted, politically motivated, and in many ways a quite different animal from anything that had come before. (The Industrial Workers of the World—IWW, or "Wobblies"—had done something similar back in the teens, but with the difference that singers like Joe Hill and T-Bone Slim were of the folk and generally set their lyrics to pop melodies or church hymns rather than to anything self-consciously rural or working-class.) It was part of the birth of "proletarian chic"—think about that the next time you slip into your designer jeans.

The urban folksingers acquired their repertoires from books, records, collecting trips, and one another, and unlike the traditional singers, they made their commitment to folk music consciously, for political and aesthetic reasons. As a result, they generally had to adopt personae not their own, singing and writing about experiences they knew only secondhand. This made for a very unstable synthesis, full of internal contradictions, but in the late 1930s such complications were ignored in the heat of political battle and the joy of musical discovery. (Besides, introspection was a petit bourgeois luxury.) Those were urgent times, and the song for tomorrow night's rally had to be written now, at once, immediately.

By 1939 this movement had its nexus in a sort of commune on West 10th Street in Greenwich Village called Almanac House. The residents included at one time or another, Pete Seeger, Alan and Bess Lomax, Woody Guthrie, Lee Hays, Millard Lampell . . . the list is long and impressive. All were songwriters to one degree or another (many collaborations and collective efforts here), but Guthrie was by far the most talented and influential of the lot. Taking pains to conceal his considerable erudition behind a folksy facade, he became a kind of proletarian oracle in the eyes of his singer-songwriter associates, who were, of course, incurable romantics. With Guthrie exercising a very loose artistic hegemony (Seeger and Lampell seem to have done most of the actual work), Almanac House became a kind of song factory, churning out topical, occasional, and protest songs at an unbelievable clip, as well as hosting regular "hootenannies."

While the Communist Party played a notable role in midwifing this musical movement—Guthrie even had a regular column for a while in the *Daily Worker*—it also presented a few problems. For one thing, there were the political shifts that found the Almanacs singing things like "Plow Under Every Fourth American Boy" and the other songs they recorded opposing U.S. entry into World War II during the Hitler-Stalin pact, then having to throw those songs out the window and replace them with "It's that UAW-CIO that makes the army roll and go," once Germany invaded the Soviet Union. However, I do not want to overstate the old bugaboo about "singing the 'party line.'" While the folksingers were certainly responsive to party positions, the Central Committee not only failed to exercise tight control over them but showed a discouraging lack of interest in the whole business. The main obstacle to musical growth presented by the CP was not a matter of committee directives or party discipline but a matter of attitude. Among Progressives of the time, personal expression in music was discouraged. Art was considered to be a tool. (Or a weapon: the famous sign on Woody's guitar, "This machine kills fascists," is a perfect example.) As odd as it may seem to us now, many of these people were embarrassed to write a love song, because the Spanish Civil War was going on, or the steelworkers were on strike, or Mussolini was invading

Ethiopia. Thus, while the songwriters around the CP had some magnificent moments, they were unable to exploit the full range of their experience, and their compositions ended up being as obsessively focused on one subject (politics) as the commercial music they despised was on another (romantic love).

My purpose is not to chart the fortunes of the Almanacs and their various heirs and assigns through the 1940s, but only to note that their influence was fundamental and continued to grow. People's Songs was formed as a sort of central clearinghouse for progressive folksingers, and it published a regular bulletin that was the direct ancestor of *Sing Out!* magazine. Then, in 1948, the Weavers reached the top ten on the Hit Parade, putting the folk revival squarely into the mainstream of American music. By this time, a good deal of ideological mellowing had been going on, and the group was—dare one say it—fun.

It is impossible to determine what further evolutions the Weavers' success might have sparked if the Cold War and its attendant anti-Communist hysteria had not intervened. The Red Scare that began in the late 1940s involved this country in one of the most disgracefully psychotic episodes in its history, and the blacklist damn near killed the folk revival in its tracks. The full extent of the witch hunt is rarely acknowledged even today. Most people believe it affected only public figures—people in government and the entertainment world—but that is completely wrong. Trade unions and the professions in the private sector were all profoundly affected, and for a while no one to the left of Genghis Khan could feel entirely safe. Thousands of people lost their jobs and were harassed by the FBI and threatened by vigilante anti-Communist crusaders. I had to sign a loyalty oath to get a job as a *messenger*, for chrissake, and I have already mentioned Lenny Glaser being fired from his job as a waiter after the FBI came around and asked the restaurant manager some pointed questions about his political affiliations. The right-wing press—which is to say, almost all of it—was running stories like "How the Reds Control Our Schools," and the whole country was in a paranoid panic that lasted almost two decades. Leftists and intellectuals were terrorized, many essentially unemployable, not a few in prison, and a couple (the Rosenbergs) executed *pour encourager les autres*. Thus the cheery atmosphere of the Golden Fifties.

When I began haunting the Village, I knew from radical politics like a dog knows his grandmother. I had read about the Wobblies and thought of them as my spiritual forefathers, but assumed that the IWW had vanished along with the five-cent beer. (As it happened, I could have found them by simply looking in the phone book: they kept a hall down on lower Broad Street.) The contemporary left was a vague and mysterious concept to me—but with McCarthy, Nixon, and their sleazy band of creeps rampaging across the land, it was clear that whatever radicals remained were in deep shit. This appealed to my contrarian streak, and I could hardly wait to get involved.

The Communist Party was the first and most obvious candidate for my attention: it had a certain underdog appeal, and its minions were relatively easy to locate—they were as hard to find as Washington Square on a Sunday afternoon. The young CP-ers, called the Labor Youth League or LYL, would be spread out all across the park, five-string banjos and nylon-string guitars in hand, singing what they called "people's songs." They were very serious, very innocent, and very young, and except for talking (and singing) a lot about "peace," their political opinions were generally indistinguishable from those of liberal Democrats. They all seemed to go to Music and Art High School, and their parents all seemed to be dentists. I remember once coming across a covey of them sitting cross-legged around a bespectacled banjoist who struck a dramatic chord and earnestly explained, "This is a song the workers sing when they're oppressed." In retrospect, I think they were kind of sweet, but at the time I was scornful: "*This* is the Red Menace?"

A few of the CP's older and more politically conscious people were usually on hand as well, and these I found evasive, dishonest, and ignorant. After listening to them recite their catechism, I concluded that however loathsome and psychotic the Red-baiters were, they had got one thing right: the CP was the American arm of Soviet foreign policy, no more, no less. They were stolid organization men, and a revolutionary looking for a home might as well have checked out the Kiwanis or the Boy Scouts.

I was in search of a movement that somehow combined socialism with individualism—a tall order. The model in my mind's eye was the old IWW, which had no use for government as we know it, but thought the whole shebang should be run by democratic workers' councils. As a workable blueprint, this sounded pretty far-fetched even at the time, but that bothered me not a bit. The important thing was that the world had fallen into the hands of a bunch of insane greed-heads and obviously needed a thorough overhaul.

So there I was, sitting in Johnny Romero's bar on Minetta one night with some of my fellow refuseniks from Richmond Hill, and we fell into an amiable political argument with some people at the next table. "What *are* your politics anyway?" one of them asked me.

"I'm an anarchist," I said. That usually shut them up.

"Oh yeah? Have you read Kropotkin? Bakunin? Nechaiev?"

I was caught flat-footed. This was the first I had heard that you had to *read* anything to be an anarchist. It sounded distinctly unanarchistic. And who were all these Russians he was talking about? They sounded like fugitives from an obscure novel. With patient condescension, he informed me that they were essential anarchist theoreticians, and that all would be revealed to me if I showed up Friday night for the weekly forum at the Libertarian Center, 813 Broadway, third floor. I wrote down the address.

The center turned out to be a big loft on the corner of 12th Street, which they would set up on forum nights with long trestle tables and folding chairs for about thirty people. I went down that Friday, and within a few weeks was signed up as a full-fledged member of the Libertarian League. (In those prelapsarian days, the word "libertarian" was still in the hands of its rightful owners: anarchists, syndicalists, council communists, and suchlike. The mean-spirited, reactionary assholes who are currently dragging it through the mud were not even a blot on the horizon. We should have taken out a copyright.) The league was a loose-knit anarchist group run by an elected steering committee. Discipline was voluntary—hell, everything was voluntary. It was almost purely a propaganda operation, mainly concentrating on running the forum and publishing an eight-page newsletter, *Views and Comments*. Unlike the Marxists, who expected "History" to descend like a deus ex machina and pull their chestnuts out of the fire, the anarchists knew how long the odds were, and they went about their business with a kind of go-to-hell, cheerful, existential despair.

They were quite a group. Of course, there were a few old guys down there who were just lost souls looking for something to do on a Friday night, but there were also genuine firebrands who had fought in the Spanish Civil War, people who had been forced to flee Europe because of their revolutionary activities, veterans of the IWW strikes. "Mitch" Mitchell, for instance, who later got me my seaman's papers, was the brother of H. L. Mitchell, who had been the main founder of the Southern Tenant Farmers Union. He had fought in Spain as well, and came out of that experience an extremely bitter anti-Communist. He was convinced that he had returned alive only because he had been taken prisoner by the Fascists—that otherwise he would have been purged by his more orthodox comrades. (Tom Condit, one of my young cohorts in the league, recalls meeting a couple of people who felt this way, and if we knew two, there must have been quite a few others.)

Listening to those guys talk provided a unique education in the ups and downs of the international left. There was a Bavarian named Franz who had been in the shop stewards' movement in Germany, and he told me about being in Munich when they were storming the parliamentary building. Someone yelled out, "Comrades! We must preserve revolutionary order. Don't run on the grass." And all of these guys, with their rifles and whatever, duly filed off the grass and onto the walkways. Meanwhile, down at the other end of the path, the machine guns were waiting. Franz saw this happening, and he just threw down his rifle and walked in the other direction. Went to Hamburg, got on a boat, came to the States. But after that experience, he said, he always had a special place in his heart for the German working class . . .

There were a lot of amusing stories around the left in those days. Tom Condit tells about going as a delegate of the Young Socialist League to a meeting to plan the 1958 May Day rally. There were people there from all the different factions, and these old guys from the Jewish organizations were getting up and making speeches in Yiddish. Things were dragging on and on, and at one point the chairman got up to say, "I must ask the comrades not to repeat what has already been said." So Dick Gilpin sticks up his hand and says, "Excuse me, comrade chair, but what *has* already been said?" It was a fair question, so the chair ruled that from now on everyone must speak in English. The next guy who got up was another of these old characters, a guy named Seymour, who was a Socialist Party right-winger but also a hard sectarian who hated the Democrats and had no truck with mushy stuff. He began speaking in Yiddish, and the chair banged his gavel and said, "I must remind you that we just agreed to speak in English." So Seymour says, "I am going to speak in English. This is the preamble."

Among the older members of the league, the ones I remember best are Sam and Esther Dolgoff, both very forceful characters. (At the time we knew Sam as Sam Weiner, which was his alias in the movement. Esther went by their married name, but they pretended that they were just living together, because they were very hard-line anarchists and ashamed to have gone through an official marriage ceremony.) Sam was a house painter who had taught himself six languages so that he could do translations from the anarchist press around the world. Esther had known Emma Goldman, and the story was that she had been arrested trying to smuggle Emma back into the United States, coming across the border from Canada. They had two children, Abe, short for Abraham Lincoln Brigade Dolgoff, and Dets, short for Buenaventura Durruti Dolgoff. (Durruti was a leader of the Spanish Anarchists.)

Sam was something of a mentor to me, and would give me long lectures about the history of anarchism. He also presented me with a big, black, wide-brimmed fedora that had belonged to Carlo Tresca, the Italian American anarchist who had been assassinated in New York in the early 1940s, which I wore with great pride for several years. Unfortunately, Sam and I had a bitter falling-out over an attempt by some of us to build an alliance with the ACTU, the Association of Catholic Trade Unionists. At that time, there was a whole slew of unions in New York that were more or less run by the mob and did nothing for their members; they existed for the sole purpose of signing contracts with the bosses. The ACTU people were starting a program to organize the Puerto Rican membership of the gangster unions, and some of us thought we should get involved, but Sam vehemently objected to us having anything to do with any Catholic organization, because he was a firm anticlerical. It did not even occur to him—or to us at the time, since we were all hard-core sectarians and hated the Communists like poison—that the real reason not to work with the ACTU was its role in the Red-baiting attack that had destroyed the core of industrial unionism in the United States.

In any case, Sam hit the ceiling, and he blamed me for the whole thing. He considered me the Judas Iscariot of the anarchist movement, and he would get shit-faced drunk and come into meetings and curse me up hill and down dale. It got incredibly abusive, and there were several times when I had to be physically restrained—all in all, a very ugly situation, which hurt both of us. I remember one night he had just finished denouncing me as a tool of the Vatican or something like that, and he sat down, and then he staggered to his feet and shouted, "And furthermore, I want that fucking hat back!"

Sam and I finally managed a sort of reconciliation, but only after several years of not speaking to each other. When Terri and I got married in 1961, I called Esther on I forget what pretext, and she asked us to come by. They were living in Co-op Village, on the Lower East Side, so we went over there and Sam gave me a book of posters by Sin, the watercolorist from the Spanish Civil War. Peace was made, but things were never the same. He was getting more and more bitter as he got older, and the liquor wasn't helping any, besides which by that time I was becoming involved with the Trotskyists—but that's another story.

The politics and the music overlapped in a lot of ways, not all of which have been understood by people who have written about the history of the folk scene. For example, some writers have concluded that those of us who chose not to sing political songs did so because we were apolitical. It is true that in some cases this choice was a reaction to the previous generation and their political affiliations, but for many of us it was a purely aesthetic decision. For myself, I was always ready to go to a rally or a demonstration or a benefit for this, that, or the other cause, and to sing my songs, but I did very little political material. It did not suit my style, and I never felt that I did it convincingly. I just did not have that kind of voice or that kind of presence. Also, although I am a singer and have always had strong political views, I felt that my politics were no more relevant to my music than they would have been to the work of any other craftsman. Just because you are a cabinetmaker and a leftist, are you supposed to make left-wing cabinets?

That said, a great many of us drew a particularly strong distinction between ourselves and the Stalinist singers. The left was so miniscule at this point that you knew pretty much who everybody was and what their politics were, and there was a very clear split between the singers who were associated with the LYL and those who were not. The nonpoliticals and the non-Communist leftists tended to coalesce, by and large, the exception being Hashomer Hatzair the Zionist youth group, which was a big element at that time and tended more towards the LYL-ers.

Overall, the CP was still the dominant influence on leftist politics. In terms of membership, it was probably bigger than everybody else combined, from the Social Democrats all the way over to the anarchists. But it was also extremely vulnerable. The Communists had been slapped silly during the witch hunt, and in that three-year period from the time of the Berlin uprising through to the time of the Hungarian Revolution, more and more of the dirt from the Kremlin was being exposed. In a way, I almost sympathized with them. I mean, put yourself in their shoes: here you are, you've spent thirty or forty years of your life peddling poison that you thought was candy—think what that can do to somebody's head. On the other hand, we could see what was happening in Eastern Europe, and many of us had also had our share of run-ins with authoritarian, Stalinist die-hards in one group or another, and we knew them for the assholes they were. We of the non-Communist left, whether we were revolutionary socialists or anarchists or whatever the hell we were calling ourselves that week, felt that, as Trotsky once said, between ourselves and the Stalinists there was a river of blood. So even though we had a certain admiration for the singers who had stood up to the Red hunters, when you got right down to it we wanted very little to do with them.*

Of course, there were some issues on which we and the Communists formed common cause. We all opposed the blacklist, for example. But even there, our situations were quite different. The singers who had made a name for themselves in the 1940s had national reputations and careers as nightclub and concert artists, and the blacklist was a direct threat to their livelihoods. Pete Seeger had been cited for contempt of Congress and had a sentence of I don't know what hanging over his head. So that generation was very hard beset and very scared. If the American Legion got word of a performance by someone who had been cited as a Communist or a Communist sympathizer in *Red Channels* or some other blacklisting publication—and a lot of people

---

*I still go back and forth on this issue: sometimes I think we were right to distance ourselves from the CP when and wherever possible, and sometimes I think we were a bunch of McCarthyite leftists and, given the situation, we should have been supporting those Stalinist swine right up and down the pike.

got cited who had only the vaguest left-wing tendencies—there might very well be a picket line of legionnaires out in front of the place. If it was a nightclub, that sort of publicity could shut the place down, since even if they only booked that performer for a week, people would remember the pickets and be nervous about being seen there. If some group tried to rent a hall for a Pete Seeger concert in Akron, Ohio, or someplace like that, whoever owned the hall was likely to get a phone call saying, "Did you know that you're renting your hall to the Communist blah, blah, blah?" and all of a sudden the deposit would be returned. That kind of harassment was going on all the time, both from government agencies and from self-appointed vigilantes.

Those of us in the younger generation, though, had essentially nothing to lose. We didn't have to worry about somebody pulling a concert hall out from under us, because no one in his right mind would have put us in a concert hall in the first place. We opposed the blacklist for ideological reasons, but it had no effect on our musical careers, because we had no musical careers. So in a sense, the justifiable paranoia that was common in some sectors of the folk music field in the 1950s left us pretty much untouched. In the long run, that was a good thing because it meant we were not cowed. Some of the older performers—Josh White, for example—got to feeling, "Once burned, twice careful," and tended to shy away from anything that might be construed as political. We were very open about our radicalism, and when the Civil Rights Movement and the antiwar movement came along in the 1960s, we jumped in with both feet. Had we gone through what the older generation went through in the 1950s, I wonder if we would have been quite so gung ho. But I am getting ahead of myself.

4

Washington Square and Beyond

By 1956 or so, I had worked out the basics of fingerpicking and become a regular at Washington Square. That was the golden age for that particular scene, because a whole new generation of us was coming in but it had not yet gotten so big that it was out of hand.

The regular Sunday musical get-togethers had actually started sometime in the mid-1940s when a few friends took to meeting in the park for loose song sessions. These had grown until the police began taking notice and there were all sorts of arguments, leading eventually to an inner core of musicians arranging to get regular permits. Naturally, a lot of us despised the idea of needing an official permit, but it did have one advantage: the rule was that everyone was allowed to sing and play from two until five as long as they had no drums, and that kept out the bongo players. The Village had bongo players up the wazoo, and they would have loved to sit in, and we hated them. So that was some consolation.

When I first made my appearance on that scene, the permit holder was Lionel Kilberg, who played a homemade "brownie bass" with the string band crowd. Lionel was already considered an old-timer, along with Roger Sprung, whom he played with in a trio called the Shanty Boys. (The third member was Mike Cohen, brother of John Cohen of New Lost City Ramblers fame.) As for the other veteran regulars, an article Barry Kornfeld wrote for *Caravan* magazine gives a pretty good idea, though as I recall, a few of the names were gone by my time: Bob Claiborne, Tom Paley, Ray Boguslav, "Prof" Joe Jaffe, Stan Atlas, Rod Hill, Dick Rosmini, Erik Darling, Jean and Joe Silverstein, Ed Jancke, and on occasion, Pete Seeger. I do not remember Pete coming around, but I saw Woody Guthrie there a couple of times—I understand that it was John Cohen who brought him down. By that time, though, he was in very poor shape. He could still play a little, and we were introduced, but speech was coming very hard to him and it was impossible to communicate or strike up any kind of rapport.

As a general thing, there would be six or seven different groups of musicians, most of them over near the arch and the fountain. The Zionists were the most visible, because they had to stake out a large enough area for the dancers, and they would be over by the Sullivan Street side of the square, singing "Hava Nagilah."* Then there would be the LYL-ers, the Stalinists: someone like Jerry Silverman would be playing guitar, surrounded by all these summer camp kids of the People's Songs persuasion, and they would be singing old union songs and things they had picked up from *Sing Out!* Sometimes they would have a hundred people, all singing "Hold the Fort," and quite a lot of them knew how to sing harmony, so it actually could sound pretty good. Very few of those people stayed around for more than a year or two, though. Most of them came down because they belonged to these various youth groups, and when they dropped out of the youth groups, they dropped out of the music.

The bluegrassers would be off in another area, led by Roger Sprung, the original citybilly. As far as I know, Roger single-handedly brought Scruggs picking to the city—not just to New York but to any city. Lionel Kilberg would be playing bass, and there would be a little group around them that gradually grew to include a lot of people who would go on to spearhead the bluegrass and old-time string band revivals.

Then there were various people singing ballads and blues, and we would split into a number of smaller circles around whoever felt like singing. The individual singers varied over the years, but they might include me, Dick Rosmini, Barry Kornfeld, Luke Faust, Jerry Levine, Happy Traum, Paul Clayton, Gina Glaser, Roy Berkeley, Roger Abra-

*Have another nagilah. Have two nagilahs, they're small.

hams . . . The ballad singers and the blues people tended to hang around together, because there were not many of either, comparatively speaking, so we banded together for mutual support. We did not make as much noise as the other groups, and we hated them all—the Zionists, the LYL-ers, and the bluegrassers—every last, dead one of them. Of course, we hated a lot of people in those days.

Those were roughly the divisions, though different people might have developed slightly different taxonomies: Paul Clayton at one point decided that the whole movement could be divided into two essential tendencies, which he called bluegrass and greensleeves. He included the blues singers among the greensleevers, and if one leaves out the political singers, that was about how I saw it, as well. Which is not to say that the greensleevers did not have politics—some did, some did not—but there was a consensus among us that using folk music for political ends was distasteful and insult-ing to the music.

That Washington Square Sunday afternoon scene was a great catalyst for my whole generation. It kept getting bigger and bigger every year, and by the late 1950s it had become a tourist attraction as well. That was kind of a drag, on one hand, but on the other it meant that we had an audience, which was good for those of us who were, in effect, learning our craft. If you were a soloist, you would just sit down—at least I always sat—and start to play, and people would gather around. You would stake out your own little bit of private turf, where you would not have to sing "Hey Lolly Lolly" with a bunch of people, and then you would keep singing for as long as you could hold an audience. Just as in the jazz world, I had an advantage because of my volume—whether or not I was any good, I could always make myself heard—so I usually had a pretty good crowd around me. In-cidentally, there was no money involved in any of this. I never saw anybody pass the hat or collect a cent in Washington Square Park. Some of us could have used the extra money, but most of the singers were still living at home and did not really need it, and in any case it simply was not done.

As with my migration to the Village, or my involvement in trad jazz, my assimilation into the Washington Square scene happened over a period of time and there was never any clear break between that and what I had been doing before. In fact, a great part of what attracted me to the folk scene was that I could hear the tie between what some of those people were doing and the music that I was already playing. There had been a good deal of inter-action between jazz and some of the older folk styles, at least during its first twenty or thirty years, which was the period that most attracted me at that time. When Bessie Smith sang something like "Backwater Blues," was it jazz or folk music? I would hate to have to answer that question, because there simply is no clear distinction, no firm line dividing the two.

When I heard Leadbelly, I immediately fit him into the music that was already familiar to me. Except for the fact that he sang over his own guitar rather than a band, there was not that much difference between his singing and what I was hearing on a lot of trad records. So for a while I developed a huge crush on Leadbelly, singing a bunch of his numbers and doing them as closely as I could to the way he did them. Josh White was another one. I probably started to listen to Josh when I was still living in Queens, because he was the big star at that point, and to this day when I listen to a tape of myself, I can occasionally hear some of Josh.

Because of those links, blues was my original door into the folk world, but I was never really a blues singer, in the sense of devoting myself exclu-sively to that. I never stopped doing jazz material, and I also picked up all sorts of other stuff in one place and another. I still have some tapes I recorded in the mid-1950s, and they include songs like "If You Miss Me Here, You Can Find Me at the Greasy Spoon," an old vaudeville thing that I learned off a record by Coot Grant and Kid Wilson. Now, that is material you did not hear every day, but I had a lot of stuff like that, as well as dozens of Bessie Smith tunes, and I found that with a little work I could fit all of it into the fingerpicking and country blues format. So I had a unique repertoire, and I think that gave me something of a jump start compared with the people who had gotten involved entirely through the folk scene.

Of course, I also got a lot from the folk crowd. While I never thought of myself as a folksinger, I would harmonize along with whoever was singing, and I learned a lot of those songs just through osmosis. Later on, when I started to perform regularly, I used some of that material, too, because I would have been crazy not to. One thing I need to emphasize is that the folk scene at that point was a lot more varied than it became later on. We were a small enough group that the bluegrass players knew the flamenco guitarists, the flamenco people knew the blues singers, the blues singers knew the ballad scholars, and all of us knew the Irish musicians. And there was a great deal of cross-pollination. For example, during that period I acquired a little knowledge of flamenco singing and guitar playing, I developed a decent repertoire of Child ballads, and I even learned parts from Dowland's *Airs for Four Voices*. We were all hanging out together, and if you were any kind of musician, you couldn't find enough hands to pick all the pockets that were available. So I ended up with a very broad musical base, without even thinking about it, simply because of the range of people I was associating with. And while I did not continue to play much of that material, a lot of it was adapted and incorporated into other things I did, and I am musically much the better for it.*

Later on, when the scene got bigger, the niches became more specialized and the different groups didn't mix as much, which was a real pity. The musical world became segregated, and today people no longer get that broad range of influences. There is also this constant pursuit of the new, the search for the next big thing, which is very limiting. It's like, if you want to be a painter—I don't care if you want to be a representational realist or an op artist—you still go back and study the old masters. You look at Correggio, you check out Titian and Rembrandt. A while ago, I went to a retrospective show of Arshile Gorky, the early abstract expressionist, and it starts out with Gorky when he's fourteen doing Cezanne, and then there's Gorky at age sixteen doing Picasso, and so on. Eventually, you get to the later works, and there is Gorky doing, by God, Arshile Gorky. But if you begin there, you miss the opportunity to profit from the experience Gorky acquired. And it's the same with music, whether it's me or Dylan or a jazz trumpeter. You have to start somewhere, and the broader your base, the more options you have.

For a while there, we were all learning from each other, and there was relatively little recorded music coming into the mix. What with the blacklist, the folk record business had slowed way down in the early 1950s, and anyway, my crowd did not have much interest in the sort of folk music that

---

*There were also some serious academic folklorists on that scene, people like Roger Abrahams and Ellen Steckert who were en route to their doctorates, and that created yet another sort of cross-fertilization: the folklorists would also perform, and for a while it was de rigueur for everyone to present their material with long, scholarly introductions. You had to explain the song before you could sing it— the song itself was an anticlimax. Some of the Cambridge crowd were still doing that in the 1960s, but after a while even they realized how deadly it was.

would have been recorded at that point. That whole thing with the Weavers and the cabaret folksingers—Cynthia Gooding, Susan Reed, Richard Dyer-Bennett, Theo Bikel, Oscar Brand—we might see some of those people occasionally, and often got along with them quite well personally, but their approach to the music did not interest us at all. It was obviously related to the "art song" tradition, very genteel and refined, which to us was the antithesis of everything that true folk music should be. It always used to tickle me to see Richard Dyer-Bennett sing "John Henry" in a tuxedo, or someone get up in an evening gown and perform an Appalachian ballad. We considered all of that slick and fake. Of course, to a great extent, it was a generational thing: we thought of them as the old wave and conceived of ourselves as an opposition, as is the way of young Turks in every time and place.*

We were severely limited, however, because much as we might consider ourselves devotees of the true, pure folk styles, there was very little of that music available. Then a marvelous thing happened. Around 1953 Folkways Records put out a six-LP set called the *Anthology of American Folk Music,* culled from commercial recordings of traditional rural musicians that had been made in the South during the 1920s and '30s. The *Anthology* was created by a man named Harry Smith, who was a beatnik eccentric artist, an experimental filmmaker, and a disciple of Aleister Crowley. (When he died in the 1990s, his fellow Satanists held a memorial black mass for him, complete with a virgin on the altar.) Harry had a fantastic collection of 78s, and his idea was to provide an overview of the range of styles being played in rural America at the dawn of recording. That set became our bible. It is how most of us first heard Blind Willie Johnson, Mississippi John Hurt, and even Blind Lemon Jefferson. And it was not just blues people, by any means. It had ballad singers, square-dance fiddling, gospel congregations. It was an incredible compendium of American traditional musics, all performed in the traditional styles. That was very important for my generation, especially those of us I consider the "neo-ethnics," because we were trying not only to

---

*In this context I must also mention John Jacob Niles, one of the key people in the American folk revival going back to the 1920s, a marvelous singer, and a truly memorable character. There are a few things that make me glad I'm old, and one of them is that I saw John Jacob Niles perform "Hangman, Slack Your Rope," running around the stage with his dulcimer and playing all the roles. It was gorgeously awful.

sing traditional songs but also to assimilate the styles of the rural players. Without the Harry Smith *Anthology* we could not have existed, because there was no other way for us to get hold of that material.

We did not all like everything on those records; some of it was terrible. But it was all important to us, simply because it showed us what was out there and how it really sounded. For almost the first time, it gave us a sense of what traditional music in the United States was all about, from the source rather than from second- and thirdhand interpreters. The *Anthology* had eighty-two cuts on it, and after a while we all knew every word of every song, including the ones we hated. They say that in the nineteenth-century British Parliament, when a member would begin to quote a classical author in Latin, the entire House would rise in a body and finish the quote along with him. It was like that. The *Anthology* provided us with a classical education that we all shared in common, whatever our personal differences. And it also started the whole reissue business—pretty soon Folkways had out an album of Uncle Dave Macon, one of Blind Willie Johnson, and then other labels picked up the ball.

Once again I have to stress that none of us was just listening to blues, or just listening to old-time music. Someone would go off to Mexico or Greece and come back with a few new songs, or someone would stumble across an album of African cabaret music and learn a couple of tunes—that's where I picked up one of my favorites, a Liberian song called "Chicken Is Nice." And all of this was going into the same meat grinder. The one limiting factor was the insistence on "authenticity," on reproducing the traditional ethnic styles, all the way down to getting the accents right. It did not matter if you were ethnic à la Furry Lewis, or à la Jimmie Rodgers, or à la Earl Scruggs; that was a matter of personal taste. But that it should be authentically ethnic was a matter of principle.

As an erstwhile mouldy fig, I was right at home. The neo-ethnics were in exactly the same position vis-à-vis folk music that I had been in jazz—with the key difference that this was a new movement, while in jazz I had arrived too late to get in on the excitement. With the benefit of hindsight I can see that we were making a lot of the same mistakes, but we also gained some of the same benefits. When you listen to the early New Orleans revivalists, people like Lu Watters and the other West Coast players, they were trying to recreate the music of the teens and twenties, but what actually happened was that they unwittingly created a new kind of music. It was not the music they set out to make in the first place, but it stands on its own merits, not on whether or not it is an accurate reflection of King Oliver and the Creole Jazz Band. And that is a good thing, because King Oliver's music had already been made. Now, the same thing was happening with us on the folk scene. I was taking these old records as my models, but what was really happening—though I might well have denied this at the time—was that I was developing a style and approach that was quite different from what I was hearing. Even when I tried to sound exactly like Leadbelly, I could not do it, so I ended up sounding like Dave Van Ronk. And that process was happening to a lot of us, just by playing the music, listening to each other, and finding out what worked for us and what didn't.

Of course, all of this was not just happening at Washington Square. There was a constant round of parties, jam sessions, song swapping, and hootenannies. The interest was obsessive, to the point that for a while there, except for my political friends, I did not associate with anyone who was not involved in folk music in one way or another. That kind of passionate attention pays off, in terms of being able to learn songs, play, sing, or whatever one needs to do. I was learning more music, and learning it faster, than I have ever done before or since.

The most regular venue for our get-togethers was a coffeehouse on MacDougal Street called the Caricature. This was not like the later coffeehouses that would emerge on that block, in that it was by no means a performance space. It was a tiny place, with an even tinier back room where we were permitted—permitted, mind you—to pick and sing, as long as we did not disturb the marathon bridge games out front. It was a snug, I suppose you would call it, with just room enough for two tables and some benches. The owner was a woman named Liz, and she had the patience of a saint. She would be out there trying to play bridge, with all of us flailing and wailing in the background, and just once in a while she would come back and say, "We've got a very, very difficult rubber going. Could you keep it down a little bit?" She did like the music, though she rarely commented on it, and she was very good to us. If it had not been for her cheeseburgers on the cuff, I probably would have died. She made great cheeseburgers, and the free ones were the biggest and the best. She was altogether a great lady, although she also could be tough when she had to be.

She ran me out once or twice, and I remember her running other people out as well.

As best I can recall, the person who brought me down to the Caricature was Roy Berkeley, the Traveling Trotskyist Troubadour. At that time, Roy was hanging out with the Shachtmanites, another fringe-left group, and I was with the anarchists, and the Shachtmanites were among the only people who would talk to us. He was also one of the central figures over at the Caricature, and there were several people who started to hang out there because they were drawn to the Shachtmanites, for whatever reason, and then followed Roy down to the scene. As usual, it was a constantly shifting crew, but some of the regulars in that circle whom I have not mentioned up to now would have been Pete Goldsmith, Paul Schoenwetter, Perry Lederman, Curly Baird, Marty Jukovsky, Dorothy Carter, Bruce Langhorne, and Dave Woods. Dave was a big influence on me, because he was a real musician, a jazz guitarist who had studied with Lennie Tristano and did some country blues picking for his own amusement. He knew theory, knew how all the chords worked and how to build an arrangement, and he was only too happy to show me or anyone else who asked. I latched onto him, and it was like having coffee with Einstein a few times a week.

Quite a few of the regulars did not play but just enjoyed hanging out and listening to the music. There was Roland Dumontet, for example, who was something of a Mack the Knife character—God knows what all he was mixed up in. He was part of the motorcycle crowd, and always got the best-looking women. Women did not say Roland's name, they swooned it. He was just perfectly creepy, with one drooping eyelid and an air of lurking menace. (Which is as good a moment as any to mention that one of the advantages of both anarchism and folk music was the number of young women who seemed to be attracted to the scene. Some were singers, but a lot just hung out on the fringes, and the anarchists were all deeply committed to the principle of "free love." The Caricature drew a bunch of girls from Music and Performing Arts High, and there were pregnancy scares at least twice a month—some girl would come rushing in, grab another by the arm and drag her outside for a consultation.)

Weekends were the big party nights, especially since a lot of the musicians were still living over in Queens or Jersey. We would start partying on Friday, and it would all kind of build to Sunday. On Sunday we would crawl out of bed sometime after noon and make our way over to Washington Square. We would play there until five o'clock, when the permit ran out, and then we would grab a bite to eat at Mother Hubbard's or a place on 8th Avenue that we called "the secret deli" because it had a back room that could not be seen from the front room. Then we would shoulder our guitars again and head over to the American Youth Hostels building on 8th Street, where the old Whitney Museum used to be. Mike Cohen had a job with the AYH, and arranged for them to host a regular hootenanny every Sunday from seven to nine. Mike ran it some of the time, and then Barry Kornfeld took it over. So we would spend a couple of hours there, and then all of us would troop down to 190 Spring Street, in what is now SoHo, where the real party would begin. Roger Abrahams, who would later become a prominent folklorist, had an apartment there, and after a while some other people moved in and it became a sort of rat's nest of folk singers. (I also remember a Peruvian guy named Inti, who was living there with a pet monkey. God, I hated that monkey.) On Sunday nights we would be distributed through two or three floors. One apartment would be all blue-grassers—the shit-kicker ghetto—and then there would be rooms full of blues singers and ballad people, usually taking turns and trading off with the same guitar. The rooms were small and ill lit, very crowded, and insufferably stuffy, and the music would go on until four or five o'clock in the morning.

Those Spring Street parties led directly to the opening of the first Village folk music venue, and the beginning of my professional career, but before I get to that I must make a brief digression.

Much as I loved playing music, it was not earning me a penny. The jazz gigs had dried up and no one was hiring blues howlers from Brooklyn. At this point I was mostly crashing at what we called the Diogenes Club, named for the place where Mycroft Holmes held court in the Conan Doyle stories. A bunch of us from Richmond Hill had chipped in $5 a month each to rent a loft at 350 Bowery, between 3rd and 4th, so we would have a place to hold parties, bring girls, or to crash if we got stuck in Manhattan. We had all brought our record collections and pooled them into a sort of common library; we had a rule at that time that no one was supposed to buy a record that anyone else had bought, thereby maximizing our group purchasing power. Since this was common space, nobody was supposed to actually live there, but of course a number of us did, particularly me and one of my political buddies, Lenny Glaser. No one cared much, and people like my jazz pals Danny Frueh and Eddie Kaplan were happy that there was somebody around regularly who could keep an eye on their record collections, since after a while, there were a lot of people with keys, and stuff began to get ripped off. So I crashed there, or over at the Libertarian League hall, or with one or another girlfriend.

I was managing to keep body and soul together, but it was pretty lean pickings, and eventually I decided that I needed a real job. Since I was itching to see a little more of the world, my solution was to ship out with the merchant marine. Mitch Mitchell, whom I knew from the Libertarians, was a member of the Masters, Mates, and Pilots Union, and he pulled some strings for me and got me my papers. For a week or two I had to get up at eight-thirty every goddamn morning and go down to the union hall in Brooklyn and throw in my card. Eventually I got a berth on a tanker, and over the next year or so I shipped out twice, once to New Orleans and once to Wilmington, California.

I liked that life a lot, though it had some disadvantages from a musical standpoint. I was a messman, and I had brought a guitar on board, an old Gretsch. One night I was standing my watch, and some big seas came up and I could not get down to my cabin in the fo'c'sle to close the port. When my watch finally ended, I went down and there was my guitar, gently bobbing up and down in several inches of water. I wiped it off as best I could, but as it dried out, the back just peeled up like a window shade. So I had to get another guitar, which I did in New Orleans. I was walking down the street and saw this beautiful Gibson J-45 in the window of a secondhand shop. I had planned to sign off the ship and spend a couple of months there, soaking up what was left of the jazz scene, but I had to have that guitar and it cost $150, which was more than I had saved up. So I got hold of the radio operator and borrowed a couple of hundred from him, and then I had to sign back on the ship to pay him back.

That period in the merchant marine was the most regular work I ever did, and also my first chance to do any real traveling. Except for that summer in Shaker Heights and a couple of times when a radical companion and I hitched out to Chicago for one reason or another, I had never been out of the New York area. It was all new to me, and I have believed ever since that the best way to see a town for the first time is to come in on a ship. I will never forget my arrival in San Francisco: we came in through a huge fog bank, and suddenly there was a cutoff, just as if somebody had drawn a line in ink, and the sky was completely clear, and looming up over us was the Golden Gate Bridge. As an introduction to San Francisco, you just cannot beat that.*

We docked across the bay in Richmond, but I had a little time off, so I took my duffel bag and my recently acquired Gibson and got a lift over the Bay Bridge into San Francisco. Walking up the Embarcadero, I passed a saloon where a traditional jazz band was playing "Ace in the Hole," a song I had never heard before but that became one of my favorites. I went in and introduced myself to the band. I had just picked up my pay, so I was relatively solvent. Not for long, though. In one wonderful afternoon they introduced me to the mysteries of steam beer and poker dice, and I remember very little else.

That was my second trip, and it kept me out of New York for almost six months. Now, the great advantage of seafaring as a profession is that if you steer clear of the poker tables or if you're lucky at cards, you accumulate lots of cash. I have always had the card luck of Wild Bill Hickok, so in self-defense I started up a small blackjack game in the crew mess room—the point being that if you play by Las Vegas rules and have enough capital to ride out the occasional bad night, the dealer simply cannot lose. On the home journey, I made out like a bandit, and I paid off the S.S. *Texan* with $1,500 and a six-ounce jar of Dexedrine pills provided in lieu of a gambling debt, not to mention a half kilo of reefer scored off a Panamanian donkey-man for $20 while trundling through the Canal. In short, I was loaded for bear.

Coming back from a long stint at sea is a kind of Rip Van Winkle experience. Old friends have left town, old girlfriends have new boyfriends—it is all familiar places and strange faces. Most seamen deal with this situation by taking another ship, which only makes the problem worse the next time they come home. Before you know it, shipmates are calling you "last-

---

*I must note that my pleasure was somewhat soured by the fact that the bridge is painted with industrial red lead rust-proofing paint. Sailors, for reasons of excessive familiarity, loathe red lead. I have never understood why they don't gild the damn thing.

tripper" or "chicken farmer"—as in "Boys, this is my last trip; this time I'm gonna save my money and buy me a nice little chicken farm in Georgia." It's a trap.

After a few days of aimlessly banging about the Village, spending money like a drunken sailor (apt metaphor, that), I decided that I had no place here anymore, that there was a big world waiting for me, and that as soon as my money ran low, I would ship out again. After all, what kind of future could I expect from music? I had been hacking away at it for three years, and all I had to show for my trouble was a taste for Irish whiskey and a borderline case of malnutrition. What's more, I really liked the sea. The work was hard, but I got a kind of masochistic satisfaction from being able to cut it— besides which, it was actually a healthy way of making a living, something I had never dreamed existed. Obviously, I did not want to spend my life working in the mess, chipping rust, and painting on layers of red lead, but I was sure that I could move up pretty quickly and was already dreaming of becoming first mate. The money was good, and I liked the men I worked with and the sleazy gin mills in the sleazy refinery ports where we blew our paychecks. In short, I was hooked.

Even if I had still been intent on a musical career, it was obvious at that point that folk music was not a serious option. I was not about to jettison all my hard-earned prejudices, and in any case I could never have made it as a slick cabaret artist à la Josh White or Theo Bikel. And for us neo-ethnics, there simply was no place that wanted us onstage. Not a single venue in all the greater New York area.

Nonetheless, when Sunday afternoon rolled around, force of habit took me to Washington Square. Force of habit, hell—I couldn't wait to get there, in my bell-bottom dungarees and Lundeberg Stetson from the ship's slop chest, brown as a nut and hard as a nail. I was looking forward to pulling rank on my middle-class folkie friends.

My reception was the very model of Village cool: "Oh, hi. You've been away?" There was a lot of excitement in our small circle of balladeers manqué, but it had nothing to do with the return of Ishmael from the seven seas. Rick Allmen, who was the landlord at 190 Spring Street, had taken note of all the folksingers hanging out there—probably while desperately trying to collect his rent—and he was opening a coffeehouse in a big old garage on 3rd Street that supposedly had once been Aaron Burr's stable. As the troops explained: "We're sort of helping him fix it up, laying down a cement floor and painting and like that. He's going to feature folk music, and we'll have a place to play."

"Wrong," I said. "Fattening frogs for snakes," I said. "The only time you'll get on that stage is when you build it," I said. But for once my knee-jerk skepticism failed me. From time to time I would drop by the site and there they would be, troweling, whitewashing, hammering, and sawing. I had to admit that it was starting to look pretty good, but I still didn't believe there would ever be a payoff. Then the job was done, and good as his word, Rick offered a spot in the opening night's show to any of the crew who was interested. He even extended the offer to me. Of course, payment was another matter. If the club took off, there would be plenty of money for everybody, but in the meantime it would have to be on spec. "It's a con," I said. "Not one of us will ever see a nickel out of this . . ." and I immediately accepted. What the hell—it took a long time to spend fifteen hundred bucks in those days.

The Café Bizarre, which was what Allmen called his room, was the first Village coffeehouse to feature folk music—or any formal entertainment at all for that matter—and it became a howling success that shortly begat clones all over the country. In concept and design, it was a tourist trap, selling the clydes (customers) a Greenwich Village that had never existed except in the film *Bell, Book and Candle*. The ambiance was cut-rate Charles Addams haunted house: dark and candlelit, with fake cobwebs hanging all over everything. The waitresses were got up to look like Morticia, with fishnet stockings, long straight hair, and so much mascara that they looked like raccoons. I swear I even saw some poor clown in a Frankenstein outfit wandering around the set.*

The Bizarre opened to the public on August 18, 1957, and the entertainment was no slapdash affair. There was a real stage, a sound system, a light script, a suitably spooky MC, and we even had a director: Logan English. Poor Logie had recently graduated from the University of Kentucky as a drama major and was a fine, if somewhat mellifluous, folk singer. His

---

*I have never understood why the rubes insist on equating the Village with *Tales from the Crypt*. Maybe they figure, "Bela Lugosi is weird, Greenwich Village is weird, therefore . . ."—a neat suburban syllogism. But the phenomenon persists to this day. I have for years lived less than a block from the Jack the Ripper Pub and the Slaughtered Lamb, which has a werewolf motif. I guess burbies are just weird.

problem was that he took his job seriously. More to the point, his problem was us. We thought all of his elaborate stagecraft was a crock of shit, and took sadistic delight in deliberately missing our cues, tripping over the furniture, and provoking him into screaming fits of rage. We couldn't help ourselves; he was so funny when he blew up.

In fact, the Café Bizarre and the rigid formalism of the show were such flatulent frauds that we might have walked out in a body had it not been for the fact that the opening night headliner was to be Odetta. We had heard the *Odetta and Larry at the Tin Angel* album, and by then I think I had her first solo album as well, and she had made an incredible impression on us. Her presence lent the program an artistic legitimacy that—at least to our way of thinking—no other performer could have done, except perhaps Pete Seeger.

I am not certain who all was on that bill. The one review I can find mentions me, Logan, Bob Brill, Luke Faust, and Ellen Adler, as well as an unnamed "skiffle" group, but there were certainly other people involved, including Roger Abrahams, Roy Berkeley, and Judy Isquith. We each took a turn, doing four or five songs apiece, with a full set by Odetta to close the show.

My set opened the second half, and I was scared out of my bird from the minute the house lights went down. This was my first experience with the real thing. Damn, it was exciting! I snuck out to stage center in the dark and was "discovered" by a single spotlight a few seconds after I had started my first song. The effect was stunning—at least it stunned the bejesus out of me. I was so dazed and scared and exhilarated that when I came off the stage, I had no recollection of what I had done while I was up there.

I still do not know what I sang or said, but I remember very well what happened immediately afterward. I was shaking like someone who has narrowly missed a fatal car crash, and just as happy, when up came Odetta herself with a great big smile on her face—and she has a smile that could melt diamonds. "That was wonderful," she said. "Do you do this for a living?" I told her, no, I was a merchant seaman on the beach and I meant to ship out again as soon as my money ran low. Well, she said, if I was interested, she could take a tape of mine out to Chicago to Albert Grossman, the owner of the Gate of Horn. Of course, she could not make any promises, but there might be a gig in it for me.

On the face of it, me at the Gate of Horn seemed pretty far-fetched. That was where the big kids played: Josh White, Theo Bikel, Odetta herself. On the other hand, I was a pretty arrogant young dog, so why not? Was I not a vessel of the Great Tradition, a Keeper of the Flame? In any case, I had nothing to lose. I thanked the nice lady profusely and told her I would get a tape to her directly.

With some difficulty, I got a demonstration tape made—tape recorders were expensive, and thus rare in my circle—and a mutual acquaintance volunteered to get it to Odetta before she left for Chicago. I remember thinking the tape was pretty good, and by this time I had convinced myself that within a few short weeks Destiny would summon me to the Windy City and my rightful place as King of the Folkniks. (That word had not yet been coined, but you get the idea.)

My money was still holding out, so I was in no great hurry. The days passed. I was sleeping on couches and floors—no point in getting an apartment, since soon I would be in Chicago surrounded by worshipful acolytes (mostly female) or, barring that, back at sea. Parties almost every night. Songs sung and learned. I worked on my guitar playing. I was drinking a lot. No word from Chicago.

Weeks passed. This was getting downright embarrassing. I had been telling everybody who would listen that Odetta had taken my tape to the Gate of Horn and I would be following it forthwith. I offed the remnants of my half-key of dope to a friend for a hundred bucks, but the end of my money was still visible on the horizon. Chicago remained mute.

Finally, I could stand it no longer. I was almost broke, I was drinking like a fish, and my nerves were stretched like piano wires. This thing had to be settled once and for all. I made up my mind to hitch to Chicago and find out what the hell was going down.

Why didn't I just pick up the phone and call Grossman? And why hitchhike? I had enough money left for a bus or even a train. (It would never have occurred to me to fly out there; I had never been on a plane in my life.) As to the first question, this was far too important a matter to be handled over the phone, and in any case my association with the radical left in those McCarthyite days—not to mention the fringes of the underground drug culture—had given me the firm conviction that all telephones were tapped and thus not to be used for anything but casual chitchat. As to the second, hitchhiking was the way we traveled. We had all read Kerouac, after all. Money would be saved for food and drink.

Hitching to Chicago was easy. You just stuck out your thumb near the entrance of the Holland Tunnel, headed west, and switched to public transportation when you got to the Illinois suburbs. The main problem was sleep. It was about 900 miles and took roughly 24 hours, depending on how many rides you needed to get there. There were some rest stops on the recently completed Ohio Turnpike, but if the cops caught you sleeping, they would roust you, and when they found that you had no car, they would run you in. You could get thirty days for vagrancy, so it was a good idea to stay awake.

I girded my loins with a huge meal at the Sagamore Cafeteria and set out with high hopes, my Gibson, a spare shirt and some clean underwear in a shopping bag, and fifty bucks or so in my pocket. For good measure, I brought along a handful of Dexedrine pills to keep the sandman at bay and for the edification of the fine fellows who were going to pick me up. I think they were already illegal then, but I had never heard of anyone being busted for them.

I got lucky with my first lift in New Jersey: a trucker going all the way to Akron. I gave him a couple of Dexies and took a couple myself, just to be sociable, and before I knew it we were pushing that semi 85 miles an hour down the Pennsy Turnpike, babbling at each other like happy lunatics. It was like that all the way, one long ride after another, right to the outskirts of Chi.

I took a bus to the Loop and taxied from there to the near North Side and the Gate of Horn. The whole trip had taken about 22 hours—great time—and I was still wide awake. In fact, I was jazzed out of my skull. It was midafternoon. I was unannounced and unexpected. There was nothing for it but to try the door and, if no one was home, wait until somebody came to open up. The door was open, so I stepped inside.

The room had that seedy, impermanent look that all nightclubs have when the house lights are on. The staff was taking chairs down from the tables and setting up for the night. At the bar, a heavy-set man with graying hair, in a too-tight suit was talking to another guy. The stage was unlit and empty. I figured that tight-suit was in charge, so I walked up to him: "Excuse me, but are you Albert Grossman?"

He wore glasses and had a blank, unblinking gaze. "Yes," he said. "What can I do for you?"

"I did a show with Odetta a few weeks ago and she brought you a demo tape of mine. I'm Dave Van Ronk."

A gray voice, no inflection at all: "I never got a tape of yours from Odetta."

Suddenly I wasn't high anymore, just tired. I was on my own in a strange city, and the vibes were spooking me plenty. (To keep the record straight, I later found out that Odetta had never got the tape in the first place. My intermediary had blown it.)

So I told him my sad tale, how I had hitched all the way from New York, blah, blah, blah. He heard me out noncommittally. "Well," he said, "you've come all this way . . . Why not audition right now? There's the stage."

This wasn't going according to my script at all, but maybe I could still pull it out. I got onstage and launched into a set of my biggest flag-wavers: "Tell Old Bill," "Willie the Weeper," "Dink's Song," and suchlike. I could see Albert plainly—the house lights were still on. His face had the studied impassiveness of a very bad poker player with a very good hand. All around me chairs and tables scraped and thumped, glasses and silverware clinked and rattled, but I forged on. This was D-Day, goddamnit, and I was showing this hypercool Chicago hick how we did it in Washington Square.

I'm afraid that's just what I did.

When I got off, Albert still had not batted an eyelash. "Do you know who works here?" he asked. "Big Bill Broonzy works here. Josh White works here. Brownie McGhee and Sonny Terry play here a lot. Now tell me," he went on, "why should I hire you?"

I could have killed him on the spot, but I contented myself with screaming in his face, "Grossman, you son of a bitch, you're Crow-Jimming me!"

Back out on the street, where I belonged, I made some quick decisions. I had planned to call some friends on the South Side and hang around Chicago for a few days, but I was so bummed out that all I could think of was getting back on the road and holing up in New York until I could find me another ship—Tasmania or Tierra del Fuego sounded about right. A life on the rolling waves was beginning to look good again.

My first ride going east was with a bunch of young guys who were doing some serious partying. A jug of bourbon was being passed around, and I gratefully took my turn when it got to me. Just what I needed—a few belts of that rotgut and I crashed like the Hindenburg. The next thing I knew, someone was shaking me awake: "Hey, we're getting off the thruway; you'll have to get out here." Groggily, I grabbed my guitar (I had almost given it to a wino back in Chi) and got out of the car somewhere in Indiana.

There I stood, half loaded and half hungover, coming down off speed in the middle of the night, in the middle of nowhere, with my thumb stuck out like a gooney bird's beak. I stuck my other hand in my pocket—it was chilly—and, sure enough, my wallet was gone. It was a perfect moment.

Now this is the hook: it wasn't the thirty or so bucks—those would have gone anyway in another few days—but my seaman's papers were in that wallet. The Coast Guard issues those papers and waxes very suspicious when someone reports them missing. It seems they fetch a good price on the black market, and sailors are not always immune to temptation. I would have to testify before some kind of board, and there would have to be an investigation before I could get those papers replaced. It might take six months or a year before I could get a new set and ship out again, or so I had been told when I first got them. Furthermore, with my politics and all my Commie friends, it had been a small miracle that I was given them at all. Hearings and investigations were simply asking for trouble: the powers that be would probably assume I had handed my papers over to some filthy Red who was on the lam from the forces of freedom and righteousness. A big mess all around. I was on the beach permanently.

So that's how I became a folksinger. Like most great career choices, it was a decision by default.

5

The Guild and Caravan

For better or worse, I was going to have to make a living in folk music. The problem was, how? Most of the other musicians on the scene had jobs or were students getting money from their parents. I had never had any regular work aside from my stint in the merchant marine, my family had no money, and I hadn't even finished high school. I had nothing to live on except what I could beg, borrow, steal, or—less frequently—earn as a singer. There were no clubs that would hire me or anyone like me, and no one insane enough to sponsor me for a concert.

For a while, I took to busking, playing for tips in bars. That was something that most of the people I knew refused to get into, but I ran into a guy in Washington Square Park who had a voice that was even louder than mine, a tall black man from Maryland named Andrew. He sounded a lot like Vaughn Monroe, and his specialty was things like "Mule Train" and "Ghost Riders in the Sky." He and I would hit the bars up on 8th Avenue in the 40s, and on a good night we might pick up as much as seventy-five or a hundred bucks each, which was incredible for that time. Unfortunately, after a month or two the city started one of its periodic cleanups, and since the bars had no license for live entertainment, the cops started to descend on them. The bartenders would see us coming in, and they would take us aside and say, "If you even take that guitar out of the case, we're gonna have to throw you out." We tried to sing in the streets, but that was no better—the cops moved us along immediately. So that was that. Andrew hopped a freight and I never saw him again.

There were, however, some rays of light on the horizon. As I was walking down MacDougal during those first days back from the sea, I noticed a tiny storefront with a new sign saying "Folklore Center." I thought, "What the hell?" and went right in, and that was when I met Izzy Young, who would be a key figure in the Village scene for the next decade or so. I guess Izzy was in his mid-twenties at that point, and the first thing I remember noticing about him was his ears, which stuck out like mug handles. He had rented this place on the block between Bleecker and 3rd, and it was exactly what the name said: the folklore center. It was a place where you could buy folk music records, books, and accessories. People would leave guitars or banjos to be sold on consignment, and he had strings, picks, capos, odds and ends. But more than anything else, what it almost immediately became was a sort of clubhouse for the folk scene. Izzy was the switchboard: if anything was happening to anyone on the scene, Izzy would find out about it and broadcast it to the world—whether you wanted him to or not. If you came into New York and needed to know how to get in touch with somebody or to leave a message, you would go into the Folklore Center and ask Izzy, and he would probably know all about it, or failing that, he would let you leave a note on his bulletin board. If you had no fixed address, you would have your mail sent care of the Folklore Center. So everybody on the scene was coming by on a regular basis to get mail or check the notes on the bulletin board, and that made it even more of a central meeting place.

There had been places where musicians met before that, like 190 Spring Street, but different crowds went to different places. When Izzy opened that little hole, there was suddenly a place where everyone went, and it became a catalyst for all sorts of things. There were picking sessions, and Izzy even held a few concerts there to help out singers who needed a gig and couldn't find one elsewhere. I did two or three of those, and a review of one in *Caravan* says the crowd was so big that "the back room was well-filled with standees who, from there, could only listen"—which, if memory serves, would not have required a very big crowd. I first ran into Moe Asch of Folkways Records at the Center. In fact, by the next year, I was living on

MacDougal Street and I must have met hundreds of people there. It became so much like a club that there was a sort of running joke that Izzy never actually sold anything. A few years later, Dylan wrote "Talking Folklore Center Blues," and the tag line to one of the verses was "You don't have to buy anything. Do what everybody else does. Walk in, walk around, walk out."

Izzy was not a musician himself; the closest thing he did to performing was English harness dancing. Every once in a while, he would put on his harness and bells and take off down MacDougal Street. It was a wonderful sight, and he was actually pretty good at it. He was extraordinarily energetic, and constantly organizing—concerts, get-togethers, projects of one sort and another—and he was a real asset not only to the New York scene but to the whole folk music world. By the mid- to late 1960s, there were folklore centers all over America, and every single one was inspired by Izzy Young. At the same time, he was constantly scuffling to make ends meet. I think it was because, although he had incredible enthusiasm and a lot of good ideas, he was too diffuse. He was the kind of person who was great for a one-shot deal but had trouble sustaining anything. So no matter how popular the Center got, it was always in trouble financially. Still, he kept it going for years and even made a living out of it. Not a great living, but those were easier times—otherwise, none of us would have made it through. I knew people who were paying $25 or $30 a month for a two-person apartment. Not a good apartment, but it could be done.

Another ray on the horizon was the beginning of *Caravan* magazine. In a way, it was not really a magazine—it was a mimeographed fanzine, run off on 8½-by-11-inch paper stapled together at the edges. That was the brainchild of Lee Shaw, formerly and currently Lee Hoffman but then married to Larry Shaw. Lee and Larry had been editing a sci-fi 'zine, and Lee had dedicated a couple of issues to her favorite folksingers. At that point, there was a great deal of overlap between folk fans, the fringe left, and the sci-fi crowd—all three offered new, interesting ways of looking at the world and a chance to mingle with like-minded souls who were equally frustrated with the monochrome oppressiveness of Eisenhower America. Of course, not all of us became fans; Roy Berkeley says that he avoided ever picking up a sci-fi book, because he was sure that he would become so addicted that he would never leave his room. Nevertheless, sci-fi provided us with another kind of common language, and the attraction worked both ways: for a while, Harlan Ellison was one of *Caravan*'s record reviewers.

The first issue of *Caravan* appeared in August of 1957 and opened with a diatribe by one "Blind Rafferty" titled, "The Elektra Catalog—A Sarcophagus." This was an all-out attack on the old-guard folk scene as represented by the label that was home to Bikel, Brand, White, Gooding, and so forth, and it read as follows:

> Sitting in front of me, I have a copy of an Elektra Records catalog. Somewhere in the background an LP of folksongs by Clarence Cooper—also on Elektra—is warbling innocuously. Since I write better when I'm annoyed, and since both the catalog before me and the ditties in back of me annoy the bejesus out of me, I might as well take this as a starting point for my favorite kind of essay—a diatribe.
>
> A casual thumbing through Elektra's catalog gives one the impression of wide scope ingeniously combined with selectivity. Obviously the people in charge know their folk music and have worked tirelessly to disseminate this knowledge to the world at large. Certainly there is no lack of variety—Israeli folk songs, Old English and Haitian, Turkish, Spanish, Mexican, Blues, and Mountain Style, and God knows what else. But a good catalog is nothing more than a good catalog, and before we pat its engineers on the heads for a job well done, let's examine some of the records.
>
> For example, *Festival in Haiti* (EKL-130). Since I have neither the record nor album notes at hand, I will have to go chiefly by memory, but I have heard and read the contents of same thoroughly.
>
> Jean Léon Destiné, the star performer on this album has a rather pretty voice, sort of a Harry Belafonte type. Most of the accompaniment is supplied by drums. Like everything else on this record, the drumming is remarkably smooth and proficient, and if we are to believe the jacket notes, this is the REAL AUTHENTIC music of Haiti, in all its primitive vigor. Fortunately, this is not the case and you can settle the matter for yourself with little effort. Listen to some of the records cut on location in Haiti by Harold Courlander, and released on Folkways (P-403, P-407). After fifteen minutes with these field recordings turn again to Destiné. Pretty pallid? Sounds like a chic niteclub act? Exactly. The guts have been deftly extracted

and the corpse neatly stuffed, tied with a pink ribbon and placed on exhibit in Elektra's marvelous museum.

The article continued for a couple more paragraphs, ladling out similar encomiums to the Cooper album and to Josh White, "who should know better." Then it concluded:

> As I said before, I have chosen these records as examples. I honestly believe that they represent the overall approach of the record company in question—at least in those areas of folk music that I know well enough to judge. Moreover, I think that this approach is very much in keeping with the zeitgeist of the so-called "Folkmusic Revival" in America.
>
> Even at my angriest, I cannot truthfully say that many of Elektra's records are actually "bad." They lack even that much character. The aim of the A and R [Artists and Repertory] men seems to be to avoid frightening or offending anyone. Whether or not this is literally true, I am amazed at Elektra's ability to turn out one innocuous little album right after another—genteel, sophisticated, and utterly false.
>
> —*Blind Rafferty*

Rafferty was me. The pseudonym was both a holdover of my occasional writing for radical newsletters—we all assumed colorful noms de guerre to avoid unnecessary hassles from the official snoops—and a sensible precaution for an ambitious young folksinger attacking what was, from our perspective, one of the giants of the industry. At last, the young Turks had a platform from which we could lob fiery invective at the battlements of the folk establishment, and a number of us proceeded to vent several years of pent-up frustration. Looking back, I am amused at the undergraduate snottiness of our prose, but I still agree with many of our basic arguments: we threw some babies out with the bathwater, but bathwater—comfortably warm and bubbly—was exactly what a lot of our targets were purveying.

Caravan became our forum, with page upon page of theoretical argument about the correct stance of the modern urban folk musician or listener. Barry Kornfeld was a regular and frequently vituperative columnist, writing under the pen name "Kafka" and calling his column "From the Dead." Roger Lass, a quite good musician and one of the sharpest tongues in the east, wrote some very controversial pieces, and Roger Abrahams violently disagreed with him, and all the cats jumped in on one side or the other. Lionel Coots, a possibly pseudonymous wag from Richmond Hill, wrote in to inquire whether Rafferty's appellation "Blind" was based not on a physical disability but on his critical acumen. Altogether, it was a tremendous foofaraw, and looked at one way, a lot of it was pretty silly. But we were defining ourselves. The identity of the folk revival was being established at that time, and *Caravan* was a critical nexus.

It also served as a sort of club newsletter, with gossip, in-jokes, and commentary about whatever was happening on the Village scene—the March 1958 issue, for example, notes that "Dave Van Ronk, like so many other Village characters, has affected a beard." There were concert announcements and advertisements for guitar and banjo lessons, which Lee printed free of charge. (The magazine's cover boasted that it was a "nonprofit, great-cost amateur publication," and the first half-dozen issues were free. After that, the circulation had grown too large to be paid for out of Lee's pocket, and she was forced to start charging ten cents per.) Lee was an impressive figure and had a great influence on the scene. She could walk up to Roger Abrahams or Aaron Rennert or me, or even Paul Clayton, that incredibly pigheaded man, and say something and we would listen. She was the pope, the final authority. Izzy thought he was the pope, but in fact his opinions were often not taken very seriously, while Lee's were. Izzy would say whatever came into his head, but Lee thought everything through very carefully before she said it, and we listened to her in a way we did not listen to anyone else, because what she said made sense. She was a writer, not a musician, so she was capable of a kind of detachment that we were not. (Lee also did me another service: for several months after I got back from my hitch in the merchant marine, she and Larry let me sleep on their couch.)

Running *Caravan* must at times have been incredibly frustrating. We were all eager to put our opinions in print, but often a good deal less eager to show up when help was needed to collate and staple. So Lee deserves a lot of credit simply for sticking with it and keeping the magazine going. She ran it from August 1957 until the end of 1958, by which time it had become a much more professional-looking object, a small-format magazine that looked a good deal like *Sing Out!* It had ceased to be a little Village newsletter and was taking up so much of her time that she decided to quit, handed it over to Billy Faier, and shortly started another informal, mimeographed fanzine called *Gardyloo* (named for the shout that British housewives would give before emptying chamberpots onto the street, from the French "Garde de l'eau!").

With *Caravan*, there was finally a place where the arguments that had previously been limited to barroom colloquies could be set down in print. The first Rafferty piece drew some predictably outraged responses and led Lee to add a note to the cover of issue no. 2, to the effect that "the opinions expressed herein (especially those of Rafferty) are not necessarily those of the editor," and also that "parcels containing small poisonous objects and/or explosives should be marked clearly 'to Rafferty' and 'personal.'" That issue's lead article was a three-page review of the Café Bizarre show, with a complimentary paragraph about my performance, and I weighed in with another Rafferty column. In good anarchist fashion, I chose a theme guaranteed to perplex those readers who assumed they had my number after the Elektra diatribe—my admiration for Pete Seeger:

A few days ago someone handed me the latest copy of *Sing Out* and told me to turn to Pete Seeger's column, "Johnny Appleseed, Jr.," if I wanted to work up a really fine rage. I accepted the proffered magazine and my friend stepped back a few paces and waited for the explosion. There was no explosion. Of course, I disagreed with the article as expected (the contents of same are of no importance here) but I got no satisfaction out of disagreeing with Seeger. I think that the man is really great, in almost every sense of the word, and it saddens me to constantly find myself in the opposition camp every time he ventures an opinion. But when he sings—

Artists of Seeger's genre are hard to come by in this day and age. He is, in my opinion, taste and honesty personified, and a Seeger concert is a lesson which no singer of folksongs can afford to miss. When he speaks on the stage, his voice rarely rises above a conversational level, and yet he is heard. There is no phony upstaging at all. As a matter of fact, "stage presence" of the Broadway variety is entirely absent. Seeger does not act; he is.

I think that this is the key to his entire greatness. The man has no need to act in order to establish contact with his audience. He genuinely respects the people who are listening to him and refuses to insult their sensibilities with insincere theatrics. And they respond, not to an actor or stage personality, but to the man.

He treats his material in much the same way. I doubt if Seeger considers himself a "folklorist" per se; but rather he looks at folkmusic as a human being, subject to love, hate, enthusiasm, sorrow—in short, all of the emotions with which folkmusic deals. He is not "preserving" folklore but living it, and so are we, and he knows it. He neither sings up nor down to his material but with it. And there is no dichotomy between the performer and the content of his songs. This is the reason why one never gets the "isn't this cute" or "how quaint" impression from Seeger's singing. When he sings, *all* of him is involved. Which is another lesson that many singers of folksongs could profit by.

Again, I can't say I think much of Pete's point of view on many subjects. He is forever espousing causes which at best leave me cold. But I can't say that I think he would be better off without his causes and opinions. However wrong I happen to think they may be, they reflect a genuine concern with the real world which, to my way of thinking, is an indispensable part of a whole person, which I think Pete Seeger is.

The tragedy is that there are almost none like him. He is almost unique and insofar as such people in folkmusic are rare, then it becomes necessary to form "societies for the preservation of folklore"—or perhaps the word should be "embalming."

Naturally, this piece did not attract as much response as my attack on Elektra, but at least one person took me to task for calling Pete a "real" folksinger. What can I say? He is the man who invented my profession. When his first solo album, *Darling Corey,* came out, it was like a clarion call: this is the real stuff, played the way it should be played. What is more, I always thought Pete was a much better musician than most people appreciated—including most of his fans. He phrases like a sonofabitch, he never overplays, and he dug up so much wonderful material. Whatever our disagreements over the years, I learned a hell of a lot from him.

In *Caravan* no. 3, Rafferty provided an article on "The Singing IWW," a subject dear to my heart, along with a plug for the Kossoy Sisters' album. They were a pair of identical twins with marvelous, perfectly matched voices, and I still think that was one of the most lovely albums to come out of that period. In the same issue, under my own name, I answered a reader's request for the lyrics to Wynonie Harris's R&B hit "Don't Roll Those Bloodshot Eyes at Me" and gave high marks to two albums of field recordings, Alan Lomax's collection of *Negro Prison Songs* and a Jean Ritchie album in which she presented various traditional English ballad singers, juxtaposing their performances with her American versions of the same songs.

By contrast, *Caravan* no. 4 noted in the contents page that "Mr. Rafferty has not been heard from," and the following issue described him as having "disappeared." Being a regular columnist was getting to feel too much like work, and the pleasure of seeing my opinions in print was not enough to keep me in harness. However, I continued to devote myself to other literary ventures, acting as editor of a slim, mimeographed folio titled *The Bosses' Songbook: Songs to Stifle the Flames of Discontent*.

The genesis of *The Bosses' Songbook* began with Roy Berkeley, who had written a series of parodies of old folk chestnuts in the Almanac–People's Artists style, but turned around to make them the targets. His masterpiece was "The Ballad of Pete Seeger," a viciously funny reworking of "The Wreck of the Old 97" that began "They gave him his orders at Party headquarters, / Saying, 'Pete, you're way behind the times. / This is not '38, it is 1957, / There's a change in that old Party Line.'" It had a couple more verses, ending with a quip about how the People's Artists were going on with "their noble mission of teaching folksongs to the folk." Among Roy's other gems was "Way Down in Lubyanka Prison" (to the tune of "Columbus Stockade"), which he had composed for the Young Socialist League's May Day show. He would introduce these songs by saying that they came from "The Bosses' Songbook," a capitalist parallel to the IWW's "Little Red Songbook" of "Songs to Fan the Flames of Discontent." (There had been a similarly satiric collection, called *Ballads for Sectarians,* recorded in 1950 by a singer named Joe Glazer, with songs like "My Darling Party Line" and a reworking of the Admiral's song from *The H.M.S. Pinafore* that began "When I was a lad in 1906, I joined a band of Bolsheviks . . . ")

I put Roy's efforts together with a few additional songs by people like me and Barry Kornfeld, and Dick Ellington served as publisher—which is to say, he organized and printed the thing. Dick was a friend from the Libertarian League and a fellow sci-fi addict (he was one of a group of sci-fi-reading lefties who called themselves the Fanarchists). He was also a professional printer and got out the League's paper, *Views and Comments*. He was living in a big apartment called the Dive up on Riverside Drive, where I crashed on occasion and attended many memorable parties, of which I naturally remember nothing—except that it was at one of them that I first got together with Terri Thal, who shortly became my girlfriend and eventually my first wife.

The Bosses' Songbook was mildly popular in our circle and caused a fair amount of irritation in others. I was told on good authority that Pete was thinking of suing us, and for our second printing we changed the title of "The Ballad of Pete Seeger" to "Ballad of a Party Singer." (Dick Ellington remembered this quite differently. He heard that Pete found the song funny and actually performed it a few times, and as proof presented Pete's order for three songbooks.)

What with one thing and another, my corner of the folk scene was getting a lot more active, and among the new developments was the birth of our own organization, the Folksingers Guild. This was formed in the winter of 1957–58, largely as a response to the screwing we got at the Café Bizarre. After the first two or three concerts, Rick Allmen had the Bizarre up and running, so he did not need us anymore. He was quite an unprincipled man, and he did not pay the performers; he would make an exception for someone like Odetta or Josh White, but whoever else was on the bill was doing it for the "exposure" (which, as Utah Phillips points out, is something people die of). Those of us who had developed a local reputation, if only from our Washington Square performances, would have cost him a few bucks. No more than a few bucks, but as far as he was concerned, there was no reason even to pay that.

It was cold-blooded exploitation, and that was essentially what got the Folksingers Guild started. We had been promised pay and we were not paid, and we foresaw a big folk boom coming, so we wanted to get a union started forthwith to prevent that kind of thing occurring again. As it happened, the boom would not come for another three years or so—at least to an extent that affected us—but by 1958 it was clearly on its way. The college folk clubs were starting, Harry Belafonte and the Tarriers had some hit records, Elektra was doing good business, and to our way of thinking it could not be long before discerning listeners had got their fill of slick folk-fakery and must turn to us, the true keepers of the flame. We had no doubt that we were the cutting edge of the folk revival—though bear in mind, we were in our late teens and early twenties, and if you do not feel you are the cutting edge at that age, there is something wrong with you. Of course we were the wave of the future—we were twenty-one!

As it turned out, we were premature, but we had the basic idea right, and we started the Guild to protect ourselves from the capitalist exploitation that we were sure was right around the corner. I cannot remember exactly how we first got together, but I was in on it from the outset, along with a crew of the usual suspects: Roy Berkeley, again; Roger Abrahams, again; Roger Lass, Bob and Sylvia Brill, Luke Faust, Gina Glaser, Jerry Levine, Judy Isquith, Al Foster, Dave Sternlight, Silvia Burnett, Ben Rifkin . . . We held our meetings at Dick and Kiki Greenhaus's loft on 17th Street. Dick was a remarkably good guitar player, and Kiki was a modern dancer who also worked as a belly dancer in the clubs on 8th Avenue in the 20s, and they had this big loft where Dick taught guitar and Kiki taught modern dance.

The obvious problem with forming a protective organization for workers in the folk industry was that at that point Rick Allmen was the sole capitalist on the scene, and even he was only rather fecklessly exploiting anybody. We were basically a trade union with no bosses, and we realized pretty quickly that we would have to be our own bosses, and began putting on concerts. That was where Lee Hoffman Shaw came in again, and also Lee Haring. Roy Berkeley and a few other performers were actively involved, but in my recollection we were more in the form of window dressing as far as actually running things was concerned. We attended meetings and made a lot of noise, but the real work—renting the halls, printing up posters—could not be left to the performers. (Years later we were trying to organize a union down on MacDougal Street, and when I told John Mitchell, who was running the Gaslight Café, he said, "You?! You're organizing a union? If you were a dog you couldn't organize a pack of fleas." And he was right.) There were some other people as well: Aaron Rennert was the official photographer and Ray Sullivan did the sound system.

We had a concert committee, and since the main function of the organization was to produce concerts, that became in effect the executive committee. The concert committee would decide who would be on the bill for each concert, and there was a great deal of "Well, we can't pick so-and-so, because he was on the show before last ... Why don't we give so-and-so a chance?" The weighing of the bills was a delicate matter and had to be handled with a great deal of diplomacy, because a lot of egos were involved. There were always at least three or four people on a bill. Somebody would be up there for fifteen or twenty minutes, then would get yanked off before everybody walked out, and we would hit them with the next screecher. As things went on, we occasionally added a somewhat bigger name—Paul Clayton, say—to bring in more people. With Paul you could have a whole bunch of relative unknowns, because Paul could pull. If you were going to book it strictly from within the group, then you would have performers like Roy and myself and Gina Glaser, who had some following—if we could bring down twenty or thirty people each, that was already a big deal. On a good night, the audience might have been as big as two hundred people, but it was often more like ninety, and out of that we would pay the production costs and divvy the rest up among the performers.

Roy recalls that he arranged for the YSL to let us use their hall for our first concert, and with the money from that one we rented a room in Adelphi Hall, on 5th Avenue. *Caravan* lists what may have been our first concert there, in February 1958, featuring Roy, me, and a "surprise guest," all for the sum of fifty cents. Once we were a little bit established, we moved over to the Sullivan Street Playhouse, just south of MacDougal, renting it for midnight shows or on nights when the theater was dark. We would have three or four performers, introduced by Jock Root—John Schuyler Root—a very dignified-looking, slightly built man with a little dark mustache. Jock did not play or sing, but he was very well-spoken and traditionally acted as master of ceremonies, and he often presided over our meetings as well. There was one show, I believe at Joan of Arc High School, where Doris Stone and Pat Foster were on the bill, and while they were waiting in the dressing room, they got into some sort of argument, and Pat went one step too far over the line, so Doris picked up a jar of cold cream that caught him right between the eyes. He was knocked completely unconscious, and poor Jock Root was out on the stage and introduced them to a thundering patter of applause, and nothing happened.

One way and another, the Guild was a way for us to pick up a few bucks, to establish ourselves, and to learn our craft. There were a lot of fans and amateurs involved, but there was a core of people who really wanted to be professional folksingers, and the Guild was essentially our support group. Obviously, some of us took ourselves a good deal more seriously than others. I remember one committee meeting where Paul Clayton threw a beautiful scene. I do not remember what set him off, but he was on his feet, screaming, "I am a professional, and you have to treat me like a professional!" Paul was such a professional that he never actually joined the Guild. He would come to meetings, but he made a very sharp distinction between himself and all of us wannabes, because he had already recorded a bunch of albums. There were a few people like that, who were around and very influential, but who I do not think actually joined. John Cohen would have been one, and I think Tom Paley.

Frankly, Paul had a point. While most of the Guild performers might not have thought of themselves as amateurs, that is what they really were. A lot of them were in college or living with their folks, and their time on the Village scene was essentially their *Wanderjahr,* after which they went on to their real careers as doctors, lawyers, and Indian chiefs. So the Guild was a professional organization of amateurs, and in retrospect, I am surprised at how much good work we got done. Not that it was all so monumentally great: I have, for historical purposes, listened to a tape of one of my shows from this period, and I can testify that this is something no one should be forced to do. Judy Isquith was pretty good, though, with a big, rich voice; Bob Brill was fine; and Roy could sing Jimmie Rodgers songs very convincingly. Mostly, though, we were trying too hard, and I sometimes think that the best of us was Luke Faust, because he was a much quieter, more subtle musician. The rest of us were huffing and puffing, trying to compensate for our inadequacies with volume and enthusiasm, while Luke was a minimalist. We all got better, though, and along the way some pretty good music got made. The Guild even assisted at the birth of the New Lost City Ramblers, who were the first of the New York neo-ethnics really to be successful, either artistically or commercially.

Those Guild concerts and the shows at the Folklore Center were not earning enough to pay anybody's food and rent, but it made a big difference for us to be in front of a real audience and to be taken seriously. If you look through the *Caravan* event listings for that period, there are always these concerts at Carnegie or Town Hall with people like Jean Ritchie, Theo

Bikel, Pete Seeger, Cynthia Gooding, Richard Dyer-Bennett, Leon Bibb, Brownie McGhee, and Sonny Terry, or "international" acts like Marais and Miranda; and then there will be the Folklore Center and the Folksingers Guild, with all of the Village crowd—and never the twain did meet. Over the next couple of years, the first Newport Folk Festivals were held, and the only Village musicians invited were the Ramblers. (The Clancy Brothers were at Newport as well, and we saw them around the Village a good deal, but as drinking partners, not because we were working any of the same stages.)

The only place where the two strains crossed was on Oscar Brand's radio show. Oscar had a regular show every Sunday on WNYC, which went back to the mid-1940s and continues to the present day. He was incredibly important to the whole scene because for many years his show was the only access that folk music had to the general public. I used to listen to him when I was still back in Queens, and that was how I was first introduced to all kinds of people that I subsequently met and became friends with, like Roger Sprung, Erik Darling, Eric Weissberg. Oscar knows 575 trillion songs: if any living human being has a larger repertoire than Pete Seeger, it could only be Oscar, and I would like to see them slug it out toe-to-toe on that one, only it would take at least fifteen years of straight singing. To give you an idea: I remember David Greenhill telling me one time that he got into an argument about American history with someone at a party somewhere in California. It was around midnight out there, so 3:00 A.M. in New York, and they were just loaded enough to pick up the phone and call Oscar. The question was, who had been Henry Clay's running mate, and Oscar, woken out of a sound sleep, burst straight into "Hurrah! Hurrah! The country's risin', for Clay and Frelinghuesen!"

Oscar always managed to tread a middle ground, both politically and in terms of musical approach. His own work was certainly in the cabaret style, without any of the guts and rawness that we demanded, but his repertoire was so huge that we had to respect it. Besides, he was always very supportive of what we were doing, and clearly had a genuine love for the more traditional styles. He also was one of the few people to have been a steadfast member of the non-Communist left—People's Songs used to parade him as proof that they were not a Communist organization. For a while there, with the HUAC investigations and the blacklisting, everything got polarized to the point that the Stalinists did not really trust him, but his show remained the one place that would always put them on the air. (Years later, I was talking with him and expressed my disgust that he, or maybe someone else, had put on a show with Burl Ives, who had outraged all of us by naming a string of names in front of HUAC. Oscar just quietly said, "Dave, we on the left do not blacklist." Put me right in my place.)

Oscar would let us sing on his show occasionally, and by the late 1950s, there were a couple of other people who would let us on the air. Billy Faier hosted a show called *Midnight Special,* from midnight to 2:00 A.M. on Saturday nights, and George Lourie had a show that parties of us used to descend on from time to time. Lourie's engineer was this kind of strange guy named Dave, a real loser who had taken up karate. One time I was on there, and Dave had some young lady in the control room whom he was trying desperately to impress with his karate, and he gave the console a chop that knocked me right off the air—it was about fifteen minutes before they could get any signal.

All in all, things were looking up. I was still living hand to mouth, but I was at least playing fairly regularly and beginning to have some sort of reputation, and so were quite a few of my friends. The changes were small, taken one by one, but they were straws in the wind.

6

Where the Real Money Was

There was, of course, more to our lives than the folk scene. There is no way I can cover it all, but to broaden the palette a little I append the following vignette.

It was the summer of 1958. Big Judy was off to Provincetown for a few weeks, and her one-room apartment would be standing empty. Good Samaritan that I was, I offered to move in, keep an eye on things, and fend off the burglars. (We knew from burglars; some of them were our friends.) The place was on 12th Street between avenues A and B, in what rent-gouging real estate agents would soon rechristen the East Village, but was then still known as the East Side, except to some old-timers who called it "Mackerelville," from the French *maquereau*, meaning pimp. I happily ensconced myself and settled into a routine of uproarious nights at Stanley's bar down the block and days spent idling in Tompkins Square Park or watching the locals practice their quaint native crafts: there was a chop shop right out on the street in front of my building, where stolen cars were disassembled to be sold off pushcarts. Pigeon rustling was also pretty popular.

Then, early one fine day, as I was sleeping off Stanley's rotgut, there came an insistent pounding at the door. "Nobody but a cop could do this to me at eight o'clock on a Sunday morning," I thought. There was nothing for it, though, so fearfully I lurched to the door. "Who is it?" I croaked.

Two names, unfamiliar, but at least they didn't sound like cops: "Judy sent us."

"Oh, in that case . . . "

I opened the door, and there before my wondering eyes stood two citizens whose outfits would have raised a double take in the most depraved boho saloon in the Village, or even in a frat house. Specimen A was wearing women's pedal pushers that were so tight I wondered how he had squeezed himself into them, and filled out the ensemble with a middy blouse, short enough to expose his bare midriff, and bare feet. Specimen B wore a terry-cloth bathrobe, period. "This better be good," I muttered, whilst fumbling through the routine of building a pot of coffee.

Fortified with their first cups, they launched into the following saga. Like Herodotus, the Father of History, I set it down without comment:

They were characters of a type that has been with us since Caesar was a pup: army hustlers. Until a few months back they had been stationed in Tokyo and Seoul, respectively, and had been running some kind of currency scam involving fluctuating exchange rates between the Japanese yen and the Korean won. I did not understand the details, but I believed them when they told me it was "beautiful." However the grift worked, it had made them a pile, and as soon as they mustered out, they began casting about for some kind of swindle that would parlay their nest egg into a real fortune.

Now, as it happened, at just about this time the powers and principalities of Japan had decided to demonstrate to the world how progressive they were by prohibiting the manufacture and sale of "green ruin"—absinthe. In the interval between enactment and enforcement, it was possible to buy a warehouse full of the stuff at fire-sale prices, which is what our future tycoons had proceeded to do. They loaded this cargo aboard a Filipino rust bucket, booking passage for themselves on the same ship.

The voyage back to the Land of Opportunity ("where the real money is," as they put it) was a hairy one. Somewhere in mid-Pacific they ran into a storm, and fearing for the merchandise, which was none too securely stowed, they raced down to the hold, where they spent the better part of two days running back and forth, propping up mountainous stacks of crates with their bare hands while the ship pitched and heaved. To make things merrier, they were seasick the whole time, but they lost only a few cases. What prodigies of fraud and effrontery got them and their cargo of liquid vice past customs in San Francisco I never found out, but somehow they pulled it off and stashed the stuff in a loft somewhere near the Embarcadero.

Personally, I could not imagine a better place than San Fran to unload a cargo of absinthe. The natives there so pride themselves on their worldliness that they would probably drink it even if they hated it. But our heroes decided, inscrutably, that "Cape Cod is where the real money is." They acquired a used pickup truck, loaded it to the gunwales with samples, and headed east.

The cross-country trip was blessedly uneventful, and once they hit Provincetown, they made the rounds of the tourist bars. Unobtrusively, they buttonholed the saloon keepers, offering them cases and cases of very illegal booze at very reasonable prices. No takers. Universally, the response was "Look—you know what the stuff is, and I know what the stuff is, but nobody else has ever heard of it. Who am I going to sell it to?" Concerned but not yet panicking, they repaired to yet another bar to take council and a few slugs of government-approved solace—which is where Big Judy came in. They got to talking with her, and upon hearing their sad tale, she suggested they try their luck in New York. Helpful soul that she was, she even gave them her address, told them I was staying there, and said I might know someone who would be interested in their wares.

"Right," they said. "The Big A. Plenty of action. Everybody knows that's where the real money is."

After a few more convivial glasses, they hopped into their pickup, which was still piled high with contraband, and took off for 12th Street. They were somewhere on Route 6, outside of Wellfleet, when disaster struck. Two big black cars forced them off the road and four thugs with guns waved them out of the truck. Efficiently they were stripped to the buff and trussed up like Christmas turkeys. The four gunmen then drove off, taking the truck and its cargo with them.

Our heroes felt that this treatment added an unnecessary complement of insult to the injury: "They didn't have to tie us up and take our clothes. I mean, what were we going to do—go to the cops and say, 'Some meanies stole our absinthe?'" I explained that these procedures are time-honored, and that hijackers, like any other artists, set high store by tradition. They were not mollified.

Where the Real Money Was   79

It had taken them an hour or so to get un-hog-tied, and then there was the matter of clothes. These were the days before the ubiquitous washer-dryer, so there was always the clothesline option; but apparently it was not wash day on Cape Cod, and the pickings were very slim indeed. The threads in which they stood before me were the very best they could do.

"But how did you get here?" I asked.

"We hitched."

"You hitched in those outfits?"

"It was easy. We certainly didn't look like muggers."

No doubt about that. "But what did you tell the people who picked you up?"

"We said we were Shriners on our way to a convention and had dressed this way on a bet. They loved us." I had to admit it, these guys were good.

I had no trouble figuring out who Judy had in mind when she said I might know a prospective buyer for their goods. An acquaintance of ours, a low-level associate of George Lefty's (reputedly the local capo for one of the Five Families), held court at Stanley's most nights. A word in his ear, and who knew? As a general rule, I tried to avoid getting mixed up in this kind of convoluted skullduggery, but ever since I was a teenager, I had been reading about Lautrec and absinthe, Modigliani and absinthe, Swinburne and absinthe—naturally I was dying to find out about Van Ronk and absinthe. Also, there was the sheer joy of conspiracy for its own sake. What can I say? I have always been a hopeless romantic.

I told them I might be able to set up a meet with some wiseguys I knew. They were ecstatic. "Oh boy! The mob—that's where the real money is!" One might have thought they had already had one too many meetings with such types, but the boys were so happy that I kept my counsel. It would take a week or two for them to get more "samples" sent from the Coast, and in the meantime I would see what I could do. I lent them some of my clothes, and they went blissfully on their way.

The sit-down was easily arranged: "No harm in talking," the guy said. "Bring them around." A couple of days later, I brought them around to Stanley's, made the necessary introductions, and having performed my good offices as honest broker, discreetly took my leave. For services rendered, I received five bottles of the stuff.

So, what was it like? It is simple to describe: If you subtract the worm-wood from absinthe, you get Pernod. It is licorice flavored, sweet, the wormwood gives it a pleasantly bitter undertaste—a bit like quinine—and it is green in color, turning opalescent on contact with water or ice. I drank a couple of glasses, and found that it gave a strangely lucid high. I liked it a lot, though it delivered a hellish hangover. So, that was what all the fuss was about.

The next day my two smugglers dropped by Judy's place, and over glasses of guess what, I got the discouraging word: my guy had bought a few cases for himself and his friends, but basically his position was, "Look—you know what it is and I know what it is, but nobody else ever heard of the stuff. Who are we going to sell it to?"

"Gee," I said, "the Mafia sure is hard on honest crooks."

By way of consolation, I took five more bottles off their hands. Hell, they were selling it cheaper than Irish whiskey. For the next few weeks, the nabe was awash in absinthe. Everybody I knew must have picked up a few jugs. Then it was gone. My dynamic duo had shifted their operation to the Village, I heard. I suppose that was where the real money was.

A couple of months later I shifted my own operation back to the Village. I got hold of a sixth-floor walk-up on MacDougal Street, and took to spending my evenings in the Kettle of Fish, which was right downstairs, and my afternoons down the block at the Figaro.

One fall afternoon I was sitting over coffee at the Figaro when a glassy-eyed derelict who looked vaguely familiar hove into view. It was Specimen A, looking like an advance man for the bubonic plague. He was going from table to table, whispering a few urgent words to whoever was seated there, receiving an emphatic negative, and moving on. Al, the day manager, watched this action briefly and balefully before he swooped. He grabbed the guy by the collar and gave him the bum's rush right out the door, but not before I overheard the whispered pitch to the tourist at the next table: "Would you like to buy a bottle of absinthe for a dollar?" When we had finished admiring Al's technique, the rubberneck turned to me and said, "What's absinthe?"

It must have been about ten years down the line that I happened to be doing a gig in Provincetown, and a publican in Wellfleet invited Paul

Geremia (the world's best blues guitarist and singer) and me to a high-class bash at his Victorian Gothic "cottage." Paul and I were sitting there jamming, when our host approached us with two glasses of a familiar-looking opalescent fluid. I thought "Wellfleet! Absinthe! Ah-hah!" It was, as Yogi Berra would say, "Déjà vu all over again."

"I'll bet you guys'll never guess what this is," our host said, as he handed me a glass.

I took a sip, ostentatiously rolled it around my tongue and replied, "It tastes very much like Japanese absinthe."

"Jesus, how could you tell?"

I arched my eyebrows in my very best William F. Buckley imitation. "To the truly sophisticated palate," I intoned, "there are no mysteries."

7

Friends and Recordings

The last years of the 1950s were a great time to be in the Village. It was not too crazy yet, but there was an exhilarating sense of something big right around the corner. As for the folk scene, it was beginning to look as if it might have a future, and me with it. Admittedly, a great deal of my concertizing was still at benefits, a clear case of the famished aiding the starving. Roy Berkeley and I were working together fairly often, and we would play for the Libertarian League, for the Shachtmanite magazine *Handbill*, for the Committee to Save the World on Friday, the Committee to Blow Up the World on Saturday, and the Locofoco Party of Baluchistan on the first Monday of each month. I enjoyed it and felt that in an atheistic sort of way I was doing the Lord's work. And, though I have typically found that working for Reds is the pits—they all learned about labor relations from book two of *Das Kapital*, "Chain them to the factory bench!"—they were not entirely heartless and would usually slip us a few bucks. And a few bucks was really all I needed. Rent was next to nothing. I could always get a cheeseburger on the cuff down at the Caricature, and I had a humongous tab over at the Figaro as well. For extras, every now and again somebody I knew would come into some money, and we all borrowed a lot from each other and sometimes even paid it back.

Still, I had seen a vision of better things and was sure that places like the Gate of Horn would be just my meat if only they could be persuaded to put me onstage and do a little promotion. As I saw it, the problem was that I still did not have a record. I had worked out an equation that might be thought of as "*in vinyl veritas*": no record equals no work; therefore a record would equal jobs, fame, fortune, wine, women, and song. Simplistic as this may seem, it is not just a dumb mantra from the theologically incorrect 1950s. Most unrecorded musicians continue to subscribe to something of the sort.

Throughout the previous year or so, I had been gradually edging closer to my objective. The first nibble was an offer to record two songs for an anthology called *Our Singing Heritage*, to be issued by—of all companies—Elektra Records. As I remember, this offer came by way of Paul Clayton, who was pulling together a varied crew to present a reasonably well rounded picture of traditional American song. My contributions were an old Christmas carol, "Mary Had a Baby," and "Nobody Knows You When You're Down and Out." I chose "Nobody Knows You" because, of all the songs I was doing in those days, that was my mother's favorite—which always puzzled me, because Bessie Smith was by no means considered a respectable singer and should hardly have appealed to Grace Van Ronk, the backbone of the Rosary Society. It is only with the experience of age that I have come to have a glimmer of a hypothesis: Any number of friends of mine from the roaring sixties—alcoholics, druggies, sex maniacs, complete social lepers—have gotten married, built careers, moved to the suburbs. They keep up some of their old friendships, but there you are, sitting in the living room with them, and you hear them remonstrating with their children, telling them to stick to the straight and narrow, and to "just say no" to pretty much everything that could give a young person pleasure. I sit there, smothering my guffaws, and I have to think: we'll never know about our parents, either, will we?

As for Paul Clayton, he was one of my closest friends and also something of a mentor at times. There can have been few singers as unlike one another as Paul and myself, and yet he had a considerable influence on me, as he had some years later on Bob Dylan. He was a brilliant man and had thought through a lot of musical questions very carefully. His voice was a smooth, midrange baritone, almost a Burl Ives sound, which was not usually to my taste, and while he could play quite effective accompaniments on guitar or dulcimer, he was not an expert instrumentalist. His great strength as a musician was that he phrased marvelously, quite unlike anyone else. He had a very personal way of reading a lyric, and gave you the feeling that he was talking to you directly, so you listened with an attention you would not have paid to another singer. In that sense, he had the same sort of skill that Frank Sinatra had, though in a totally different style.

Paul was also a folklorist and collector of songs in the field, and made some quite important finds. He was the first person since the 1920s to record Pink Anderson, one of the great old medicine show guitarists and singers, and he also found a blues guitarist named Etta Baker and innumerable ballad singers. He had a unique repertoire of songs that he had come across on his collecting trips in the Appalachians, and I learned several of them, including the version I do of "Duncan and Brady." God knows where he collected that, but I never heard another version like it, with that great refrain "He's been on the job too long." It is one of a kind, and I have to wonder whether it was at least partly his own work. Paul was a serious folklorist, but when it came to his performance repertoire, he had no qualms about combining verses from different songs and changing words around to suit his taste. He had a beautiful thing called "I'm Going to Georgia," which I am quite sure he had done more with than just collect. And he had found a song called "Who'll Buy Your Chickens When I'm Gone," which he changed to "Who'll Buy You Ribbons"—not a masterpiece, but it got to be a great point of contention later on when Dylan copped the melody and a couple of lines for "Don't Think Twice, It's All Right."

Paul was one of the most delightful human beings I have ever met, a marvelous guy to go out and have a few drinks with and argue about whatever came to mind. At that age we were prepared to debate almost anything. For example, after the Kingston Trio hit, a bunch of folksong collectors and singers filed a class action suit against them for all the supposedly "public domain" material that they had slapped their names onto. A few of these songs had actually been written by professional folksingers like Cynthia Gooding, and a lot of the others had clearly been collected in specific versions from particular sources—Frank Warner had acquired "Tom Dooley" from a banjo player named Frank Profitt, and even if Profitt had not written the song, it was certainly his version that the Trio had made into a number-one hit. So there was this huge suit, and one of the trio made some comment that got widely quoted to the effect that "Jean Ritchie should wear looser shoes and eat more roughage." It was adding insult to injury, and we were all righteously incensed. Jean and Frank Warner were not exactly our people, but when you put them up against the Kingston Trio, we were in full solidarity with them. As someone who had collected a lot of material in the field, Paul was hotly engaged in this debate, but he was also pretty funny about it. He had put his own name on a good many of his arrangements of older songs, and began saying that his motto was "If you can't write, rewrite. If you can't rewrite, copyright."

Like all of us, Paul had strong political opinions, and he had spent some time in Cuba, so when Castro and company were in the Sierra Maestra, he decided that he wanted to get up a bunch of volunteers, call it the Patrick Henry Brigade, and head over there like the Abraham Lincoln Brigade in Spain. That was when I took to calling him "Pablo." I remember one night sitting around at the Village Gate and telling him, "Well, I can go along with you up to a certain point, but what we really need to do is to take the Patrick Henry Brigade up to the Sierra Catskills and liberate Grossingers, and turn it into a folk music room."

Paul was quite a character in other ways as well. He had a collection of walking sticks—it was one of his passions—and he wore some pretty extraordinary getups. I remember once a friend of ours had borrowed a book from him—a rare volume titled *The Short History of Sex Worship*—and had failed to return it. After dunning this fellow off and on for a few weeks, Clayton lost his patience and developed a scheme to deal with the situation. (I don't know if this actually came to fruition, but I certainly like to think it did.) As it happened, the borrower was one of the few of us who was respectably employed; he had some sort of job where he worked at a desk in a sea of desks in this huge office. So one day Clayton put on shorts, sandals, a pith helmet, two or three overcoats one over the other—this was in the middle of summer, mind you—and took one of his most ornate Malacca walking sticks. Then he went charging down to this office, ran up to the man's desk, and started pounding on it with his cane, screaming, "Where's my *Short History of Sex Worship?!*"

Occasionally I would see Paul with Phil Perlman, who weighed a good 300 pounds and was the first man with a ponytail I ever saw outside of a pirate movie, and it was quite something to watch the two of them walking down the street, wearing these bizarre outfits, to the awe and amazement of absolutely everybody. Back then, most of us dressed pretty conservatively. Not only was it the 1950s, but we were paranoid about the beatnik connection—I remember myself onstage saying, "Please excuse the sunglasses."

Paul used to bill himself as "the world's most recorded young folksinger"—the "young" had to be in there because of Pete Seeger—and he had already made well over a dozen albums. A lot of them were thematic collections: *Songs of Love and Marriage*; *Songs of Hate and Divorce*; *"Hunt the Cutty Auk" and Other Auk-Hunting Ballads from the Inner Hebrides*. He sometimes had to stretch a point to find material that would fit these programmatic slots, and a certain amount of garbage was laid down, but some really nice stuff was done as well, and he was recording like a madman. For a while there, every time he needed a few bucks, he would go to the library and thumb through some obscure folklore collection, then go up to Moe Asch at Folkways Records and say, "You know, Moe, I was just looking through your catalog, and I noticed that you don't have a single album of Maine lumberjack ballads."

Moe would say, "Well, I guess that's a pretty serious omission. Do you know anyone who can sing enough of those to make a record?"

And Paul would say, "Well, as it happens . . . "

Paul was originally from New Bedford, Massachusetts, the old whaling port, and he had a huge repertoire of sailing songs he had learned from his grandfather. He had recorded some of these on his own, but in 1958 he or Moe—or maybe it was Kenny Goldstein, who had produced a lot of his records—decided that he should do an album with a group, singing mostly unaccompanied, the way the songs would actually have been done on the ships. He rounded up a gang of the usual suspects: me, Bob Brill, Roger Abrahams, and Bob Yellin, a good singer and bluegrass banjo player who could also do some nice, simple picking of the sort that a sailor might have done while relaxing between watches.

We held our rehearsals at the Village Gate in the afternoons. Art D'Lugoff had just opened the club and was having trouble obtaining the necessary license to hire entertainment. He was a Jew in an Italian neighborhood where liquor licenses had traditionally been acquired only by becoming somebody's son-in-law, so everything he did in that place had to be done two or three times, because the other bar owners had the inspectors coming back again and again. D'Lugoff is a very ballsy man, and he stuck to his guns, but they harassed the shit out of him.

It being a brand new place, Art was more than happy to have some people in there, so he invited us to do our singing in his downstairs room and even supplied pitchers of beer to fend off dehydration. The only problem was that after a few pitchers, we were so well fended that our attention was apt to wander, and after a diligent hour or so of "Haul on the Bowline" and "Santa Anna," we would find ourselves harmonizing to "Friggin' in the Riggin'" or "D'Lugoff Fill the Flowing Bowl." Then other singers would drift in, and shortly the whole thing would devolve into impromptu barbershop octets or dodecatets, and on to the usual arguments about politics and the future of folk music. Finally, it was time to make the record, and we had only eight songs worked out. We went into the studio and, aided by a goodly supply of Demerara rum—very appropriate to the material—somehow improvised our way through enough songs to fill out the album. We traded off leading the chanteys, with everybody joining in on the choruses, and I suspect we sounded more genuine, and certainly more enthusiastic, than we might have with more practice. The LP was issued as *Fo'c'sle Songs and Chanties*, by Paul Clayton and the Fo'c'sle Singers, and has remained in the Folkways catalog. I still think it is one of the best records I have ever been involved in making, though it attracted very little attention then or since.

My next recording venture was less satisfactory. By that time, I was living in Gina Glaser's old apartment on MacDougal Street, a sixth-story railroad flat that she had left to me when she went off to Europe. It consisted of three tiny rooms, and I was sharing it for much of the time with Sam Charters, a friend of Bob Brill's who had recently come up from New Orleans. Sam would shortly emerge as one of the most important figures in the blues revival, because he was the first person to take the trouble to really research blues history. Before that, blues had been treated pretty cursorily, either as a primitive form of jazz or as a corner of the folk tradition. Sam wrote a book called *The Country Blues*, which had an effect that still resonates today. To begin with, he actually went to the libraries and pulled out copies of newspapers from various black communities in the 1920s, so he had some idea of how that music had been treated at the time. Who would have thought that there would be big advertisements for records by people like Blind Lemon Jefferson and Charley Patton in the *Chicago Defender*? But there they were. So Sam put blues research on a serious basis, and as a result of his work and the work of other people standing on his shoulders, we now know more about that music than any of us would have dreamt possible before he wrote that book. Also, he was the first person to stop assuming that the people who had made those records were dead. If he had not found an obituary of, say, Blind Willie Johnson, he saw no need to assume that Blind Willie Johnson was dead—and when he went to see if he could find Blind Willie, he missed him by only a year or so. A lot of other people were still alive, and he found some of the old jug band players in Memphis and recorded an album of them for Folkways, then tracked down Lightnin' Hopkins, still going strong in Texas. Sam hunted these guys up and wrote about it, and that started everybody else off on the trail of older, vanished singers. He is a marvelously prescient man and has one of the best sets of ears of any critic or music producer I know.

Sam also fooled around with music himself. He sang, played some guitar, some trumpet; he had been involved in the trad jazz scene out on the West Coast and had spent time in New Orleans interviewing the older jazz musicians there. We used to play together at parties, messing around with jazz stuff, which I was not getting much chance to do on the folk scene, and some jug band songs. Right around that time, an English singer named Lonnie Donegan got a hit playing a jug band version of Leadbelly's "Rock Island Line," so there was a brief flutter of interest in the style, which the English called "skiffle." As a result, we ended up with a deal to make a skiffle record for a label called Lyrichord. We put together a group that included Sam's future wife, Ann, on washboard and one of our trad buddies, Len Kunstadt, on kazoo, and rehearsed a bunch of tunes—I recall a truly unique version of Beethoven's Fifth Symphony. I still maintain that we were a pretty good band, but no one would ever know it from that record. Those were the days when stereo recording was still a neat new gimmick, and Lyrichord decided to wrap up two hot trends in one package by making an album called *Skiffle in Stereo*. The problem was that back in the mono days, there had been no need to separate musicians onto different recording tracks, and hence microphones were designed to capture the full range of sound in their area. We were still using this old microphone technology, so to get separation, they had to put all of us in different rooms, and for the same reason that there were no directional mikes, there was no such thing as recording with headphones. The upshot was that each of us could just barely hear the two nearest players, but none of us could hear the whole band. We were constantly getting away from each other, and the result included some of the most appalling moments I have ever heard on record. To crown the whole debacle, I pulled rank on my lesser-known associates, and the band was billed on the album cover as The Orange Blossom Jug Five with Dave Van Ronk. Talk about the punishment fitting the crime . . .

Far from teaching me a lesson, this experience just whetted my appetite. I wanted my own record, and I decided that the key was Kenny Goldstein. Kenneth S. Goldstein was a serious folklorist, then working toward his Ph.D., but he was also a freelance producer. He had produced records by Pat Foster, the Kossoy Sisters, and all sorts of other people, along with a bunch of Clayton's albums, for Folkways, Riverside, and Tradition, which aside from Elektra were about the only labels on the scene at that point. I figured if he could record them, he could damn well record me, so I got on his case and pestered him mercilessly. He kept telling me, "You're not ready," and I kept thinking, "Ready, schmeady—I need that LP so I can get some work, or I won't live long enough to get ready." I bugged him and bugged him, until eventually he must have concluded that a Van Ronk record would be a lesser evil than Van Ronk. The poor man caved completely and brought me out to his place on Long Island, where he had a little recording studio in the basement. I think we did the whole record in one session, though it might have taken two. Basically he just sat me in front of a microphone, and I sang a couple dozen of the things I was performing at that point, and that was that.

Hindsight being what it is, I have to say that Kenny was right and I was not ready to make that record. I have always referred to it as "Archie Andrews Sings the Blues," which about sums up my feelings. I was still essentially a living room or Washington Square singer. I did not know the first thing about using a microphone, and my singing sounds high and forced. I continued to play some of those songs, and to play them in the same key, so

I was not really singing higher than I did later, but it does not sound like the same voice. I developed more control and I learned a lot more about phrasing, how to come in ahead of or behind the beat. As for the guitar playing, it makes me want to crawl under a rug. I have often thought how nice it would be if I could buy the master of that record and use it for skeet shooting. (There were also other problems: When the album came out, someone at the *San Francisco Chronicle* gave it a nice review in which he described me as "a very promising young black singer." Kenny immediately wrote a letter to the paper, giving him the horselaugh, with the result that when I played San Francisco a few years later, the guy came down and gave me one of the nastiest reviews I have ever received in my life.)

All of which said, I was right as well: having a record out made an immediate difference in terms of getting jobs, and the fact that it appeared on the Folkways label gave me the equivalent of the Good Folksinging Seal of Approval. This was the label that Woody Guthrie was on, that Leadbelly was on, that Pete Seeger was on. Moe Asch could be an exasperating man, and he would never pay you ten cents if he could get away with five, but he really loved the music. That was the most important thing to him, and we all knew that, and we loved him for it. In all the years he kept that record company going, he did not cut anything out of the catalog. Every album that he made was like one of his kids, and he loved all of them, including some of the most cockamamy things you ever heard. There was one, *Sounds of a South American Rain Forest*, and it turned out that this was a complete put-on, that it was Frederic Ramsey and a friend standing in the shower and making bird noises—but Moe kept it in the catalog. So that was the label I wanted, even though I was well aware that I would not make a lot of money from it.

As it happened, Moe paid me a couple hundred bucks, which was very welcome, and over the years I managed to hit him up for handouts from time to time, but on the whole I always found his accounting mysterious, to say the least. It must have taken a fair amount of financial wizardry to keep that operation afloat for all those years, and I am convinced that, rather than chain himself to the legal niceties of his contractual agreements, he was cooking his books with the élan of an Escoffier.

It actually got to be kind of entertaining, because when I really needed some money, I would head up to Folkways, and I worked out a whole routine for dealing with Moe. I had a special outfit that I used to put on, which I called my "Folkways suit." It consisted of a jacket that I had worn when I was shipping out on a chemical tanker, which was incredibly filthy and smelled of acetone, and these old, worn jeans—no holes in them, but they were transparent. I would go up to his office in the West 40s and give him a whole spiel about how I was broke and I needed money, and blah blah blah, and he would come up with something like fifty bucks or maybe even a hundred. First, though, he would always go through the ritual of checking his ledger books, and one time he got called out of the room for some reason and I took the opportunity to glance over what he was checking. I could not make head or tail of it, but am quite certain that nothing I was seeing had anything to do with any record of mine.

This was a regular routine, and there was one time when it was a particularly cold day and I thought I would use that to improve my rap, so I said, "Moe, you gotta lay some bread on me; I don't even have a winter coat." Moe got up from behind his desk, walked out to the reception room, came back with this beautiful camel-hair overcoat, and said: "Here, Dave, take this." He called my bluff, absolutely—it was a gorgeous coat, but not something I would have been caught dead in even if it had fit me, and I'm quite sure he was aware of the fact. So I mumbled some excuse, and he gave me the usual fifty bucks.

Jumping ahead a few years, there came a time when I was doing pretty well. I was on another label by then, but my Folkways records were still around and Moe had even reissued them with new covers, so he was clearly doing all right with them. Presumably my royalty payments should have been growing along with this situation, but when I would occasionally get a statement from him, the sums were tiny. Finally, around 1964, the day came when I got a check from Folkways for something like $3.98, and I flew off the handle. I thought, "Goddamnit, if this guy's going to steal, that's one thing. But to steal and insult my intelligence—there, I draw the line!" At that time I was doing some business with Bill Krasilowski, the music industry lawyer par excellence, and I was in his office one day, ranting about this letter from Moe. Bill said, "Let's shake the tree a little bit." He wrote off this really nasty letter on his legal stationery, chuckling all the while, in which he threatened to sue Folkways for every penny it had. Lo and behold, three or four weeks later I got a check from Moe for several hundred dollars. I could not believe my eyes, but I must admit that I felt a little sorry to have sicced the big dogs on good old Moe. No more than two days after that I happened to wander into the Village Gate, and I was sitting at the bar, and I suddenly realized that there on the adjacent stool, buried in a large camel-hair coat, was Moe Asch. I thought, "Oh, shit. Now he's really going to take my head off." Moe had spotted me at the same moment, and he slowly turned to me and said, "I got your letter, Dave . . ." Then he smiled, slapped me on the back, and said, "So, you're finally getting smart."

To return to 1958, a few other stories come to mind. Before I moved to the MacDougal apartment, I had been living in a loft on Monroe Street with Richie Fox, one of the old Richmond Hill jazz crowd, and Chuck Freudenthal, who I knew from the Fanarchists and the Riverside Dive. I was going with Terri by that time, and she remembers that we had this big Christmas tree that we set out on the fire escape, and all through the spring she could see it as she came in over the bridge. During that period I was hanging out quite a lot with Roland Dumontet and his motorcycle crowd, and thanks to them I had one of the closest calls of my life. One night we were lounging around, just shooting the breeze, and a couple of them decided that they would go racing on the West Side Highway. A guy named Johnny Mocklin invited me to ride along as his passenger, which normally would have sounded exciting, but I was having a deep conversation with Jennifer, Roland's girl, and did not want to be bothered. As a result, I sat up all night talking with Jennifer, and someone else went as Johnny's passenger instead of me, and he never came back. They were racing right down the middle of the West Side Highway, which was completely empty at that hour of the morning, and a cop came after them. To throw the cop off, they split up, and Johnny took an exit ramp at top speed and collided with a taxi, and his passenger went flying off the back and was killed.

I was also keeping pretty active in the political world. A few of us had started a sort of offshoot of the Libertarian League called the Carlo Tresca Club. It was an organization with only three requirements: you had to be opposed to both capitalism and Stalinism, had to believe in direct action as a way of accomplishing social change, and had to participate in some activity that the group agreed constituted direct action, and report back on what you were doing. At its height the Tresca Club had about seventy-five members, almost all of them around my age, and people were involved in all sorts of things, including groups like CORE, the Congress of Racial Equality.

I fulfilled the third requirement through my work with the Folksingers Guild, though I also was involved in some other minor actions. For instance, this was when the United States had officially declared an embargo on arms to Cuba, but the CIA was still shipping weapons to Batista. There was this Cuban freighter that was docked in town, supposedly with a cargo of agricultural implements, and the word went around that it was actually carrying weapons to prop up the dictatorship. I am not sure how we got that information, but it came from a fairly reliable source, so some of us went down to alert the crew to what was going on. Well, talk about "doing well by doing good"! We walked off that boat loaded down with *añejo* rum and Havana cigars. Nobody we knew was smoking anything but the best Cuban cigars or drinking anything but the best fifteen-year-old rum for a couple of weeks. I do not really know what happened to the freighter, but the story went around that the crew mutinied and deep-sixed the whole cargo, and it would certainly be nice to think that was true.

At some point I also joined the IWW—me and Lenny Glaser hitched out to Chicago to sign up—and Tom Condit, who has a much better memory for this than I do, remembers that in December of 1957 he and Nan Kern and I also joined YPSL, the Young People's Socialist League. (This was pronounced "yipsel," which I recently learned is Yiddish for squirrel— explaining why the older Jewish party members always grinned when we were mentioned.) The three of us went down to Socialist Party headquarters, and there was this huge office with only one person in it, way in the back. That was Irwin Suall, who was the national secretary at the time, and when the three of us came in together, he instantly became very suspicious, because it was probably the largest group that had come to join the Socialist Party in years.

My dedication to syndicalism and political organizing made me particularly impatient with the attitudes of a lot of people on the folk scene who were so eager to be heard that they completely ignored the fact that they were being used as unpaid labor. The Café Bizarre experience continued to rankle, and other bright young entrepreneurs were by now poised to learn from Rick's success. The Guild was doing what it could, but as is always the case, there was a constant supply of kids with guitars who were more than happy to take any work we might reject. My feelings about this were summed up in another *Caravan* piece, which I titled "Ethics and the Folksinger" and signed, for a change, with my own name:

Recently a flurry of activity in the folkmusic field has spotlighted a problem which seems to be almost unique in the arts; that of the professional non-professional. That is to say performers who allow themselves to be jimmied by any petty promoter who comes along, just in order to "be heard." Aside from the stupidity of this attitude, this is a serious breach of ethics.

There are quite a few singers of folksongs floating around and very few job opportunities open. So few in fact that a great many accomplished artists must earn livings in other fields or starve. Add to this the arty entrepreneur with a shoe-string budget looking for free, or cheap, talent, and a musicians' union that devotes its time to taking your money and telling you where you *can't* work, and the confusion of the folksingers' professional world starts to become apparent.

I know several folksingers who have taken jobs without pay, not quite understanding that aside from its artistic nature, singing in front of an audience is work like any other job and that even if they do not need or want pay a great many of their colleagues do and that in any other line of endeavor their practices are referred to as *scabbing* and its practitioners are known as *scabs*. "But these people are as poor as we are and they can't afford to pay us." In some cases this is quite true, but businessmen who have no cash have absolutely no right to employ singers, and entrepreneurs who cop the poverty plea would have their faces laughed in if there weren't so many militant victim-types around this field. Dishwashers, waiters and janitors demand wages for their work. They rarely contribute their talents free to help some small businessman line his pockets. Why should you?

I went on to point out that there were plenty of opportunities available for those who wanted a chance to play for free in front of an audience, such as concerts at hospitals and charity benefits. "The pay is the same as at

Sherri's Loft (none) and no one is lining his pockets at anyone's expense." There was also Washington Square, where no money was made by anyone, and if people wanted to play in a more formal setting, they could pool their resources and hire their own hall.

> If there was less irresponsibility and more understanding among folksingers more of us might be able to eke out a living at it, and even if we continue to sit on our haunches at least we would not be known as easy marks for professional welshers. If you must sing without pay, sing for non-profit enterprises. Don't make another man's living for him, if it doesn't help you and only hurts the rest of us.

I had reason to be acutely aware of the financial deficiencies of the expanding folk business. I was making a little money teaching blues guitar, and a little from concerts, but the light on the horizon remained frustratingly dim. All of us were sure that there was a folk revival on the way, and as it turned out, we were absolutely correct—but any airhead can predict a future event accurately; the trick is to get the tempo right. (My Trotskyist comrades began predicting the collapse of Soviet Stalinism in 1928, but when it finally went belly-up, they were caught just as flat-footed as everybody else. They've been predicting a major depression since 1945, and they'll get that one right too . . . eventually.) Meanwhile, there I was with a reputation as New York's premier young blues interpreter, and nothing to do with it. Great days were a-comin' and a new dawn was in sight—but for the present, as my sainted great-grandmother would say, "Live, horse, and you'll get oats."

My colleague Phil "Dusty" Rhodes (né Perlman), faced with the same problem, had lit out for the territories. Within a startlingly short time, he was holding down a regular gig in Hermosa Beach, California, and he dropped me a note saying, in effect, "Come on in, the water's fine." It sounded too good to be true: He was working five nights a week in a coffeehouse called the Insomniac, getting something like $125 a week with a free apartment right upstairs thrown in for sweeteners. He was less than a block from the beach, he had taken up surfcasting and miniature golf, it was warm, they paid you to take marijuana off their hands, and the women were gorgeous and not vulgarly overdressed. Furthermore, he wrote that he had told the club owners about me and they could hardly wait for me to show up so they could give me the same deal. I had heard yarns like this before, and it really sounded like the Big Rock Candy Mountain, especially since Phil was never given to small enthusiasms. Still, by now it was clear that if I stayed in New York, running in ever narrowing concentric circles, I was bound, sooner or later, to disappear up my own asshole. So what the hell, it was Horace Greeley time . . .

8

Lewis and Clark Revisited

California! It was a continent away, but I talked the matter over with Terri, and we hit on a scheme to get me there for next to nothing—precisely my capital holdings. We were active members of YPSL, and the organization was having its annual conference in Chicago. We could get elected as delegates and get a lift that far with whichever other delegate had a car. From there, Gary Craig, a political accomplice from Seattle, planned to get one of those "Triple-A Drive-away" deals, where you got paid gas and expenses for driving somebody's car from point A to point B, point B in this case being San Francisco. I would join him for that leg of the journey, then Gary would proceed north to Seattle and I south, by hook or by crook, to Hermosa Beach.

I remember almost nothing of the drive to Chicago. There were six of us in a VW Beetle, and I recall dreaming wistfully of the roomy semi cabs and sleek bourgeois bombs I had traveled in when I made that same trip hitchhiking. Hitching cross-country in winter, however, was out of the question; people literally froze to death on the road out there in the wide-open spaces.

The conference was the usual stew of bellow-and-drang and clumsy Machiavellianism to be found wherever young ideologues gather. I loved that stuff, and had a fine time. We stayed at a comrade's apartment, which Terri later described as having "polka-dot wallpaper that moved"—even as a cockroach connoisseur and veteran of countless East Side crash pads, I had to admit it was pretty impressive. Two other things that I remember: I heard Howlin' Wolf for the first time, and Gary and I acquired a passenger, A.K. Trevelyan, age twelve, known forever after (by me) as "Red Chief."

I do not recollect exactly how we got A.K. for a road buddy, but he was the son and heir of an old friend who was sending him to spend some time with his mother in the Bay Area. I did not envy the poor woman. Red Chief had the intellect of an Einstein and the temperament of a pissed-off wolverine.

The arrangement Gary had with Triple-A gave us only four days to get the car to San Francisco. That meant doing about five hundred miles a day, a solid pace but not unreasonable if the roads were clear. Gas money and a small per diem were thrown in, which made a big difference since Gary and I had only about a hundred bucks between us. A.K. had some bread, as well, but he categorically refused to tell us how much.

We left Chicago early in the morning to get as much daylight driving as possible. Gary had to do all of it—I did not have a license, then or ever. The weather got right down to business as soon as we got into Iowa: a regular "blue norther," snow so thick you had to squint to see your windshield wipers, shrieking winds, the works. There was not another car in sight. We crawled along at 20 miles an hour, losing the road from time to time since the terrain was flat as a pancake and there were no tire tracks to follow. When this would happen, I would get out of the car with a tire iron, poke a hole in the snow, and if I hit dirt we would back up and repeat the procedure until I struck pavement. Clearly, this was not a good system for getting to Omaha by early evening. "Gary," I said, "if this keeps up, we'll be lucky if we can reach the next town. We'd better find ourselves a motel and hole up until this blows over."

"We can't afford it," he said. "We only have enough money for three nights of motel."

"It's warm in Nevada," I said. (I was thinking of Las Vegas, not Reno, which was where we were headed, and which gets as cold as the ninth circle.) "When we get there, we can sleep one night in the car. Or else," I continued, "we could always stay right where we are until they dig us out, sometime in April. That wouldn't cost a cent."

Red Chief was in favor of pushing on. He was having the time of his life. Gary was having no fun at all, but he kept driving until somewhere west of Iowa City, at which point my fatuous reasoning, with a strong assist from the blizzard, prevailed. Next morning, bright and early, we were back on the road. In the brilliant sunlight, the world was a vast, flat, blinding snow-field from horizon to horizon. The roads had been sanded, though, and we could do fifty or better—Gary was a superb driver.

The car was a Chevy Impala, which was a pretty hot little number, and we were just waiting to get some dry road under us so we could really boo-gie. We stopped somewhere around Omaha, but only for gas and a bite to eat. I was beginning what would become a lifelong fascination with "real American chow." Heretofore, my idea of a Lucullan feast was the kasha varnishkes with mushroom gravy at the Garden Cafeteria on East Broad-way, lo mein at Sam Wo's, or the arroz con pollo the Spanish anarchists used to dish up at their loft on Broadway and 12th. Chicken fried steak? You've got to be kidding. Country ham with biscuits and redeye gravy? Hush puppies? Give me a break. Mostly it was awful, but I gradually real-ized the problem was not the dishes themselves but the fact that the hash slingers in those truck stops were unbelievably lousy cooks. I have since had chicken fried steaks that could stand toe-to-toe with the best *filetto di manzo* I have ever eaten in Italy.

Whatever may have been wrong with the food, they gave you plenty of it and it was cheap. Gary was a westerner and knew from this stuff, and cu-riosity led me to experiment. A.K. made faces at it and stuck to BLTs. He was also beginning to develop a parody of a midwestern accent that dripped venom. He would try it out on everybody we talked to, and I was sure it was only a question of time before some no-neck behemoth took of-fense and killed all three of us on the spot. He especially loved to say "You betcha!" which he seemed to think was the most hilarious thing he had ever heard in his life. We were getting some pretty funny looks.

Our beards did not help a whole lot. The culture wars of the sixties had not yet begun, but the battle lines were forming and one of the great, burn-ing issues was to be "the beard." You could see it coming—"Hey feller, what's that growing on your chin? Spinach? Hee, hee, hee." You smiled po-litely and disengaged as quickly as possible.

The road opened up in Nebraska; snowbanks six feet high along the shoulders, but the blacktop was clear and dry. Gary was determined to make up lost time, and dropped the hammer. Seventy-five, eighty miles an hour—we were really rolling. Just after dark, we hit a patch of black ice that was slick as greased glass. The car pinwheeled, executing two or three complete spins while we watched helplessly. Somehow Gary managed to get some control, and miraculously brought us to a stop almost gently, against a snowdrift on the side of the road. A quick check of body parts turned up nothing broken, but we were firmly wedged into that snow bank, with our front end three feet deep and nothing but ice under our rear wheels. Gary tried his best, but could not move the damn thing an inch.

So there we sat. Every now and then we would hear a car approaching, and we would pile out, flagging wildly. A couple of guys actually stopped, but lacking tow chains there was nothing they could do. Salvation finally appeared in the form of a local farmer in a pickup with studded tires. "You boys've got yourselves in a pickle, fer sher!"

"Yew betcha!" said Red Chief.

Our Good Sam matter-of-factly produced a tow chain, and quick as it takes to tell, we were on dry land again. Time pressure was weighing heavily on us now, so we had to turn down his offer of supper and beds for the night, and directly were tooling down the road again, doing eighty-five. (Incidentally, further research has confirmed that if you *must* have a disaster, have it happen in the Midwest. Whatever their cultural quirks, those folks can be really nice.)

Night driving in that part of the world is an entirely different thing from what I was used to. Back east there is always some kind of man-made light: a house with a colicky baby, a neon sign, the horizon glow of a distant town, *something*. But here, out beyond the power lines, especially when the sky is overcast, there is a surreal quality, an isolation that at once numbs the mind and fills it with a vague sense of apprehension.

We raced across the Nebraska plains, preceded by our little cowcatcher of light, in a kind of hypnotic trance. Occasionally, the lights of an oncoming truck would appear, brights clicking on, off, on, off: "Cop ahead," "Shitty coffee up the line," or just "Hello, are you alive?" Truckers' signals. I used to be able to read them, but they have pretty much died out now that all the drivers have radios, and I have long since forgotten.

Maybe we were too spaced-out to notice, or maybe the son of a bitch just materialized like a phantom trooper in a Stephen King novel, but the next thing we knew we were being pulled over by Dudley Do-right. The usual routine: high-powered flashlight in the eyes; license, registration; "Do you know how fast you were going?" The fine, he informed us, was based on the number of miles per hour over the speed limit the culprit was clocked at, and since we had been caught red-handed doing 600 miles per hour, we owed the people of Ignominee County $60. At least that was the gist of it. Then he produced a new wrinkle: since court was closed for the night, we could either go with him into town and wait—in jail, naturally—until it convened, which would be two full days since tomorrow was Saturday, or we could waive the hearing and pay the fine on the spot. Just to guarantee that there was no hanky-panky involved, he would watch while we placed the cash in an envelope, addressed it appropriately, and dropped it into a mail slot at the courthouse. This had all the earmarks of a well-oiled scam, but what could we do? We drove into town with him close behind and stopped in front of City Hall, where with the cop watching, A.K. dug an envelope out of his Boy Scout knapsack and I stuffed the sixty bucks (almost all we had) into it, addressed it, and dispatched it as ordered. A galling and nerve-wracking experience.

Over shitty coffee in an all-night truck stop up the line, we reviewed our position. Gary and I had about $30 between us, there was another $30 or so of gas money from Triple-A, and that was it. Red Chief had some money, but still refused to say how much, and announced that he would pool it with us "over my dead body." (To myself I muttered, "Ah yes, the scenic route.") It was a dilemma: we were pressed for time, and if we proceeded legally and sedately at the speed limit, it would take us forever to get out of Nebraska; but if we continued tearing up the pea patch, we ran the risk of having the same rip-off pulled on us again, and that would leave us too broke to continue, sedately or otherwise.

"I say, give 'em the old 'bait and switch,'" said A.K. with a conspiratorial smirk.

"The old what and which?"

"Here," he said, "let me show you." He delved into his knapsack and fished out a box of stationery, did a bit of scrawling on a sheet of letter paper, and before folding it into an envelope, let us take a look. It read,

"Deed to the Brooklyn Bridge"—I think he even signed it, "Peter Minuit." He addressed the envelope to "Town Clowns—Fishfart, Neb.," and handed it to me. "If we get stopped again and they try that same routine on us, all you have to do is switch envelopes at the last minute."

"Oh, is *that* all? And what's the cop supposed to be doing while I'm prestidigitating? The last one was watching me like a hawk."

"Don't worry," he said. "I'll think of something." How a twelve-year-old could come up with a scheme so devious and baroque filled my heart with wonder, but he explained: "Oh, I got it out of a kid's book." It is the only time I have heard the *Newgate Calendar* described as a "kid's book."

In any case, what were the odds on getting popped the same way twice in one night? Lightning doesn't strike etc., etc. Well, just ask any lightning rod about that old saw. Sure enough, not far from the Wyoming line, it happened again. It was still dark. Different cop, but exactly the same routine. As we drove, hangdog, into town, Red Chief said, "When you get out of the car, leave the door open. I'll divert him." What the hell was he going to do, throw a brick at the guy? He giggled, and would say no more.

As I trudged, scared shitless, toward the municipal building, one envelope in my hand, the other in my pocket, I suddenly heard a piercing yell: "Hey! Shut that door, I'm freezing to death back here!" The kid had lungs of steel, and I don't know about that cop, but it sure diverted the hell out of me. I was so startled that I almost botched the substitution, but the thing came off without a hitch. We laughed hysterically all the way to Wyoming.

I guess we must have stopped for gas and even had some breakfast, but other than that we drove straight on through the night. We were rolling merrily along, some fifteen miles east of Cheyenne on a sunny Saturday morning, when we blew a gasket. The Chevy was still ambulatory, but just barely. Gary howled obscenities as we limped down the road at five or ten miles an hour, looking for an open repair shop. At that speed, it took us a while to get into town, where we finally spotted one. "Yep," the fellow agreed that it was a head gasket. "Nope," he couldn't fix it today. The garage closed at noon on Saturday, and it was almost eleven o'clock. The best he could do would be to have it ready early on Monday. Gary explained that Triple-A would be footing the bill, and showed him some papers that seemed to satisfy him. We walked the rest of the way into the center of town.

"First," said Gary, "we get a cheap room. Then a call to Triple-A for some money, and then some sleep." The sleep part sounded especially good. We had been going for at least 24 hours and were walking around in a co-coon of daze.

Cheyenne was the state capital, but first and foremost it was a cow town. Ranch hands, who worked half days on Saturday, crowded the sidewalks looking for ways to spend their week's pay. The atmosphere was festive, al-though almost nobody was drunk yet.

So we're walking along, taking it all in, when up steps the Marlboro Man and says (I swear to God), "You boys new in town?" With one hand he flipped open a wallet and flashed a badge, and with the other he pro-duced a cannon that looked to me like Big Bertha. We were so surprised, and so zonked with fatigue, that we could only stand and stare: was this joker for real? All too real, as it turned out. In seconds he had Gary and me handcuffed together, and A.K. cuffed to his left wrist. "I think we'd better go down to the station and have a little talk." He kept Gary and me in front of him, with A.K. at his side, and he kept that damned bazooka pointed right at us all the time. That hombre didn't take no chances.

It must have been quite a sight: there we were at high noon, being marched at gunpoint down the main street of Cheyenne, Wyoming, by Wyatt Earp. The locals were enjoying it immensely. They gasped with de-light and craned their necks, probably looking for the movie cameras. Nor did they remain silent onlookers: "Hey Bud, looks like you finally caught up with the Dalton boys! Hee, hee, hee." I must confess, the carnival atmos-phere was lost on me at the time, but Red Chief got right into the spirit. He kept looking up at our grim-faced captor and asking, "Air yew the fastest gun in Cheyenne, Shairroff?" I could tell this was going over real big.

At the cop shop, they separated us and grilled us one at a time, with no hint of what the hell it was they were after. Over and over: "What's your name? Where do you come from? What are you doing here?" and "Who's the kid?" I kept explaining to them: "His father is a friend of mine. We're giving him a lift to his mother's place in San Francisco." I had his pop's number with me, and they let me try calling him. No answer.

After the third round of questioning, everybody was getting pretty exas-perated, and they started to slap me around a little, on general principles, just to let me know they weren't too happy with the way things were going.

It was looking like things could get very nasty indeed. They let me try the phone again, and—Praise God!—A.K.'s father was home. "Bert," I said, "we've got a bit of a problem here." I ran down the story for him, and one of the cops got on the line. After some palaver he hung up and said, "We've got to check on this. Wait here." I had a lot of choice. Twenty minutes later he was back: "OK, you can go. Your friends are waiting outside."

"Just like that?" I said. "Wait a minute. What was this all about?"

He looked a little embarrassed. "We kind of thought you two might have kidnapped the boy."

I started to laugh. "Why didn't you ask him?"

"We did," he answered, "but he wouldn't tell us a thing."

"But his I.D. must have checked out."

"Yeah, it did, but it said he was from New York, and he talked like a shit kicker from Iowa. Now get out of here. It's coming on Saturday night, and we're gonna need all the jail cells we've got."

Out on the street, I confronted the little swine: "Why didn't you just tell them the truth?" I screamed.

All of a sudden he was Humphrey Bogart: "I don't talk to cops."

Post mortem in a ratty railroad hotel. Dave: "They hit me a couple of times—nothing serious."

Gary: "That big bastard with the Stetson kicked me in the shins with those pointy-toed cowboy boots." He raised his pants leg, and displayed a bruise that was beginning to look like a Turner sunset.

A.K.: "Yeah, they brought me a cold cheeseburger."

Killing the weekend on a shoestring was no problem at all: We slept. Cheap eats were easy to come by, as well. I continued my culinary research with a substance called "son-of-a-bitch stew" ("S.O.B. Stew" on the lunch-room's "Daily Specials" blackboard), made from beef unmentionables and seasoned with nasty little bird's-eye chilies. Good, though.

Monday morning, refinanced by Triple-A by way of Western Union, we picked up the car and were tooling down Route 80 singing—what else?— "Goodbye, Old Paint, I'm Leavin' Cheyenne."

That stretch of highway across the high plains of Wyoming can be a traveler's graveyard in the winter, but this trip it was like a superfast conveyor belt. Gary had previous experience with the route, though, and wanted to get over into Utah and the Great Basin before the shit hit the fan, which at this time of year was almost inevitable. Hitchhikers were few and far between—hell, people were in short supply, period—so when we saw a guy standing on the road with his thumb out, I was usually inclined to give the poor soul a lift. Gary, on the other hand, was really in the slot now and did not want to stop for anything. But this time was different: "Gary!" I yelled, "Stop the car! That guy has a *beard!!*" He hit the brakes, and it was a lucky thing the road was dry—we must have been doing ninety. We backed up for what seemed like ten miles, and met the guy partway as he trotted to meet us.

Now, the beard factor had been an ongoing irritant in our dealings with the natives since we had left Chicago. Almost every stop we made, there would be comments about our facial hair, and once or twice, only our hasty departure had averted mayhem. Cops seemed especially hostile; both of the times we had been stopped in Nebraska, we had to grin and bear it while Ol' Smokey trotted out his nimble wit at our expense, and remarks dropped at the station house in Cheyenne suggested pretty strongly that we would not have been collared had we been clean shaven. So it was a question of solidarity. There was no way we were going to leave that poor bastard out there to face the tender mercies of the aborigines.

As it turned out, the poor bastard *was* an aborigine, and an honest-to-God cowboy to boot. Andrew ("not Andy, goddammit") could rope ("some"), ride ("pretty good"), and bulldog the kiyoodles ("huh?") with the best of them. But mostly he wanted to get the hell out of Wyoming. The problem was his beard. He was not trying to make any kind of statement, but had grown it on a whim, and when it came in full, he kind of liked the way it looked—understandable, as it was a fine specimen of what I believe is called a "scup," full around the edges, with no mustache, as worn by Horace Greeley and Abraham Lincoln. Indeed, Andrew was a handsome specimen entirely. Of medium height, and older than us (about thirty), with his battered Stetson and slightly weather-beaten look, he was the very image of that film director's dream, "The Last American Cowboy"—and he knew it.

Apparently the scheme had been percolating in his mind for a while, and the beard had finally kicked off a hegira to the coast to get into the movies. His buddies on the ranch where he worked were giving him no peace, calling him "Abe" (in reference to Lincoln, I suppose, but with anti-Semitic undertones), and perfect strangers were always trying to start fights.

"Yeah, tell us about it."

"So I figured, if I'm gonna look like an extra in *Shane*, I might as well get paid for it." I had heard tell of Will Geer's theater in Topanga Canyon, where Woody Guthrie used to crash and where, according to the grapevine, Jack Elliott was currently holing up, so I passed the word along; maybe a connection with the film colony could be made from there. He liked the sound of that. Comfortably ensconced with a bunch of fellow outcasts, he settled into the backseat with A.K. and began teaching him "real cowboy songs." As I recall, one of them went:

I am an old cow-puncher; I punch them cows real hard.
I've got me a cow-punching bag at home in my back yard.
It's all made out of leather; it's real cowhide of course.
When I get tired of punching cows, I go and punch a horse.

Our virtuous deed did not go unrewarded: Andrew had a driver's license and was only too happy to spell Gary at the wheel. Of course, the insurance on the car would not cover him as a driver, but the clock was still ticking and money was still mighty scarce. Gary proposed that he and Andrew take turns, eight hours on and eight off, driving and sleeping, all the way to San Fran. I thought this really sucked the big one; the idea of sitting in that car for eighteen hours—give or take a couple—made me sick with dread. For a change, A.K. agreed with me. He wanted to have a look at Salt Lake City and do some "real gambling" in Reno. "OK," Gary told him, "you pick up the motel bills. Besides," he added spitefully, "they're not gonna let you gamble in Reno; you're only a kid." That actually shut him up for a while. (Red Chief had never been Mr. Popularity with us, and after the "High Noon in Cheyenne" caper, Gary and I tacitly agreed that the more sequestered we kept the kid, the safer we all would be. Personally, if there had been room I would have stowed the little rodent in the trunk.)

With Red Chief silenced—there was no way he would agree to pay the motel—I was outvoted. I glumly resigned myself to an eternity of cramps and claustrophobia and let the matter drop.

West toward the Utah line, Route 80 rises with the terrain into the Wasatch Range—not exactly the Himalayas, but formidable enough—and very scenic, weather permitting. Weather did not permit. As soon as we began to climb, the snow began to fall, and with predictable synchronicity, the higher we climbed, the harder it fell. I am not sure how it happened—maybe the interstate had not yet been completed through the mountains, or maybe some half-wit (probably me, since I was the expedition's navigator) spotted a shortcut on the road map—but the next thing we knew, we were on a narrow two-lane road in the middle of the mountains, up to our asses in snow. Those were seven or eight of the hairiest, scariest hours I have ever lived through. No question of finding a nice motel and waiting out the storm; there was nothing out there but mountains and chasms with five-hundred-foot drops, and that pathetically narrow road, snaking and hair-pinning around them. We were doing fifteen miles an hour. Once in a rare while, some idiot would actually pass us, raising the tension in the car even higher. Some stretches of that route could not have had more than a few inches of clearance, but the trucks went barreling on through. Did those lunatics *want* to die? No one had spoken for hours, and I was on the point of screaming, or praying, or just gibbering like an idiot, when the road finally leveled and straightened, the snow tapered off and stopped, and we were out of it.

We slept that night in a motel, and did not even try to make A.K. foot the bill.

Salt Lake City I recall only as an oblong blur. (Rosalie Sorrels, who was living there before she took to the road as a folksinger, assures me that this is a fairly accurate description.) We zipped across the Bonneville Flats and the Great Salt Desert, on over into Nevada, where, mirabile dictu, there was *no speed limit.*

Gary had been living for this moment. Our handy-dandy road atlas had a chart listing the speed limits of the various states. Next to Nevada it said only "Reasonable and proper." It was cold out there, and there was snow off the road, but the asphalt itself was straight, flat, and bone-dry. "Hoo boy, lets boogie!" And boogie we did. That Impala was a sweet little item, and Gary put his foot through the floor and got her up to 120. "Gary," I said, the voice of sweet reason and propriety, "don't you think a hundred will do?" He grumbled a little, but moderation prevailed and we scooted on past Elko at a stately 100 miles per hour. Splat! A lump of reddish-gray goop appeared on the windshield. "What the fuck was that?" Gary yelled.

"It's a bird," said Andrew.

"Yeah sure. It's a plane, it's Superman."

"No, really," Andrew explained. "The road gets hot from the sun and they stand on it to get warm."

Sure enough, there were flocks of them now. At our approach, they would take off, but we were moving too fast for all of them to get out of the way. Splat! Splat! It was getting hard to see the road. "Fuck 'em," Gary grunted through clenched teeth. "We've gotta make time! When it gets too bad, we'll scrape 'em off." Splat.

"We" turned out to be me. Gary was the driver; Andrew was a guest of sorts; and Red Chief refused, point blank: "Oh no you don't! Slow down, and you'll stop hitting them. I'm in no hurry." So from time to time we would pull over to the side of the road, and I would trundle out, ice scraper in hand, to peel ten pounds of bird porridge off the windshield. Everybody else in the car seemed to think this a perfect division of labor. Be that as it may, we were in Reno in five hours.

In Reno, a mere five more hours short of San Francisco and blessed surcease, the word came down: Route 80 over the Donner Pass was closed to vehicles without tire chains. This was the last straw. We were just about broke again, since the unscheduled stop in Salt Lake had used up our motel money. We could just barely afford some gas and a bite to eat, and that was it. Of course, Gary *could* phone Triple-A again and ask them to wire us the money to buy a set of chains—it was certainly a legitimate expense—but the money would not get to us until tomorrow, and in the meantime where would we sleep? Gary and I looked pointedly at Red Chief, who we knew still had some cash reserves. "We can sleep in the car," he quoted, with a big evil smile. "It's warm in Nevada." I did not kill him.

I suppose I should admit that, while A.K. was something of a skinflint, he was no freeloader. When a collective expenditure was necessary, he ponied up like a mensch. If worst had come to worst, he would probably have shelled out for a cheap room in a squalid motor court—I think. But at least to my sleep-deprived mind, it seemed as if there was another way out. "Guys," I said, "we have nothing to lose. Here we are, in the gambling capital of the United States, with twenty bucks between us. Let's see if we can parlay that into some kind of grubstake for the rest of the trip." Not my sharpest reasoning perhaps, but to a bunch of young louts of the male persuasion it seemed the soul of judiciousness.

Reno in those days was even more of a stockman's town than it is now. Cattle kings and cowboys—Andrew knew the town well—Indians off the nearby reservation, Basque sheepherders, and at this time of year, very few tourists. There was no "strip." The casinos were all downtown. If you did not care for your luck in one joint, you just walked across the street. We chose Harold's, mostly because I had heard of them: they used to circulate matchbooks all over the country with a cartoon of a naked guy in a high hat, walking around in a barrel. The caption read: "I was there." On the basis of my acknowledged (by me) blackjack expertise, I was to be custodian of the treasury. Amazingly, the cards ran well. Betting no more than a buck at a time (all small bets were in silver dollars), it took me less than an hour to amass forty dollars in winnings. Time to redistribute. We divvied up the money, and Gary and Andrew went off to find their own tables. Red Chief stuck by my elbow, offering advice. By now he was calling me "Doc," and refused to budge an inch. Betting such small amounts, it takes a long time to make any kind of money, but the cards still liked me and I persisted. Then a voice hissed in my ear: "Stand on sixteen, Doc. The dealer's gonna bust." I stood. The dealer busted. I had not won enough yet to see us on our way, but I was getting close, and A.K. was driving me nuts. I handed him a couple of silver dollars. "Here, kid," I said nastily. "Go get yourself an ice cream cone." He made a face at me and took off. Ten minutes later, while I was sweating over a possible five-card Charlie, he reappeared. "Here," he said, displaying a hat full of silver dollars. "There's more in my pockets. Let's get out of here, this place bores the shit out of me."

We rounded up our coconspirators, one of whom had also come out a winner, turned our clinkers into bills at the cashiers cage (except for A.K., who liked his hat full of silver), and went our way rejoicing. As we were leaving, I stuck my hand into my pocket and discovered a last silver dollar I had overlooked. What the hell; I dropped it into a slot machine by the door, and hit a goddamn jackpot. Not of Red Chief proportions, mind you, with bells and whistles, but another forty bucks or so. We were rich! Let the good times roll!

Now we could afford tire chains, food, gas, *and* a cheap room in a squalid motor court. We proceeded to do all of the above. We gorged ourselves festively that night in the dining room of a Basque boardinghouse. All you could eat for five bucks a head, and they kept our water glasses—A.K.'s included—filled with some of the most awful sour wine I have ever tasted. What the hell did we know from wine? We loved it. And so, merrily, to bed.

Next morning, somewhat subdued (oh God, that wine . . .) but with skid chains duly in place, we proceeded up and over Donner Pass, through the Sierras and some of the most spectacular scenery in the country. There was plenty of snow on the ground, but the day was glorious and the road was fine. Our morale was improving. Coming down into the foothills, someone said happily, "Open the windows, it's stifling in here." I did so, and received a blast of warm, moist, and vegetal Pacific air that was pure bliss. An hour later we spotted our first palm tree.

9

California

Rolling down through the Coast Range and over the Bay Bridge into Frisco* was a new approach for me, and a bit of a comedown. My previous arrival, floating in under the Golden Gate, had been incomparably more dramatic. Still, right then it looked like the promised land. Gary dropped me off in North Beach, which was still the beat capital of the West Coast, albeit in sad decline from its glory days of a few years past.

This habit of showing up just in time to miss an incandescence seems to be a signature trait of mine. I am like a bellwether: "Uh-oh, here comes Van Ronk. The party must be over." There have been a couple of exceptions, but when people burble at me, "Oh what a colorful life you've led!" I am tempted to tell them, "Look, I've known people who were busted with Emma Goldman, worked the riverboats with Louis Armstrong, beat Marcel Duchamp at chess, bunked with Bix, hopped freights with Joe Hill, and shot grouse with Leon Trotsky. *That's* colorful." On the other hand, I have a sneaking suspicion that when Pericles hit Athens, everybody told him: "Boy! You should have been here last year, the joint was really jumping." You takes what you can get.

---

*Yes, I know San Franciscans hate it when people say "Frisco." I don't care.

In any case, there I was, standing outside the Co-Existence Bagel Shop in North Beach. I had heard through the grapevine that this was where "all the haps were going down," but on entering I was quickly informed that the place, an innocuous coffeehouse, had recently been raided by the cops.

This was 1959, and the city's raffishness had not yet been commodified. The cutesy boutiques and hipsey-poo restaurants that currently blight the whole peninsula were still ten years off. Ghirardelli Square was known for a derelict chocolate factory, Chinatown was a neighborhood where Chinese people lived, and Fisherman's Wharf was a fisherman's wharf. The petite bourgeoisie's unerring homing instinct for kitsch would change all that, but as yet the campaign to make Bohemia safe—and salable—had not begun. Still, the preconditions for the campaign ahead were falling into place. A kind of demographic slum clearance—"Drive the riff-raff out of North Beach"—had begun. Or as we put it at the time, "The heat was on."*

The heat took the form of harassment by the cops of anybody who looked like a "weirdo," accompanied by the occasional beating, and the aforementioned raid on the bagel shop. All of this was done to the tune of a strident crusade against "beatniks"—the word had only recently been minted by Herb Caen of the *Chronicle*, bless him—in the gutter press. Until that damned word came along, nobody noticed us, or if they did it was just "those kids." We had all the freedom anonymity could bestow—a lovely state of affairs.

What had started the current crackdown was an incident that occurred a week or two before I arrived. Eric "Big Daddy" Nord, an outstanding example of the poet-hustler type this country seems to make a specialty of (back east we had Ted Joans), had been running a series of bogus "rent parties," charging the clydes at the door and selling them drinks. At one of

---

*I have seen far too much of this: sharks note a couple of artists renovating a loft, smell blood in the water, and immediately rename the neighborhood SoHo or NoHo or HoBo and go into a real-estate feeding frenzy. It is destroying all that makes urban living a pleasure. The sad saga of my favorite restaurant in SF is a case in point: the Tortola was a neighborhood institution in the old Tenderloin. It featured the cuisine of Alta California—the *comidas* of the missions and ranches before the Anglo ascendancy. How authentic it was I can't say—I have found nothing to compare it with. God, I loved that place! Anyway, it held out through the sixties and early seventies, and then it was gone. The neighborhood had become "too dangerous" I was told, and if by "dangerous" they meant seedy and ungentrified, they had a case—but winos and panhandlers are *not* especially dangerous; they merely offended the sensibilities of the "New San Franciscans," i.e., the yuppies. Later on I heard that the Tortola had reopened somewhere out in the Western Addition, and I hastened to check it out. It was a spacious, well-lit, and comfortable vacuum. The food was OK, the sort of raspberry vinaigrette type of chow you find wherever the upwardly mobile congregate, but of the old menu, nothing remained. I never went back.

these wingdings, somebody got very drunk and fell—or, some said, was pushed—off the roof. The resultant "Splat heard 'round the world" triggered a Kulturkampf locally and, within a year or two, nationally that would simmer and flair up from time to time over the next decade.

The upshot of all this was that I was forced more or less to avoid North Beach during my stay in SF. Most of the time, I stayed with my old IWW fellow worker Al Graham in the Mission District or crashed with some college kids across the bay in Berkeley. The only scene in North Beach that attracted me was Pierre Delattre's Bread and Wine Mission on Grant Avenue. Pierre, an Episcopalian priest, had somehow conned his superiors into funding an apostolate to the freaks. It was a storefront operation, with a big room cluttered with chairs, tables, and cast-off sofas facing the street, and a couple of small rooms in the back where Pierre slept and hosted wine-swilling poker sessions every now and then. (That boy was my kind of missionary.) Besides the free spaghetti dinners every Friday night, the mission had other appeals as a hangout: the connection with Holy Mother Church rendered it, we imagined, pig-proof, and in my case it was also a source of income. On one or two occasions, Pierre produced store concerts for me on a pass-the-hat basis. I split the billing and the take with Paul Schoenwetter, a fine frailing banjoist and fellow member of the Folksingers Guild who was also rattling around Frisco with no money and nothing much to do.

Across the bay in Berkeley, I was hanging around Barry Olivier's place, the Barrel. Barry gave me a gig after I helped him unload a truck full of furniture—a somewhat unusual technique for getting onstage, but it worked fine. He also set up a couple of blues guitar workshops, which brought in a few dollars more, and meanwhile I honed my poker sharkery on the wallets of a bunch of UC students who could no more hold their liquor than they could resist drawing to an inside straight.

Compared to my situation in New York, I was performing quite a bit. I met and heard Mimi Baez for the first time at a late-night show at KPFA (one of the first "highbrow" FM radio stations), and sang there a few times myself.* I also seized the opportunity to consort with Jesse Fuller, "The Lone Cat," twelve-string guitarist extraordinaire, one-man band, and composer of

*These days, Mimi tends to be identified as Joan's younger sister, but in the Bay Area of that time she was regarded as the talent in the family.

"San Francisco Bay Blues." Jesse, like most of the rest of us, could not make a living from his music, so he was running a shoe-shine parlor on Telegraph Avenue, just over the city line in Oakland. (I think he might have been doing a little policy action on the side, as well.) In full musical harness, he provided quite a visual: along with his big twelve-string guitar, he wore a double rack around his neck with a kazoo on the upper tier and a harmonica below it. With his left foot, he operated a high-hat cymbal, and with his right he deftly tapped out a bass line on five treadles that he had hooked up to one of the damnedest musical contraptions I have ever seen. It was a piano box with five strings on it, and each treadle activated a felt-tipped piano hammer that struck one of the strings with a satisfying boom. This was his own invention, which he called a "footdella," and it was amazing how much bass he could play with just those five notes. To manage this intricate task, however, he had to remove his right shoe and sock. As I say, quite a visual.

Jesse did not keep the whole rig around the shop, but the guitar was always there, and when I stopped by, we would pick and sing a few songs, mostly blues. He taught me "San Francisco Bay," which I love but have never performed (both Jesse and Jack Elliott did it better than I ever could), and for a while I did his versions of "Linin' Track" and "Hanging Around a Skin Game." Business was pretty slow, and Jesse seemed happy for some company. He was a relentless self-promoter, and he loved to talk almost as much as he liked to perform. He especially enjoyed reminiscing about his days in Hollywood back in the 1920s, where he worked as a film extra and was taken up by Doug Fairbanks Sr. He used to perform at the monumental bashes Fairbanks and Mary Pickford threw at Pickfair, their Xanadu in the Hollywood Hills. It all sounded marvelously corrupt.

Jesse had gained a measure of local renown back in 1948, when Leadbelly appeared on a San Francisco radio program and proclaimed himself, as he was wont to do, "the king of the twelve-string guitarists of the world." Jesse picked up the telephone, called the station, and let out a squawk of rage: "Who is this bum? *I'm* the king of the twelve-string guitar, and if you put me on the air, I'll prove it." They did, and he did. Ten years later the memory still rankled. When I told a friend of his that I was going over to Oakland to visit with him, she warned me: "Don't mention Leadbelly."

Jesse was a gold mine of songs, and he painstakingly wrote down all the lyrics he knew in a series of school composition books. He let me look through one of them, and if I asked about a tune, he would pick up the guitar and run through it for me. Not a bad way to learn. He also kept a stock of the ten-inch LPs he had made for a local label called World Song, and he happily sold me one for five bucks.

Another person I was seeing pretty regularly was my old friend (personal) and nemesis (political) Bogdan Denitch, "the mad Montenegrin." Like his sidekick Mike Harrington, he had become mesmerized by the utopian notion that if enough socialists joined the Democratic Party, they could use their influence to move it to the left—a textbook example of what the sociologist C. Wright Mills used to call "crackpot realism." I held, and still do, that the only way you can influence such gentry is with the backing of a mob of screaming peasants brandishing pruning hooks. Sure enough, the Socialist Party followed Bogdan's logic, merged into the "Democracy," and vanished from the face of the earth—while my cothinkers and I went on to become the mighty political force we are today . . .

Although their supporters in YPSL were a sorry assortment of junior bureaucrats and ward-heelers manqué, Bogdan and Mike were born bohemians. Temperamentally we had all belonged to the hell-raising faction that convened regularly at the White Horse Tavern on Hudson Street in the Village, and since Bogdan had recently relocated to Berkeley, he took some time off from his job as a tool-and-die maker to show me a bit of the locale. Wonder of wonders, he actually owned a car, so we could motor down the coast to Moro Bay or over the bridge to Sausalito, where I would drink in the scenery, among other things. I am pretty sure it was Bogdan who introduced me to the No Name bar, later the scene of many fondly remembered debaucheries.

Despite all this fossicking around the periphery, my main focus was San Francisco itself. I loved its pastel-painted, bay-windowed wooden houses, the hills, the wet-wool fogs, the whole romantic concatenation—hell, I even loved those Mickey Mouse cable cars. Moreover, and a big plus for me, Frisco was a place where lefties could really feel at home. In those days, it was still a working-class town and, since the general strike of 1934 (which I heard a lot about), a union town to boot. The joint was fully outfitted with hot and cold running Reds of every imaginable persuasion.

Along with the more organized and solemn factions, anarchists and Wobblies were thick on the ground. The house where I crashed in the Mission

District was a veritable hotbed of anarchism and free love—or anyway of an-archism.* Al Graham, our boniface, was a deep-dyed Wobbly with a pen-chant for direct action and an exuberant passion for organizing absolutely everybody and everything—he had recently been popped on Cape Cod for trying to organize the lobstermen, or maybe it was the lobsters. Tom Condit, ex-marine, libertarian socialist, and that rara-est of avises, a native Californ-ian, was a walking encyclopedia of arcane social history, obscure political facts (I remember with special joy his disquisition on the Somali Youth League and its struggle for "Somalia irredenta"), and good, cheap restaurants in the Bay Area. Tom and I also haunted every low-stakes poker game we could find, and we made out pretty good sometimes.

Phil Melman, who lived elsewhere but always seemed to be around, was the real article: an *old* old Wobbly. Phil was sixty-five, and the terror and delight of the hip community, careening around the city on a big old Harley, scattering pedestrians like startled chickens and playing roller coaster on the steepest hills he could find. I used to go out with him, riding pillion—some people never learn—and I remember shouting in his ear: "Phil! Phil! Take it easy! You're going to get us killed!" He did neither.

With this cast of characters, one would think the action would be thick and fast, but as it happened, life was pretty tranquil. Al did keep a gun under his pillow, and Tom and I kept hiding it for fear that a postman or meter reader's early morning knock would set him off—in his A.M. daze, Al might see the uniform, mistake the guy for a cop, and start blazing away, thinking it was the Paris Commune or something. Admittedly, this was pretty far-fetched, but we enjoyed getting his goat. It never took him more than a minute or two to find it anyway.

At some point, Al received a notice that his phone was being shut off—for nonpayment, what else?—and he noticed that the disconnect date was the day before, and reasoned that since his service had officially been termi-nated, Ma Bell could not legally charge for any calls we made on it, despite

---

*Anyone who has read this far is probably wondering, "All this nattering on about Bohemia and beat-nikery—Where's the *sex*?" Believe me, the same question occurred to us at the time. But bear in mind, I am writing about the *fifties*. The buttoned-down, up-tight, witch-hunting, God-fearing Age of Eisen-hower. They still tossed doctors into the slammer for fitting women with diaphragms in some states, and for performing abortions in all of them. Women were understandably very cautious about dispens-ing their favors under those circumstances, and the fact that we were a pretty scuzzy bunch might also have had something to do with it.

the fact that it was still working. He promptly invited us to call anybody we wanted for free. I called Terri in New York, Tom spoke to someone in Northern Ireland, and as a collective enterprise, we decided to call the Dalai Lama in Tibet. (If this sounds like the sort of thing only a bunch of zonked-out kids would do, you're right on the money.) We actually got through to Katmandu, where an operator informed us that the phone in Lhasa was at the Summer Palace, and His Holiness was at the Winter Palace (or vice versa), but they would be happy to send a runner out with a telephone and a line and call us back tomorrow. "Nah, it wasn't important. We just wanted to chat." (Incidentally, the phone company did not appreciate Al's logic, and hounded him mercilessly until, a year or so later, we all sent him a bunch of money to cover our share of the day's entertainment.)

I was persisting in my quest for gainful employment, but was turned down at the Hungry i, which was the main folk room in SF. I was too scruffy and did not even get as far as an audition. The only gig I managed to scare up, aside from the Bread and Wine Mission concerts, was at a "poetry and jazz" evening in some dump on Grant Avenue. I sat onstage and tinkled "Freight Train," while some turkey explained to us all, at 120 decibels, the reasons for his alienation. I assume I was supposed to be the "jazz." Another ten bucks.

All in all, as far as venues for my sort of music went, it was not really all that different from New York. The Kingston Trio had first hit it big in Frisco, at a joint called the Purple Onion, but their version of the folk crowd consisted of boys in neat little three-button suits with narrow little lapels and skinny little ties, and girls in evening gowns. Crew-cuts! Crew-cuts up the wazoo. And most of the music was so precious, and so corny, you could lose your lunch. My big problem, as I was informed by several club managers, was that I didn't *look* like a folksinger. That was phase one of the great folk revival. As for phase two, I had no way of knowing this was only phase one. Who knew? Next year they might try stuffing everybody into silken doublets and hose. Then they'd *really* look like folksingers. (That ain't no joke. Twenty years later a friend of mine was picking up extra money at one of those hilariously awful "Renaissance Fairs," dressed exactly so, playing "Hell Hound on My Trail" on a lute.)

There was an obvious subtext to what these Babbitt balladeers were doing, and it was: "Of course, we're really superior to all this hayseed crap—but isn't it *cute?*" This attitude threw me into an absolute ecstasy of rage. These were no true disciples or even honest money changers—they were a bunch of slick hustlers selling Mickey Mouse dolls in the temple. Join their ranks? I would sooner have been boiled in skunk piss.

To put it somewhat less hysterically, the folk music revival that was going on west of the Hudson was pitched toward college students with pocket money from their folks, and young urban professionals just hip enough to gasp delightedly when Lenny Bruce said "shit" on stage. The popular headliners were the sort of clean-cut college types with which such an audience could identify, all singing exactly the same songs in exactly the same way. This movement was phenomenally popular and made some big record company honchos oodles of money. It had its own dress code and musical standards (basically, a diluted rehash of the old Weavers), its own circuit of clubs, and it sure as hell wasn't about to revive *me*.

The local folk establishment and I were thus locked in a circle of mutual distaste, which left me with three options: I could slink back to New York, as after the Gate of Horn fiasco; head south to Hermosa Beach, where a gig was still waiting for me; or set up shop in Frisco and try to carve out a viable niche as the vanguard of the second wave of folk revivaldom.

Going back to New York under these circumstances was out of the question. Staying in San Francisco was much more tempting, despite the fact that my only potential constituency was a bunch of penniless bums like myself—but the temptation was part of the problem. There was a "Lotus Land" quality about the place, and I had a sense that if I stuck around much longer, I would keep amiably drifting from scene to scene and lose my edge. Furthermore, how the hell would I ever convince Terri, who was as much a hard-shell New York chauvinist as I had ever been, to pick up stakes and remove herself three thousand miles from civilization? Then came a phone call from Terri. Knowing about the free spaghetti dinners at the Bread and Wine Mission, she caught me there one Friday evening and read me the riot act: No, she wouldn't move to goddamn San Francisco, and what the hell was I doing goofing off around the Bay Area when there was a stage being held for me, lo this past month, down south?

"Get your ass in gear," she told me, and her tone brooked no argument.

Besides, she had a point. I got my ass in gear.

♫   ♫   ♫

After my Bay Area experience, LA was like going from zero to sixty in 0.1 seconds. Phil's advance report had not been an exaggeration, and within a week of arriving I had more work than I could handle. Weekdays I was playing at the Insomniac on Hermosa Beach, and on the weekends I was at the Unicorn, Herbie Cohn's place on Sunset Strip. The Unicorn had a garden around the back, and I used to have to stand out there under some kind of fucking tree, which I hated, but the bread was good. As for the Insomniac, it was right across the street from Howard Rumsey's Lighthouse, so as a side benefit I had the opportunity to catch some great jazz between sets.

To be working seven nights a week was incredible to me. In a sense it was the first real test of my career plans, of whether I truly wanted to be a professional, full-time musician. And the answer was yes, without question or reservation. It also provided a lot of incentive to develop my music, build up my repertoire, all that kind of thing. It was an absolutely essential education, because you can practice playing guitar in your living room, and you can practice singing in your living room, but the only place you can practice performing is in front of an audience. Those old coffeehouses did not have to shut down early like the bars did, so they would stay open as long as there were paying customers, and you would wind up working four or five sets a night. I think that is one of the things that set the folksingers of my generation apart from the performers coming up today. There are some very good young musicians on the folk scene, but they will get to be fifty years old without having as much stage experience as I had by the time I was twenty-five. As a result, they will naturally mature much more slowly than the Dylans and Joni Mitchells and I did. We had so much opportunity to try out our stuff in public, get clobbered, figure out what was wrong, and go back and try it again. It was brutally hard work, but that was how I learned my trade: by working in front of an audience hour after hour, night after night. You can hear the difference immediately if you listen to my two Folkways albums.

The only drawback, from my point of view, was the fear that people back in New York might hear that I was playing in coffeehouses. My compatriots and I had always believed that there was no life form more protozoan than a coffeehouse folksinger. Coffeehouse folksingers were squeaky-clean optimists who brushed their teeth eighty-seven times a day, wore drip-dry seersucker suits, and sang "La Bamba." So back home, if you got known as a coffeehouse folksinger, you lost many, many points. It was an embarrassment, but I tried to shrug it off: I was singing in a coffeehouse (or two), but that didn't necessarily make me a coffeehouse folksinger, did it? Besides, I took consolation in the knowledge that New York was three thousand miles away.

Then the great day arrived when I received a record-album-shaped package with the return address marked as Folkways Records. My hours in Kenny Goldstein's basement had finally born fruit, and I ecstatically tore open the wrapping, ready to gaze for the first time on an LP of my very own. The cover puzzled me for a moment: it was one of those great old Folkways covers, a two-tone print full of tubes and vessels resembling the boiler room of the Robert E. Lee. It took a few seconds for the image to sort itself out, but then there was no mistaking it for anything but what it was: an espresso machine.

I went nuts, and if I had had the money to get back to New York right at that moment, I would have dropped everything and made the trip just to break a couple of copies of that record over Moe Asch's head. I was so enraged that it took several days before I calmed down sufficiently to notice that my name on the label was spelled V-O-N Ronk. By that time I had become philosophical about the whole business, as I have remained ever since.

As in San Francisco, I spent most of my free time in LA hanging out with New York expats. Along with Phil, there was Jimmy Gavin, whom I knew from Washington Square. He had come out a while earlier and was working at a club on the strip called the Renaissance. I went in there one night because I had heard that Jack Elliott was going to be playing, and ran into Jimmy, which was always a pleasure. Even more than the music, though, I remember being struck by the Renaissance itself. It was a real nightclub featuring folk music, and I had never seen anything like that; I had been to the Gate of Horn in Chicago, but only in the afternoon and I had never seen it function. The Renaissance made an incredible impression on me, because there was nothing comparable in New York at that point.

I should mention in this context that it has always amazed me how New York and Greenwich Village hog the credit (such as it is) for the folk music revival. In the 1950s, as far as public performance spaces were concerned,

New York might as well have been Tegucigalpa. Boston, Los Angeles, San Francisco, and Chicago were all years ahead of us, each having at least one folk club up and running by 1957 or so. In New York, there was no room dedicated to anything resembling folk music, and no possibility that anyone like me could have any hopes of working more than a few nights a month. It is true that we had some good musicians, but in terms of performance spaces we really got a slow start.

As a result, there was very little reason why a folk performer would have chosen to spend time in New York at that point, which may have been why I had never met Ramblin' Jack. Of course I knew who he was; he was already a legend to us because we had heard the stories about him going out west and becoming a cowboy, then hoboing around the country with Woody Guthrie. A lot of people idolized him, some of them with what I can only describe as a sort of wistful envy, because they were into the music and the mystique but didn't have whatever it took to pick up stakes and do that. By the time I came on the scene, though, he was long gone from the Village. For most of the 1950s he was either on the West Coast or wandering around Europe with a banjo player named Derroll Adams, and all we heard of him was some recordings for the Topic label in England. He did occasionally pass through New York—sightings were reported from time to time—but for most of us he was more a myth than a person. So meeting him was another pleasure of that LA period.

On the whole, though, I did not like Los Angeles. It was nice to be working regularly and to find some people who were interested in what I did, but there were a lot fewer weirdos than in New York or San Francisco, and I always preferred the weirdos. The kind of people who came out to the folk clubs in LA were more like regular Americans. I could go on about this, but basically the difference between New York and LA is that they are on different planets and are quite happy to be on different planets. So I hated it, mostly because I knew that I was supposed to hate it—when I went back a few years later, I got to like the place very much. Back in 1959, though, I had a chip on my shoulder like a redwood, I was an incredible intellectual snob, and I very rapidly reached the point that I could not wait to get back to New York. Terri was graduating from college in June, and I had promised to be there for that, so after a couple of months I gathered my meager savings and headed back east.

10

The Commons and Gary Davis

When I got back to New York in the summer of 1958, the work situation was about the same, but a lot else had changed. Lee Shaw had passed *Caravan* over to Billy Faier, who had turned it into a serious, scholarly periodical, and she had started *Gardyloo*. (The July issue's "Anti-Social Notes from All Over" reported that I had shaved off my beard and was "once again a bare-faced boy.") Meanwhile, the Folksingers Guild was on its last legs. It was still producing occasional concerts for a small pool of Washington Square devotees, but no great revival had yet happened, and the performers were beginning to feel as if all we were doing was taking in each other's washing. Then our newly appointed treasurer absconded with our small treasury, nobody had the heart to start again from scratch, and the outfit folded with hardly a whimper.

At the same time, it was clear that interest in folk music was spreading beyond our esoteric coterie, and not just into the crew-cut hinterlands of the Kingston Trio. About a month after I got back, we all trooped down to Newport to attend the first annual folk festival. None of the Village crowd had been invited to play, except for the New Lost City Ramblers, but nothing would have kept us away. The lineup included all the warhorses of the professional folk world, but also Memphis Slim, the Reverend Gary Davis, and Earl Scruggs. Altogether, it was an absolutely magical event, and oddly enough, what I especially remember was Cynthia Gooding's performance the first evening. Cynthia was six feet tall, with flaming red hair, and she was wearing a diaphanous green gown. As she was singing, a fog came in off the water, and the wind was blowing, and the way the lights were set up, Cynthia and her gown were reflected on the clouds. It was the most ethereal visual I have ever seen in my life. The whole weekend was like that. The next evening Bob Gibson, who was riding very high in those days, gave half of his stage time to an unknown young singer named Joan Baez. That was Joanie's big break, and anyone who was there could tell that it was the beginning of something big for all of us.

Meanwhile, Terri's graduation went off as planned, and within a couple of weeks we had settled into a fifth-floor walk-up on 15th Street.* I did not like that much—as Max Bodenheim used to say, I get nosebleeds when I get above 14th Street—but at least it was big enough for two people. Terri had a job as a substitute teacher, and I hung out my shingle as a guitar instructor, attracting maybe ten students a week, and gave occasional concerts. By and large, though, I was still out on the street in search of work. A couple of new coffeehouses had opened while I was out of town, but they were of little interest to me. This was the heyday of the beatnik craze, and what folk music was played in those places was at best a minor adjunct to the poetry. I also had a personal grudge against the main room, the Gaslight Café, because of the hassle it had made for Liz at the Caricature. It was in the basement of the same building, which had been the coal cellar, and the owner, a guy named John Mitchell, fixed it up himself. Mitchell was an incredibly abrasive man, and his construction work—converting the room from a coal bin into an armpit—played hob with Liz's plumbing and wiring, and he was not gracious about it. Liz was very upset, and she had been our patroness, so I was firmly in her camp. Plus, the place irritated me. It had started hosting poetry readings just after I left for California, with people like Allen Ginsberg and Gregory Corso, but by the time I got back, there was no one of that stature around. I checked it out because Roy Berkeley had a regular gig there, but after hearing these poets bawling and howling, I quickly concluded that it was sheer bullshit.

---

*Sam Dolgoff once said that if you shaved the top floor off all the walk-ups in New York City, you'd completely destroy the radical movement. I said, "Nah, what about the basements?"

Early Days in Queens:
My mother and me, the Harmonotes' business card, and portrait of an incipient juvenile delinquent with guitar. *(All photos not otherwise credited are from the collection of Andrea Vuocolo Van Ronk.)*

THE BOSSES 25¢
SONGBOOK

SONGS TO STIFLE THE FLAMES OF DISCONTENT

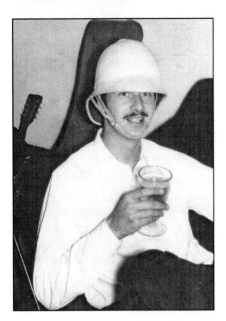

ALgonquin 5-2856

DAVE VAN RONK
Folk Blues

New York City

The 1950s: (Clockwise from bottom left) Jamming with Bob Yellin and Roy Berkeley in the Folklore Center; with Lee Hoffman in Washington Square (note the banjo); a Folksingers' Guild ad; and the Bosses Songbook; Paul Clayton in his pith helmet; my card; warring personae: the hipster bluesman and the academic folksinger. *(All photos: Photosound Associates: J. Katz, A. Rennert, and R. Sullivan.)*

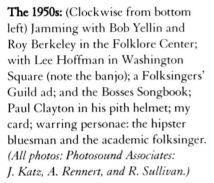

HOFSTRA COLLEGE
FOLK SONG CLUB
PRESENTS
A
FOLKSONG
CONCERT

FEATURING

MOLLY SCOTT
FRANK WARNER
BARRY KORNFELD
DAVE VAN RONK
REV. GARY DAVIS

GENERAL ADMISSION
$1.00

NOV. 20
SUNDAY

HOFSTRA PLAYHOUSE
FULTON AVENUE, HEMPSTEAD, L.I.
3:00 P.M.

The Folk Scare Begins: (Clockwise from bottom left) The Reverend Gary Davis, with fans including Happy and Jane Traum (behind unknown bass), Dick Weissman, unknown, and John Gibbon with guitar *(photo: Photosound Associates)*; me and Tom Paxton onstage at the Commons; a typical college concert poster; the blues workshop at the 1963 Newport Folk Festival, with John Hammond Jr., Mississippi John Hurt, Clarence Cooper, me, Sonny Terry, and John Lee Hooker *(photo: Dustin S. Pease)*; the cover of the *Folksinger* album, in front of the Folklore Center on MacDougal Street.

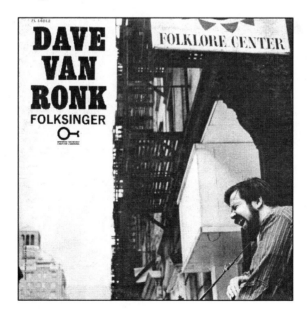

BROADSIDE JAN. 1, 1965

DAVE VAN RONK

David Ritz Kenneth Van Ronk is a gangling, bearded 28-year-old with an unruly shock of rust colored hair, usually seen trailing a huge Gibson guitar behind him. And he is usually found in New York City's Greenwich Village, the national capital of folk song, where he has become the most imitated folk-jazz singer in the country.

Although the purists may argue that Dave is a city man who learned folk music on his own (he was born in Brooklyn and grew up in Queens), he is respected for the honesty and musicality of his presentation. His sense of dynamics, from lullaby whispers to bellowing rages, carries him along with a strong sense of drama. He claims to be primarily a jazz singer, not a folk singer. His abilities as a guitarist equal his abilities as a singer.

But Dave wasn't satisfied just to be one of the best folk-jazz performers around; Dave has been one of the leading exponents of the jug band — along with his group, The Jug Stompers, who record for Mercury.

PHIL OCHS

"Singing journalist" or "Musical commentator" might best describe the work of Phil Ochs, a leader in the topical song revival. With telling lyrics and exciting music, he describes the political and social climate of the Sixties.

Phil was born in El Paso, Texas, raised in Columbus and Cleveland, Ohio. He graduated from Staunton Military Academy with Barry Goldwater's son. At Ohio State he majored in journalism and learned the rudiments of guitar playing and politics. After a year in New York earning a precarious living as a singer, his song writing brought him real recognition. Invitations to the major Folk Festivals followed. The inclusion of this twenty-three year old songwriter in the latest edition of Who's Who in America is certainly an indication that Phil Ochs has made his mark as a performer and as a songwriter. His songs have been recorded by Pete Seeger, Joan Baez, The Mitchell Trio

Glory Days: (From lower left) The Gaslight Café *(photo: Don Paulsen)*; John Hurt and Patrick Sky in the Kettle of Fish *(photo: Bob Campbell, courtesy of Patrick Sky)*; a Gaslight ad and the program for a Civil Rights concert; The Ragtime Jug Stompers at Newport, with Bob Brill, Barry Kornfeld, me, Artie Rose, and Sam Charters *(photo: Ann Charters)*; a classic example of sixties psychedelia; with Joni Mitchell.

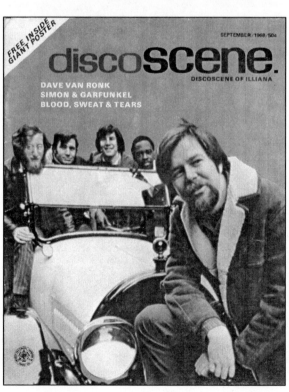

Times A-Changing:
On the street with Suze Rotolo, Terri Thal/Van Ronk, and Bob Dylan *(photo: Jim Marshall)*; going electric with The Hudson Dusters: Phil Namanworth, Dave Woods, Rick Henderson, and Ed Gregory.

I have already mentioned the degree to which we wanted to distance ourselves from the whole beatnik craze, but people who were not around at that time may have a hard time understanding what it was like. There were some smart, talented people who are, in retrospect, considered "beats," and they shared a lot of the same tastes as my friends and I: they were well-read, knew a lot about jazz, and some of them were pretty deeply into politics, at least on the arguing level. On the other hand, there were the beatniks, who were much the same sort of self-conscious young bores who twenty years later were dying their hair green and putting safety pins in their cheeks. We despised them, and even more than that we despised all the tourists who were coming down to the Village because they had *heard* about them. The whole beatnik thing had become a mass-media preoccupation: there were articles like "*Life* Goes to a Pot Party" and even a "Rent-a-Beatnik" service that advertised in the *Village Voice* for years. For a nominal fee, you could hire some clown to come to one of your parties in East Hampton or where have you, and this citizen would show up complete with beard, bongos, and beret—the three Bs—for the low, low price of twenty-five bucks for the evening, and wander around the party saying "Wow" and "Far out" and occasionally taking a feckless thwack at his bongo. It was a thriving little cottage industry, and a huge proportion of the audience in those coffeehouses was suburban tourists checking out the freaks.

To the tourists, folk music was simply part of the beatnik scene. Actually, the beats liked cool jazz, bebop, and hard drugs and hated folk music, which to them was all these fresh-faced kids sitting around on the floor and singing songs of the oppressed masses. When a folksinger would take the stage between two beat poets, all the finger-poppin' mamas and daddies would do everything but hold their noses. Then, when the beat poets would get up and begin to rant, all the folk fans would do likewise. But in the eyes of the media, folk music and beatniks were one and the same.

In 1959 the poets still had very much the upper hand. I sometimes say, and there is more than a little truth to it, that the only reason they had folksingers in those coffeehouses at all was to turn the house. The Gaslight seated only 110 customers, and on weekend nights, there would often be a line of people waiting to get in. To maximize profits, Mitchell needed a way to clear out the current crowd after they had finished their cup of overpriced coffee, since no one would have bought a second cup of that slop. This presented a logistical problem to which the folksingers were the solution: you would get up and sing three songs, and if at the end of those three songs anybody was still left in the room, you were fired.

Over the next year or two, though, the situation changed completely. I am reminded of the old tale of the Arab and the camel: An Arab is in his nice, snug, warm tent in the desert on a freezing cold night, and a camel sticks his head in and says, "Do you mind if I just put my nose inside the tent to get it warm? It's really freezing out here." The Arab, being a soft-hearted fellow, says, "Go on, be my guest." The camel sticks his nose in, but after a while he pipes up again, saying, "Do you mind if I just put my ears in as well?" The Arab allows this as well, and the story goes on and on until finally the Arab is freezing out on the desert and the camel is warm inside the tent. Thus it was with the folksingers and the beat poets. The poor bastards never knew what hit 'em.

Basically, it turned out that we could draw larger crowds and keep them coming back more regularly. This was not because folk music is inherently more interesting than poetry, but singing is inherently theatrical, and poetry is not. Even a very good poet is not necessarily any kind of a performer, since poetry is by its nature introspective—"In my craft or sullen art / Exercised in the still night," as Dylan Thomas put it. A mediocre singer can still choose good material and make decent music, while a mediocre poet is just a bore. And some of the poets around MacDougal Street were the absolute bottom of the barrel. So gradually more and more clubs phased the poets out and the singers in. It was not an absolute changeover: even into the 1960s they would keep someone like Eddie Freeman around for those occasions when a tourist would come in and say, "Hey, you got any beatnik poets?" They had to have a token specimen, just for the look of the thing, but to all intents and purposes that craze was dead. The poets probably have a quite different take on this history—I suspect their attitude is "We never lost the ball, we just got bored with the park"—but that is how it seemed to me.

When I first got back from California, Roy was the only person I knew who was playing regularly on MacDougal—frankly, one reason I disliked the Gaslight so much was probably because he had the gig and I didn't, and I was jealous. My turn came soon enough, though. A few months after my return, I ran into Jimmy Gavin, who was back in New York as well, and he told me he was booking the music for a coffeehouse called the Commons. It was right across the street from the Gaslight, and I went down there on Jimmy's invitation, and there were four or five performers working there, and I became the fifth or sixth. It was what was called a "basket house," which meant that most of the money for performers came in the form of tips. There would be a basket at the door, supervised by a young woman who would cajole, shame, or threaten the clydes into tossing in a buck or two on their way out, and however many people performed in a night, that's how many ways the basket would be split. On a good weekend night, you could actually make out pretty well, and the people who were regulars on the bill were also pulling a salary—only $100, $125 a week, but in 1960 you could live on that. As in LA, we worked hard for the money, because being a coffeehouse it did not have to shut down when the bars shut down, so after "last call" at 4:00 A.M., we would get our second straight rush and that would sometimes keep us working until 7:00, 8:00, 9:00 in the morning. I loved walking up 6th Avenue on my way home to bed, watching all the poor wage slaves schlepping off to work.

The Commons was my professional introduction to MacDougal Street and vice versa. Pretty soon I had built up something of a regular following, and in August of 1960 the *Village Voice* did a big cover piece on me. This might not be worth noting, except for the fact that the *Voice* assiduously ignored the folk scene. There had been one short piece on Carolyn Hester a few months earlier, but in general the paper was trying to be a community weekly, and a lot of people in the community thought of the coffeehouse entertainers as outsiders, beatniks, and bait for the tourists and troublemakers that were ruining the neighborhood. The same reporter who did the piece on me had just finished a three-part series on how MacDougal Street had become "a fruitcake 'Inferno'," and the beatnik equivalent of Coney Island. Thus, odd as it seems, this was not only the first cover piece on a Village folksinger but also the last. Over the next few years, which are often remembered as the high point of Greenwich Village as a musical mecca, the local press did its best to avoid the whole subject.

The *Voice* piece was very welcome, naturally, though as with all articles of that period it laid more stress on the "white man singing the blues" angle than I cared for. It began:

The occasional wanderer poking around tiny Minetta Street these summer evenings is liable to meet up with a most unusual sound. It drifts from the glass-partitioned back entrance of The Commons coffee house. Now wailing, now dropping on down to a mean, guttural rasp, it is the sound of a man belting out Negro ballads and blues. The voice, however, does not quite have the timbre associated with southern Negro singing. But it is filled just the same with all that smoky, bittersweet funk and jazz common to the musical tradition south of the Mason and Dixon line.

The reporter described me as "hunched over a table, nervously dragging on a cigarette. . . . A certain weariness and the droopy bush of a blond moustache make him older than his 24 years." After batting around the subject of my ethnicity, the reporter asked if I had spent much time in the South:

A tremendous grin breaks out under the walrus moustache. He scratches at his mop of brown hair. "Sometimes I feel like palming myself off as Homer Scragg, the banjo picker from Sawtooth, Arkansas. Actually, I'm from Brooklyn. And that low-down sound in my voice? Man, I've got asthma. The worse the weather, the rougher and raspier I sound. It's great. It hides all the defects."

The story summarized my basic bio, with some chat about the evils of southern racism and segregation, then ended with a question about my obvious musical growth since the Folkways album. The reporter suggested that I seemed to have developed a "more popular touch." I hastened to agree:

"For years I've hung around Israel Young's Folklore Center on MacDougal Street. I learned a helluva lot about ethnic music from the records and talking to the people there. Izzy, by the way, is the real unsung hero of folk music around New York. But lately I've been listening to other stuff—specifically Ray Charles. I think he's the finest vocalist for jazz or country blues around today. He represents the best of the rhythm and blues. I mean, he swings. I don't think I can go wrong learning from him."

Then I was back onstage, singing "Careless Love."

It was a nice piece, but I got awfully tired of that business about singing "Negro music." Frankly, I was puzzled by all the fuss. After all, no one had ever suggested that there was anything strange about me singing like Louis Armstrong when I was doing jazz. Copying Louis's phrasing was standard procedure for jazz singers, white and black. When I listen to my recordings, I hear an obvious debt to Louis, and on those early records to Bessie Smith, as well as to Jelly Roll Morton, Bing Crosby, Billie Holiday, and Gary Davis. Except for Gary, that is a fairly standard list that you might have heard from any jazz singer of my generation or of the generation before mine.

There was indeed a racial gap between me and the people who had originally recorded most of the material I was doing at that point, but there was also a large time gap. I was singing songs I had learned from recordings of Bessie Smith made in the 1920s, and musical fashions had changed tremendously in the intervening decades. So it was not just that young white singers were not doing anything like that; nobody had heard anything like that for thirty years except people who were into old music for nostalgic or scholarly reasons, or because they liked the music for itself as an "art form."

When I first started getting a lot of flak, I tried to counter it as best I could, and one of my strongest debating points was that so few black musicians were still doing that material. There were Sonny and Brownie, Josh White, and very few others. Certainly nobody who was going to work for what they were paying on MacDougal Street. So I would just say, "Look, if I don't do this music, who will?" A few years later, when Son House, John Hurt, and Lightnin' Hopkins resurfaced and started touring around the folk clubs, that answer was no longer valid, but by then most people had stopped asking me the question.

In any case, most of the people listening to folk music never thought much about the issue, for or against. The whole debate was a tempest in a teapot, generated by critics who needed something to write about. At the time, though, I got really annoyed by it, because these were songs, good songs, and what color is a song? But all sorts of erudite arguments were being made and ripostes being delivered, and though I was not the only white blues singer on the scene, I was sort of riding point, so a lot of the garbage landed on my head. Then I snapped back in a very surly manner and said some things that, while I do not regret having said them, were an overreaction to the overreaction. Forty years later, on somber reflection, having fully studied the arguments on both sides, I have reached what I believe to be a measured and definitive judgment on the matter: Who cares?

Whatever my tastes, my voice sounded like it sounded. From the first moment I opened my mouth to sing, people did not hesitate to tell me that I had an unusual voice—though that was not exactly the way they usually phrased it. In retrospect, I think that having a rough voice was actually an advantage, because I had to learn how to sing, not simply make pretty sounds. And it fitted well with the sort of material that attracted me, which often was sung by people who did not have pretty voices.

At any rate, the Commons was a turning point for me. Along with providing a regular place for me to play, it was where I met a lot of the people who would become my closest friends and associates over the next few years. The sheer number of people who worked there militated for that: I once counted thirteen performers on a single night. That even included some poets, and we mixed pretty well, all things considered. Bob Kaufman was reading there fairly often, and John Brent, who was better known as a comedian with the Second City and subsequently the Committee, came across the street occasionally from the Gaslight.

One of the best friends I met there was Tom Paxton. The Commons was Tom's first gig in the city; he was in the army and came in on weekend passes from Fort Dix. At that point he was not yet doing his own material. He was doing traditional folksongs, and he sounded a lot like Burl Ives—I can still hear Ives in his style. He may have already written his first song, or certainly would within a very short time, but that was not what he was doing onstage. From the beginning, though, he was a natural as a performer.

Two or three weeks after my arrival at the Commons, Jimmy decided to pull up stakes and head back to California, because his acting teacher was going out there. Some of the other performers went with him, and what with one thing and another I was shortly the only regular performer left. Then Rod MacDonald, who was running the place, asked me if I would be willing to book the entertainment, since he did not know from folk music; all he knew from was chess. That was fine with me, and of course I hired my friends. I brought Paxton in on a regular basis, Casey Anderson, Billy Faier, a woman named Neila Horne who was a great songwriter and wrote several things I have kept in my repertoire, and the Reverend Gary Davis.

I had met Gary a couple of years earlier through Barry Kornfeld. Barry was studying guitar with him and sometimes acting as his "lead boy" (Gary was blind, and though he could get around his own turf pretty well, he needed someone when he ventured farther afield), and for a while got into the practice of bringing him down to Washington Square on Sundays. Gary would stand there in the circle in the middle of the square with Barry, who would usually be playing banjo while Gary played guitar. The first time I heard him was a shock I will never forget. I still cannot believe the things that man could do. He was unquestionably a genius, and he became my idol, my guitar guru. It took me a while to assimilate any of his techniques, but he was certainly the strongest single influence on my playing.

Gary was in his sixties by that time. He was an ordained minister and had been a street singer and preacher for most of his life. He was from South Carolina originally, but he had come up to New York in the early 1940s, and when I first heard him, he was still working in the streets of Harlem. He also used to preach sometimes in a storefront church, and his sermons were really remarkable. He would set up a riff on his guitar, and then he would chant his sermon in counterpoint to the riff, and when he made a little change in what he was saying, he would make a little change on the guitar. There was this constant interplay and interweaving of voice and guitar, and these fantastic polyrhythms would come out of that—I have never heard anything quite like it, before or since. He was a great singer, and I do not think he has gotten enough credit for that. There were a lot of similarities between his singing and Ray Charles's, both in voice quality and in the way it fitted with his style of playing. He could shout when he needed to, but he could also be very sophisticated in terms of his phrasing and his use of dynamics.

As for Gary's guitar style, it was fantastically complicated and has never been successfully duplicated, even by his students. It was ragtimey more than bluesy, and he had unbelievable technique. More important, for my purposes, he was accessible. He gave lessons in his house and also had a succession of lead boys who helped him get around to concerts. The first I recall was a guy named Johnny Gibbon, and then there was Fred Gerlach, Barry Kornfeld, Stefan Grossman, Roy Bookbinder—a whole succession of people who went on to be really fine guitar players.

I never took formal lessons from Gary, but I went over to his house a couple of times and I worked with him as often as I could, and whenever he was playing, I would just sit there and watch his fingers. We used to hang around for hours, and we would talk and I would ask him how to play one thing or another. He used to say, "Well, playing guitar ain't nothing but a bag of tricks"—which I suppose is true in a way, but he had a very, very big bag. He was only too happy to show me things, and then I would try to play them, and he would cackle when I got them wrong, which was usually. He was an incredibly patient teacher when the mood was on him. Being blind, he had difficulty describing what it was he was doing, so his method was to play a thing over and over again, slow it down so you could see just where his fingers were going, and he would correct you by ear. He did not mind if it took two hours to get one lick across. On the other hand, he could be very irascible and unpredictable at times, so you would work on this lick or whatever it was, and a few days later you would run into him and play it, and he would growl at you, "Man, you're stealing my stuff."

He was sui generis, a unique man in so many ways. It was like W. C. Fields used to say about sex: "There are some things better and there are some things worse, but there's nothing quite like it." He was sly and sophisticated, he was naive and childlike, he was cheap, he was generous. He was a bundle of contradictions. And his guitar playing was the same way. He would play these incredibly complex, multipart ragtime compositions, and then turn around and do something like "Candyman," this little, repetitive song that he had learned as a child in South Carolina. He didn't often talk about how he learned, but of course Gary had his roots, too; he did not spring like Athena from the head of Zeus. He told me that when he was a little kid, he used to play a guitar someone had made for him out of a cigar box, and there was this guy that used to come through town who they called "the gittar man"—that was the only name they knew him by. He would come around once or twice a year, play in the streets, and pick up some money and move on, and "Candyman" was a piece Gary learned from the gittar man.

Gary was a very astute arranger, and thought his pieces through very thoroughly. He would take a song and analyze it, pick it apart and then reassemble it, sometimes while he was playing. It was an astounding process to watch, and I got a great deal from him, though I did not try to imitate his sound either as a singer or as a guitarist. For one thing, I knew that if I tried I would fail. But anything he did that I could assimilate and use, I would grab it. I messed around with a lot of his songs, and "Candyman" and "Cocaine Blues" became staples of my repertoire. I was particularly attracted to those because he did not perform them himself. Being a reverend, of the fundamentalist persuasion, he did not like to sing secular songs in any public situation. He especially would not sing blues, but any song that was not a religious song was the Devil's music, and those two songs were particularly sinful. (At first, I did not know that a "candy man" was a pimp, and I could not understand Gary's reluctance to perform that song. One time, I confronted him about it: "But Gary, that's a children's song." He said, "Yeah, you get lots of children from songs like that.")

Fortunately, he was a little more relaxed in private, and appropriately enough to his calling, he had no head for liquor, so after a drink or two you could sometimes put the arm on him to sing some blues or party songs. Something like "Cocaine Blues," though, was a little too much for him, so he refused to sing it; he would just play the guitar part and speak the words in a sort of *recitatif*. I thought that was a pretty tenuous legal argument—I would have hated to be in his shoes when he had to face Saint Peter with the defense, "I didn't *sing* it, I just talked it."—but nothing would move him. As a result, when I recorded my version I just recited the lyric, and by now dozens of other people have done versions, but none of us ever found out what the melody was. That melody died with Gary.

You can listen to the records I did for Folkways, and then my first recordings for Prestige, and you will hear a huge difference in the guitar playing, and Gary is largely responsible for that change. I sometimes think that if he had not come along, I might as well have stuck with the ukulele. As I have said, it was not so much a matter of direct imitation, though for a while I changed from playing a Gibson J-45 to a J-200 because that was what he played. It was more that he reshaped my whole approach to the instrument. He used to call the guitar his "piano around my neck," and I adopted that pianistic approach. When I am working out arrangements, I very rarely listen to guitarists. I listen to people like Jelly Roll Morton, Fats Waller, and James P. Johnson, and try to apply their techniques to the guitar.

That was what got me into the whole business of playing classic ragtime. In the early 1960s I worked out an arrangement of a turn-of-the-century rag called the "Saint Louis Tickle," and it provided the impetus for what became a quite thriving school of ragtime guitarists, people like Dave Laibman, Rick Schoenberg, Ton Von Bergeyk, and Guy Van Duser. I strongly suspect that something similar had been going strong at the turn of the century; the combination of elements is so logical and ragtime was so incredibly popular that it is very difficult to believe that this was not being done. But none was recorded, so I became known as the pioneer of fingerstyle ragtime. That was only possible because of what I picked up from Gary. For example, one thing that stopped fingerpickers from playing rags is that in most classic rags you have a section that involves a modulation into the key a fourth above where you started. If you start out in C—the most comfortable key for ragtime playing—by the time you get to the third part, you are in the key of F, and most fingerpickers were stuck on first-position chords and were not at all comfortable playing in F. But Gary had several arrangements in F, religious songs like "Blow, Gabriel" and one of his instrumental showpieces, John Phillip Sousa's "United States March." Once I had figured out what he was doing on that march, I simply applied that to the F section of "Saint Louis Tickle." Likewise, I would have tried to play Scott Joplin's "Maple Leaf Rag" in C, but I saw Gary fooling around with it, and he did it in A. It was like a light bulb going on: "Right, that's it!" The rest of it came kind of easy, but only because Gary had shown me the way.

Gary was to Eastern Seaboard guitar what Art Tatum was to stride piano: he was not the most successful player on that scene, but none of the others had his range or his grasp of the instrument. Blind Blake had a terrific right hand and a very nice stride piano sound, but it was very mechanical. The same is true of Blind Willie McTell, although I think McTell had a nicer sense of harmonies and voicing. But when you study what Rev. Davis was doing with his right hand, you see that he doesn't keep any pattern. He will start to go from a lower to a higher note and then switch right in the middle of a measure to back-picking, from a higher to a lower note, or strumming a full chord, and never drop the time.

He had no equals, and he knew it. He was a merciless critic—I hardly ever heard him say a good word about another guitar player—and the thing is, he was almost invariably right. I remember hearing him do a parody of Lightnin' Hopkins, just dripping acid, and what was so striking was that he knew exactly what Lightnin' was doing and the parody was correct. One time I asked him about Blind Lemon Jefferson, who I still think is one of the greatest blues guitarists and singers of all time. Gary disagreed, and he started to play a very accurate pastiche of Lemon's "Black Snake Moan," and just opened his mouth and let out with this incredible, bloodcurdling scream. Then he stops and says, "Man, he couldn't have sung no louder if someone was cutting his throat." He was utterly ruthless. He did like Blind Blake, though. He used to say that Blake's guitar playing was "right sporty." That was the highest accolade I ever heard him pay another guitarist. He liked Lonnie Johnson too.

I will never forget one night I was playing at a club in Detroit and was in the midst of my Rev. Davis period. I must have done two or three of Gary's things, or maybe even more, and when I came offstage, the owner comes and says, "There's a friend of yours here," and he leads me over to a table, and there are Rev. and Annie Davis. I thought, "Oh my God, why didn't I just sing some Leadbelly songs?" But I sat down, and Rev. Davis turns to me and says, "That was right sporty guitar." Oh, man! That was the highest compliment I have ever been paid in my life. I suspect he was just being kind, but it is one of my fondest memories.

Like most geniuses, Gary had his eccentricities, and one that sometimes drove me crazy was that he had his own sense of pitch. We were playing once at a concert in Canada, and he did his whole first set with the low E string about a quarter tone flat. It was driving me crazy, because every time he hit that note it was booming off-key, so on the break I borrowed his guitar on some excuse and surreptitiously tuned that string. He came back for the second set, started into a song, and just stopped dead, looked a little perplexed, and tuned that string right back down to where it had been. He also could have the weirdest taste in guitars. At one point I had busted my main guitar and it needed to be repaired, and Mattie Umanov, who was doing the repair, loaned me a Martin. It was the worst goddamn Martin I have ever picked up; the strings were a half-inch off the fingerboard, so it was excruciating to play, and it was almost purposeless because you could not hear it five feet away. Fortunately, after a few days Mattie called me, and I went over to pick up my Guild, and Gary was in the shop. I had brought back the Martin, and Gary said, "Let me see that guitar," and he started to play it, and he thought it was the greatest guitar he had ever played. He bought it on the spot, and he would play it out of tune just so, accurate to within a microtone, exactly the way he wanted it.

There are so many Gary Davis stories. He was given to cracking very bad jokes, and the worse the joke, the more he loved it. He was his own best audience. He could hardly get through one of his godawful wisecracks without breaking up. He was also quite suspicious because of all those years on the streets. Being blind, he was a target for people who would grab his guitar and run off, so as a result he never let it out of his hands. He used to take it with him into the bathroom—and he would play there. He also had concluded that he needed to be able to defend himself, so he used to carry this big .38 that he called "Miss Ready." He would pull out this gun and show it to me, and one time, as diffidently as I could, I said, "You know, Gary, you *are* blind. Don't you think maybe it's not such a good idea . . . "

He said, "If I can hear it, I can shoot it."

Over the years, we worked together as often as I could arrange it, and since we were both on the same circuit, we ran into each other a good deal outside New York, as well. One time around 1962, I was working up in Boston or Cambridge, and Rev. Davis was working there too, in another club. An old friend of mine named Pete Friedberger was handling the driving for him, and Pete asked me if I would like to ride back to New York with them. That sounded great to me, especially since otherwise I was likely to end up sleeping on somebody's kitchen floor, the usual accommodations for a traveling folksinger—we used to call it the "At Your Mercy Circuit." So after the show, we all piled into this big old Chevy, with me sitting in front with Pete, and Gary sprawled out in the back with "Miss Gibson."

Pete and I were yakking about this, that, and the other thing, and Gary as always was playing, and as we were leaving Boston, he started playing "Candyman." That was fine with me, of course; it was one of my favorite songs, and he had all sorts of variations he would play on it. By somewhere around Providence, though, it was beginning to wear a little thin, variations or not. By New Haven it was really beginning to bug me, but what could I say? This was the Reverend Gary Davis playing "Candyman." Bridgeport ... somewhere around Stamford, something inside me snapped. I growled, "For Christ's sake, Gary, can't you play anything else?" And I turned around, and he was asleep.

Maybe the best Gary Davis story, and one of the truly great moments in American music, happened when I was unfortunately not present, but a friend told me the whole thing in detail. It was after Peter, Paul, and Mary had recorded Gary's version of "Samson and Delilah" on their first album—which turned out to be a godsend for Gary and gave him the money to buy his house. In order to get all of his rights in order, Gary had to sign a contract with the publisher, Harms-Whitmark, which was associated with Warner Brothers, the label that Peter, Paul, and Mary were on. As I heard the story, the people in publicity at Harms-Whitmark decided that they were going to turn this into a media event, and they had reporters from all the trade papers there, and all the old-timers with Harms-Whitmark—the guy who had been Victor Herbert's publisher, the guy who had been Irving Berlin's partner, all these *alter kocker*s.

They were all seated around this long table, and Rev. Davis was seated in the center, and the ceremonial signing was about to happen. The flashbulbs were popping, and my friend, a junior executive appropriately named Artie Mogull, told me that just as they were about to hand Gary the golden pen to sign the contract, someone asked the formal question "Reverend Davis, are you the author of this song?"

Gary paused a dramatic pause, and in his preacher's voice announced: "No, I did not write that song!" No one knew what to do. The reporters were scribbling madly; elderly executives were popping nitro pills all around the table. And then Gary spoke again: "It was revealed to me in a dream!"

I always thought that was one of the funniest stories I ever heard, but I have kind of an interesting postscript to it. As I have said, I never actually took lessons from Gary, but I would sometimes ask him to show me things, and at the tag end of "Candyman" there is a little trick that he used to throw in, where he has the basses reversed and he comes out of the reversed bass into normal, forward picking, and just where he makes the changeover, there is this little three-note bass figure. Time and time again, Gary tried to show me that thing, and I always got my fingers all tied up in knots. He would slow it down and play it one note at a time, but I just had some kind of a block. I could not get it.

Well, Gary died in 1972, and a year or two later I had a dream. In the dream, Gary was onstage in a club, and I was sitting ringside. Gary was playing "Candyman," and when he got to that part in the thing, he leaned forward so I could see his hands very clearly, and played it very slowly. I woke up with a start, and I was in a motel room somewhere and my guitar was sitting right by the bed, and I just picked up the guitar and I could play it. That is the closest thing to a supernatural experience I have ever had in my life, and I generally don't put much stock in such things, but that man was so frustrated by my clumsiness that I would not put it past him to have come back and taken one more crack at it.

11

The Gaslight

As Wavy Gravy says, if you can remember the sixties, you weren't really there. We were young guys, full of piss and vinegar—not to mention bourbon—and at times in those early years it felt like one long party. There are a few dates that can be fixed from newspaper clippings, but for a lot of events even pinning down the year is impossible, and if my chronology seems confusing at times, that is at least in part because I am confused.

My base of operations for most of the next few years was the Gaslight Café, but before I get into that story I need to pick up a loose end: the appearance of the first honest-to-god folk club in the Village. That was what would become known as Folk City, but it started out as the Fifth Peg, and it was the brainchild of Izzy Young and a friend of his named Tom Prendergast. They started by approaching a bar owner named Mike Porco, who had a place called Gerde's over on 3rd and Mercer, across the street from what became the Bottom Line. Mike had been running that room for years, but he was basically just surviving on lunch business. That was the factory loft area, and by seven at night the place was completely empty; there must have been enough business for Mike to figure he might as well stay open, but just barely. So Izzy and Tom went to him and said, "Look, put in a stage and a PA system and we'll book acts. We'll charge at the door and pay the performers out of that, and the money from the bar is yours." It was pure gravy, so Mike went for it.

That was in January of 1960, and the Fifth Peg ran for the next five months. I may have worked there at least once, and I was down to see other people all the time. Brownie McGhee and Sonny Terry were regular performers, and there was also a double bill of Gary Davis and Cisco Houston. Cisco was dying of cancer, and that may actually have been his last show. I had never much liked his records—I thought he sounded fulsome and kind of slick—but he turned me into a believer. There was an honesty to his performance, underlined by the courage it took for him just to get up onstage; he was already in a lot of pain, but none of that was allowed to come through.

The club was packed most of the time, and before long, Mike realized that there was no need for him to keep sharing the take with Izzy and Tom. So about month six, he gave them the boot and took over the operation for himself, calling it Gerde's Folk City. We were all outraged, of course. Izzy was one of ours; he had kept the Folklore Center afloat in the dark days of the 1950s, and here he had finally opened a place for people like us to work and this capitalist was giving him the shaft. Out of loyalty, I more or less disassociated myself from Gerde's for a time, but the offer of hard cash was difficult to turn down, and it soon became obvious that you could have your cake and eat it, too: you could work at Folk City and still walk into the Folklore Center without violence being done to you. Actually, though he probably would disagree, I suspect that Izzy was a little relieved that the Fifth Peg ended; it was a lot of extra work, and the Folklore Center was getting busier all the time. So it was probably just as well that Mike took over, though he could have waited a few more months and been more diplomatic about it.

Mike was a nice guy and he seemed genuinely to enjoy the music, but he was very cheap and evasive about business matters. Every once in a while someone would put pressure on him to do something that would cost money, and he would immediately conjure up these mysterious partners whom no one had ever seen who would quash the suggestion. He was an Italian immigrant, and it was delightful to watch his English deteriorate when the bargaining got hot—when things were going well, that man could speak English like Churchill. It was due to Mike's parsimoniousness that Folk City was one of the only union houses on the folk circuit. The AF of M had essentially no interest in folksingers, but Mike made his room into a proper union house because the union pay scale was nice and low. By their standards Gerde's was a class B room, so he did not have to pay the full class A rate, with the result that you worked there for five nights a week and would not bring home more than $200. If you were doing really well, you could extract a few more bucks, but not many, and by 1963 I was making more money at the Gaslight, which didn't even have a liquor license.

All the while, though, I never stopped liking Mike. I used to go over a couple of times a week on a quiet night and shoot the shit with him and his brother John, talking above whoever the poor act onstage was. Musicians are a lousy audience, especially if they are your friends, because they all come down to see you but they wind up seeing each other, and it turns into a party. Folk City was not a bad room to sing in on a quiet night, but it had a problem I have found in a lot of bars, which is that the people seated in front of the stage knew that they were watching a show, but the people at the bar would act like they were in another room. When that place was crowded, it was one of the toughest rooms I have ever seen; I had a pretty devoted following by then, but I had a rough time. The people who did best in there were acts like Brother John Sellers, who gave a really rousing, crowd-pleasing show, or the Clancy Brothers.

When Mike took over, he had no idea of what folk music was or who the hot acts on the scene might have been, so for a year or two he had to book the place on the basis of an informal brain trust. The main advisers included Robert Shelton—who was the reviewer for the *New York Times*, which had some obvious advantages—Logan English, Terri, and myself. After a while Mike got to be fairly knowledgeable, but he was still feeling his way until about the time Phil Ochs showed up in 1962. At that point he discarded his training wheels and went his own way.

I played Folk City quite a few times, but my main base of operations was MacDougal Street. After a year or so at the Commons, I moved across the street and started working regularly at the Gaslight, which at that point was still owned by John Mitchell. I had actually been working for Mitchell already, since in June of 1960 the Gaslight was shut down by the Fire Department and Mitchell took over the Commons for the next three months, until he could get the Gaslight open again.

Mitchell was the world's foremost maniac, and he was like a magnet for trouble. Over the space of a few years, he had three successful coffeehouses—the Figaro, the Gaslight, and the Commons—and in one way or another he blew every one of them. He started out with the Figaro, and what apparently happened there was that he put the place in his wife's name to evade the IRS and whatnot, and then she left him and got involved with Tommy Ziegler, and the Figaro went with her. During that period we all used to go to the Figaro and drink coffee in the afternoon, but we had no idea what was going on behind the scenes. We would just sit around and shoot the bull, and sometimes we would take out our guitars and Al, the manager, would threaten to throw us out, and we would put our guitars back in the case and order some more coffee, if we could afford it.

When Mitchell lost the Figaro, he went down the street and opened the Gaslight, which was dogged by problems almost from the outset. As I mentioned earlier, this was an old-line Italian neighborhood, and all the clubs that served liquor had traditionally needed mob connections to get a license. The only bar that wasn't mobbed up was the Kettle of Fish, and that was because the owner, Guido, was highly respected by the entire Italian community, the mob included. The first coffeehouses had not really been an issue, since they were not taking any business away from the bars, but when they started having entertainment, they became competition. They also were drawing a new crowd, including beatniks and Negroes, and a lot of people in the neighborhood were not happy about that. Between the mob and the concerned citizens, there was a lot of pressure to close these places, and since Mitchell was one of the least diplomatic men on earth, he became the main focus of this hostility. The Fire Department would shut him down for some violation, and he would respond by putting signs all over the doorway attacking the fire chief for turning the Village into a police state, and the fire chief would try to tear the signs down, and Mitchell would blow his top and the cops would show up and book him for assault.

The Gaslight was not the only place having problems—the Bizarre, the Café Wha?, and most of the other coffeehouses that had entertainment were shut down from time to time—but Mitchell's insistence on fighting City Hall made him a special target. The cops had been in the habit of coming around and getting a little cash from all the club owners, and Mitchell started keeping books in which he wrote down all of these contributions to what he called the GAR, the Grand Army of the Republic, and he turned those books over to the press. That made a lot of noise, and at one point some lieutenant came down and informed John that if he kept stirring up trouble, he was going to be shot while resisting arrest. Meanwhile, he was also trying to avoid the usual payoffs to the mob, so what with one thing and another the word was out that Mitchell was not going to live to see his next birthday. It must have been just around that time that John Brent and Mitchell had a falling-out, and one Saturday night while I was onstage, Brent came charging in with this very realistic-looking cap pistol, got John in his sights, and started shooting. Mitchell thought it was a real gun and hit the floor, then tentatively started feeling his body for bullet holes. Eventually he realized that he was unharmed and got up, by which time Brent was on the floor himself, laughing.

It looked pretty serious for a while there, though, and people were actually laying bets on whether Mitchell would see another year. I was sitting upstairs in the Kettle one night when he came marching in, walked up to the bar, and said, "Ha-ha-ha, fuck you all," and bought drinks for the house. It was his birthday, and he was celebrating having made it. All in all, he led a kind of charmed life. Not only did he survive, but he survived with a degree of success that is incredible, considering the trouble he made for a lot of powerful people.

To be frank, any authorities who were looking for an excuse to shut down a coffeehouse should have had a field day with the Gaslight. Though the room had apparently once been a speakeasy, it had been a coal cellar for twenty or thirty years before Mitchell came in, and it was hopelessly filthy. When he remodeled it, he had people scrubbing and scrubbing for days, and they tried their damnedest, but there was just no way to get the grit out of that place. Hercules himself could not have cleaned that Augean stable, even if he had diverted the East River.*

The Gaslight was set up so that there were two doors at the sidewalk level, one on each side of the stoop to the tenement above it, where the Caricature was, next to the Kettle of Fish. Either door opened onto a flight of stairs that led down to the club. There was a cash register right at the door,

---

*Actually, it might have been a bit cleaner than the East River.

and the stage was all the way in the back. The room was maybe fifty feet deep and maybe twenty-five to thirty feet wide, and it was very dark—which was a fortunate thing, considering how filthy it was. When you came in off the street, you had to give your eyes a while to adjust before you could find a seat, and when you were onstage with a light shining in your face, you might as well have been completely blind. I was always covered with bruises from bumping into things while trying to navigate that space.

For furniture, Mitchell had gotten hold of a bunch of nineteenth-century oak tables, mostly round ones, which you could buy very cheaply in those days because this was the era of Danish modern. Another thing you could get very cheaply were Tiffany lamps, so there were Tiffany—or at least Tiffanoid—lamps over a lot of the tables. I took one of those lamps out with my head one night, though that was purely Albert Grossman's fault. That was after he had come to New York from Chicago and become the great folk impresario, with Peter, Paul, and Mary. He was sort of managing me for a while and became convinced that one of the reasons I was not becoming a superstar was that I performed sitting down. I took his counsel to heart, and one night I got onstage with my guitar on a neck strap and did the whole show standing up. At the end, just to give my exit a little more pizzazz, I sort of leapt off the stage, in the process demolishing the Tiffany. I actually knocked myself cold and had to be carried back to the kitchen. It was a valuable lesson. Grossman gave me some good advice over the years, but in this case I concluded that a seated Van Ronk was a safe Van Ronk, and I have stuck with that.

The Gaslight held about 110 people according to the fire codes, though with a shoehorn on a good night you could squeeze in 125 or 130. And there was this weird rule that no applause was permitted, because all these old Italians lived on the upper floors and they would be bothered by the noise and retaliate by hurling stuff down the airshaft. So instead of clapping, if people liked a performance they were supposed to snap their fingers. Of course, along with solving the noise problem, that also had some beatnik cachet.

There was no air conditioning whatsoever, and in the summer it would get to be like a Turkish bath. To add to that impression, the Fire Department had insisted that Mitchell put in a sprinkler system, and it would go off every now and again for no apparent reason. One time it went off on a

Saturday night in the middle of a show, and all the customers were drenched, yelling and fighting their way up the stairs. I was back in the dressing room with Luke Faust, and we got soaked along with everybody else, but instead of leaving, we just went out and sat on the lip of the stage, all by ourselves, racing paper boats down the main aisle.

Those coffeehouses were pretty tenuous as business ventures, because generally a club makes its money on alcohol sales and they did not have liquor licenses. There was not much money to be made selling coffee, even at $2.50 a cup, which was considered an astronomical price in those days. In a bar, people would pay that much for a drink, and in the course of a couple of hours they might have three or four each, but our customers typically just bought one cup and sat with it for an hour or two. That was all that could be expected of them, because one of the distinguishing features of those coffeehouses was that they had the worst coffee I have ever encountered. To give an idea, at the Gaslight they used to wash out the coffee urn with bicarbonate of soda, and one night Kevin, the kitchen man, forgot to rinse the urn, and they made the coffee while the urn was still caked with bicarb, and we did not get a single complaint. It tasted no worse than what we usually served. The only reason those places were able to survive as long as they did was that the rents were very low, and when the property values went up, most of them gradually folded. They sometimes made a little more money by serving food, but no one who had seen those rooms with all the lights turned on would have considered ordering anything to eat in one of them.

Even in the dark the Gaslight was pretty horrible. Along with the prehistoric grime, there were cockroaches, rats—all the usual denizens of a tenement basement. Sam Hood, who managed the club in the mid-1960s, tells a story about one night when a rat climbed up onto the stage in the middle of a show. People started pointing and giggling, and someone got word back to Kevin, who came out of the kitchen with a coal shovel. There was a performer onstage and a hundred-and-some-odd people watching, many of them trying to eat their dinner, but he paid none of that any mind. He just walked across the stage, positioned himself directly over the rat, cut it in half with the shovel, scooped it up, and walked back to the kitchen.

The Gaslight was one of the first coffeehouses to feature entertainment. Mitchell began hosting poetry readings early in 1959, and until the day the place closed, it was listed in the phone book as the Gaslight Poetry Café. By the time I began paying attention, there was very little serious poetry being read there anymore, but Hugh Romney and John Brent would both do some, along with their comedy and general MC patter. Hugh and John had come in as poetry directors, then segued from that into more general entertainment directors. They also had an apartment upstairs, where we hung out on occasion. They were both "hip" comedians, in the Lord Buckley tradition, though each had his own style. Hugh was quite a natty dresser; he used to wear this wonderful houndstooth suit with matching vest, and he became something of a cult figure. At one point, Marlene Dietrich came to hear him and gave him a copy of Rilke's *Letters to a Young Poet*. She left her lipstick print on a cup, which Mitchell kept in a glass case until one day Kevin washed it and Mitchell chased him down MacDougal Street with this antique sword that he had hung up on one wall. (It was a lovely, curving scimitar, which eventually ended up on the wall of my apartment.)

Hugh, who ought to know, says that the first folksinger to play in there was someone named Bobby Seidenberg, but Roy Berkeley is the first that I remember, and by the time I was at the Commons the regular musician was Len Chandler. They actually put out a record of Len, Hugh, and John on a one-shot label called Gaslight Records. It was titled *The Beat Generation* and is now an extremely rare collector's item. Len was a good singer and songwriter, and one of the few people on the set with a formal musical background. He was from Ohio and had played English horn and oboe in symphonic groups before winding up on MacDougal. (*Variety* referred to him as "musician turned folksinger.") When I met him, he was teaching at St. Barnabas School, and I may even have been the person who first dragged him down to the Gaslight. Len was a hell of a performer, and he remained the big weekend draw for several years. Sam Hood recalls that he was the highest paid of the regular acts, though that was also because he was more than usually argumentative and drove a harder bargain.

Len was one of the few young black musicians on the folk scene, and one time he got jumped right outside the Gaslight by a gang of Italian kids who were trying to "clean up the neighborhood." There was a lot of that shit going down back then. It had actually started in the early 1950s, and originally the main targets had been homosexuals. There were all these transvestite bars over on 7th Avenue, and at one point an entertainer who was working in one of those clubs was walking across Washington Square Park after work, and some of the Thompson Street guys jumped him with chains and tire irons. The word went out in the gay community, "Watch it on 3rd Street," and business slumped off, which did not please the mob guys who were running the clubs. This fellow they called Uncle Dominic from Jersey City came in, and there were a couple of little talks with the local guys about how their kneecaps might come in handy in the future. For a couple of years after that, the streets were pretty cool, but around 1961–62 it got nasty again, this time with the focus on blacks and especially interracial couples. In a way, the real issue was neither homosexuality nor race; it was that this had been the old residents' turf and they were losing it. The rents were going up and the locals were feeling threatened, so the kids were taking it out on the most obvious outsiders.

The next singer to come into the Gaslight after Len was Tom Paxton, and shortly after that I crossed over from the Commons, and then a whole flood of other people showed up. Some of them would become the legendary names of the folk revival, but as in the 1950s, it was a more varied scene than is often remembered. The regular acts included a flamenco guitarist named Juan Sastre, and after he left, another named Juan Serrano. Then there were the comedians: Hugh and John, to start off, and later Bill Cosby took over for a while. Noel Stookey, who became Paul of Peter, Paul, and Mary, started out there as a comedian. He was a good mimic and would do a sort of Ernie Kovacs fake German routine, but his masterpiece was his imitation of an old-fashioned flush toilet, and for a while he was billed as "The Toilet Man."

One interesting thing is how few of the people who had been around in the 1950s were involved in this scene. Most of the acts who became popular in the 1960s came from elsewhere, to the point that by about 1962 two-thirds of my close associates were people who had blown into town in the last year or so. I did not particularly notice this at the time, but when I go over the names, there is a striking discontinuity between my coworkers in the Folksingers Guild and the people who became the mainstays of the Village scene once it picked up steam. New York was slow to catch the folk wave, but the local attitude has always been "If anything is worth doing, it's worth overdoing," so once the boom began, there weren't three or five rooms to work in, but fifteen or twenty, all in about a five-block radius.

There was an unbelievable amount of work, and as a result musicians began streaming in from all points of the compass: Paxton from Oklahoma, Len Chandler and Phil Ochs from Ohio, Carolyn Hester from Texas, Patrick Sky from Georgia, Mark Spoelstra from California, Judy Roderick from Colorado, Ian and Sylvia from Canada, Dylan from Minnesota, and on and on. But with very few exceptions, my old friends who had been huffing and puffing all of those years to become professionals were nowhere to be seen.

Basically, what I think happened was that the New York singers simply were not as competitive as the newcomers. You do not stick it out in this line of work unless you are fiercely driven, and most of the New Yorkers, while they might have had the talent, did not have that competitive drive. It was simple economic determinism: they were going to college, getting money from their parents, and however much they might have told themselves that their real focus was the music, when push came to shove, they found they had an easier time doing whatever they were learning to do in school. Meanwhile, these hungry kids were coming in from places like East Overshoe, Montana, and they would claw their way into a job; they would just camp out on a club owner's doorstep until he hired them. It was not really a matter of talent, because if you walked into the Why Not? or some of those other clubs in the mid-1960s, you heard stuff that was as bad as the most dreadful performances the Guild ever sponsored. Even the people who got to be very, very good were not necessarily that way when they arrived. Phil Ochs was not a better performer than Roy Berkeley when he started working in the Village; he just needed it more. I was one of the few New Yorkers to stick it out, and that was because I was stuck with it. There were any number of times when I would have got out of this dumb business if there had been any viable alternative, but there wasn't, and in the end I am glad things worked out the way they did.

At the Gaslight most of us had a pretty good idea of what we were after. We were not into professionalism in the full, show-business sense of the term—we would never have dreamed of wearing anything onstage but street clothes, for example—but that being said, the quality of musicianship and professionalism was pretty high. Some of the people working there already had a lot of experience, and the rest were getting it fast. We were working for these crowds of tourists who were coming down to the Village to look at the beatniks, and they were a very tough audience. They usually started out at the bars, and by the time they got around to us they were completely loaded. So we would be playing for audiences of fifty or a hundred drunken suburbanites who really could not have cared less about the music. They were there to see the freaks and raise some hell, and if they did not like what you were doing, you might even find objects flying through the air in your direction—though fortunately they were too loaded to be able to hit anything. In that kind of situation, you either learn how to handle yourself onstage or go into some other line of work, and the people who stuck it out became thoroughly seasoned pros.

I was one of the Gaslight regulars for years, and crazy as it was, I enjoyed working there. In fact, the craziness helped. For instance, every few weeks there would be some kind of screaming fight between Mitchell and myself, and it would always end with Mitchell shouting, "You're fired!" I would pick up my guitar and go home, lay around the house for about a week; then I would come back down, sit there and have a cup of coffee and listen to the act, and Mitchell would come over and say, "Where have you been?!"

I would say, "I'm fired, John."

He would say, "Well, you're hired!"

I would say, "Oh no, no, no, John. Every time the game changes, the ante goes up . . ." So every time I was fired, it wound up that I was getting a raise.*

In the end, I was in and out of there pretty regularly for about four years, and it served as my office and my second home. There were a bunch of us who tended to show up there at some point in the course of an evening, whether we were working or not, and that was where I met a lot of the people who became my closest friends and musical associates. I eventually summed up my feelings in a song I titled the "Gaslight Rag":

Another damn day, aw, take it away,
I gotta make my gig on time.
Flailing guitar, being a star,
Scuffling for nickels and dimes.

---

*It wasn't just me; Mitchell loved to fire people. Once or twice I even saw him fire audiences.

Silly damn grind, out of my mind,
I'm crazy if I stay.
Leave your wife and bring your knife
If you're working at Mitchell's Café.

I had a dream that the Gaslight was clean
And the rats were all scrubbed down.
The coffee was great and the waitresses straight,
And Patrick Sky left town.
No one was swocked and Dylan played Bach,
And Ochs's songs all scanned.
I got out of bed and I straightened my head,
And started a rock 'n' roll band.

Honey babe, honey babe, let me carry you down.
Pimps and whores and grunge on the floors,
And the finest show in town.
Hot dog stands and skiffle bands,
And Pogo's buying this round.*
There's not much light, but there's plenty of fights
When you're singing in a hole in the ground.

There are some anachronisms in that lyric, because by the time Ochs and Sky showed up, Mitchell had jumped ship. That was in the spring of 1961, shortly after the famed "Beatnik Riot" in Washington Square Park.** He was sick of all the fights with the cops and the Fire Department, so as I understood it, he sold the place to Bob Milos, who had been working there,

---

*Pogo is Tom Paxton, but don't try calling him that.

**This incident had its roots in an attempt by the city to drive a roadway through Washington Square, thereby giving Washington Square Village a 5th Avenue address—that development will never be anything but "Tammany Towers" to anyone who was around then. To make this palatable, they had to create a situation where the park was less used, and step one was to drive out the folksingers. So they banned the singing, and when people did not comply, the park commissioner called out the riot squad—and of course the riot squad's raison d'être is to have riots. The headlines screamed, "3,000 Beatniks Riot in Greenwich Village!" I was playing in Oklahoma City that week and missed the whole thing. It was the only time I was ever glad to be in Oklahoma City.

and went back across the street to the Commons, which he remodeled and named the Fat Black Pussycat—for the time being without any entertainment, folk or otherwise.

During Milos's tenure I started running the Tuesday night hootenannies (what would now be called "open mikes"), which I continued through the early 1960s. I got into that because Milos was all at sixes and sevens and somebody had to run the fucking entertainment, so for a brief period I was actually booking the club. That didn't last long, but I hung onto the Tuesday night thing, figuring that an extra hundred a week never hurt anybody. It was an open stage with no auditions—there was no way I was going to come in at four o'clock in the afternoon and listen to all those bums—so anybody who wanted could get up onstage, and if they weren't good enough, they found that out pretty fast.

Once I had the hootenannies running relatively smoothly, I spent much of those nights next door at the Kettle of Fish. The atmosphere was a good deal more convivial there, so I would hang out with my buddies and just stagger downstairs every now and again and stick my head in the Gaslight to make sure that nobody needed to be thrown out. If everything was going OK, I would do a couple of tunes, then head back to the Kettle and have another drink. It was during this period that Babe, the bartender, dubbed me "the Mayor of MacDougal Street."

That bar was our regular meeting place, and it was a nice place to hang out on weeknights. Weekends could get a little rough. They had a bouncer named Ski, who was possibly the meanest man in Manhattan, and they needed him. I remember walking in there one Sunday afternoon, and Babe was behind the bar, and I said, "Jeez, Babe, you finally got some fresh sawdust on the floor!"

He said, "Nah, that's last night's furniture."

As for Bob Milos, I never figured out his exact relationship to the Gaslight. He was in and out for years, and it was often unclear in what capacity, but his tenure was certainly amusing. He was making most of his money by dealing, so he always had bales of incredibly powerful marijuana, and not only was he completely boxed all the time, but he wasn't happy unless all the people around him were completely boxed. There were two or three years in there when everybody around the place was so stoned from the time we got up in the morning till the time we crashed at night that between that and the drinking, it is a miracle that any of us can even manage a rough chronology of the period.

Even had we been fully compos mentis, it would have been pretty hard to sort out all the wheeling and dealing around that club. Milos definitely had some papers, but it was never clear to me whether Mitchell had really turned the place over to him or they were just throwing up some sort of smokescreen for the cops. Meanwhile, Milos wanted to avoid tax problems, so I gather that he put the place in the name of his wife, Juanita, but she was not hip to all the legal hocus-pocus, so once Milos was out of the picture, she concluded that she owned the Gaslight, and every once in a while she would come stomping in and try to fire everybody.

In any case, that was how I understood the situation. Sam Hood, who ended up running the Gaslight with his father, Clarence, says that Mitchell sold it to Sam's brother-in-law, John Wynn, and a guy named Harry Fry, and that Milos was just working in the kitchen and never really owned the place. Sam was a college football star down in Florida and came up to help out in the summer of 1960, and when he went back to school that fall, he could not stand it, so he moved back and took over the day-to-day management. Noel Stookey was doing most of the booking, and Sam handled all the other stuff, the kitchen and wait staff and so forth. The cops were still a constant annoyance, so after a couple of years Wynn and Fry decided they wanted out, and at that point Clarence came up from Mississippi and he and Sam became the owners from then until the late 1960s.

Clarence was one of the most extraordinary figures to come onto that scene. He had been quite prominent in the Truman administration, as well as becoming a self-made millionaire three times and each time losing it all. He was a gambler and knew how to take his losses with a smile. God, that man was a great poker player! There were regular games all the time, and one night I was bumped out early on—I was clearly in a different league from the guys he liked to play with—and Clarence let me kibitz his hand. I sat there and watched him fold hands that I would have held onto for dear life. Once he threw away a straight! And he was right every goddamn time. He had come from a completely different world, and suddenly was just picked up and dumped on MacDougal Street, in the middle of this kind of nonstop carnival, and he dealt with that situation as though he had created it. That man had more capacity for enjoyment than anyone I have ever known; he could have found something amusing about Hell.

There must have been moments, though, when even Clarence's patience was stretched to the breaking point. The battles between the city and the coffeehouses were absolutely constant, and even after Mitchell left, the Gaslight continued to be singled out. It was as if the cops had decided that if they could nail the Gaslight, the other clubs would fall like a row of dominoes. According to Sam, it reached the point that Clarence had to go into court for over a hundred consecutive days. The cop on the beat was Jimmy Burns, who was actually a very decent guy; he knew how to deal with people and handled that neighborhood very well. Jimmy was under a lot of pressure from his sergeant, though, so every night he would give Clarence a summons for running a cabaret without a license. Then every morning they would troop down to court, and Jimmy would say that he had written the summons because the Gaslight had a certain number of performers onstage at one time, which was a violation of the law. The judge would listen to this testimony, and at a certain point would ask the key question: "Did you see these performers onstage?" Jimmy, right on cue, for those hundred-plus consecutive days, would pause for a moment, give great thought to the question, and then allow as to how, no, the curtain was closed at the time he was writing, so he could only hear the performers. That was insufficient evidence, so the case would be thrown out, and the whole charade would be repeated the following day.

On one level, I could see why so many people were annoyed about the coffeehouses. MacDougal Street really did become a madhouse, and it could not have been any pleasure to try and live a normal life there. I mean, Coney Island is very nice if you come in from somewhere else, enjoy yourself for a while, and then can go home—but when you just want to go across the street for a cup of coffee, you don't want to find yourself on the Boardwalk. We used to call that block between Bleecker and 3rd Street the Elephant Walk, and it was more like a slow elephant stampede. Eventually they put sawhorses up at either end of the block because the crowds were so heavy that cars could not get through. We used to sit out on the steps in front of the Gaslight and pick out particular people, and just count how many times they went past. A lot of them never went in anywhere, they just wandered back and forth between Bleecker and 3rd Street. That was a couple of years later, though, after Peter, Paul, and Mary had hit and the Great Folk Scare was upon us.

12

Changing of the Guard

The winter of 1960-61 was a real momzer—snow up to your earballs and colder than a grave digger's butt. Terri and I were living in Chelsea, and it seemed to take forever to slog through the drifts down to MacDougal. But there was something very cozy about it. Partly because of the weather, it was to be the last time from that day to this that we had the neighborhood to ourselves. The tourist avalanche of the next summer was undreamed of, and on the street or in the joints, you hardly saw a soul you didn't know.

The afternoons were best. Sitting at a window table at the Figaro, playing chess, gossiping with friends, or just watching the snow, one felt an almost rural sense of peace. But in the circles I was running in, there was an undercurrent of electricity. We knew we were right on the edge of something, even if we were uncertain exactly what it was. Clubs and rumors of clubs were popping up everywhere, and it seemed as if every basement and derelict coal bin in the Village was about to become yet another coffeehouse equipped with a stage, all for the greater glory of us. New singers were drifting in almost daily, and the cadre was growing, as my friend Russ Blackwell put it, "by creeps and bounders."

It became a regular thing: a bunch of us would be sitting in the Figaro or the Kettle, and a colleague would come rushing in to tell us, "Hey, there's a new guy over at"—he would name one of the four or five rooms already functioning. "You've gotta hear him, he's really something else." And we would all troop off to check out the new phee-nom.

This particular afternoon, the venue was the Café Wha? on the corner of MacDougal and Minetta.* Manny Roth, the manager, had recently instituted a policy of daytime hootenannies, with Fred Neil presiding. When we arrived, Fred was on stage with his guitar and up there with him, playing harmonica, was the scruffiest-looking fugitive from a cornfield I do believe I had ever seen.

"Where did he pick up that style of harp blowing? Mars?" I said to my companions. But I liked it. There was a gung ho, Dada quality to it that cracked me up. Then Fred relinquished the stage and the kid did a couple of numbers on his own. As I remember, they were Woody Guthrie songs, and his singing had the same take-no-prisoners delivery as his harmonica playing. We were impressed.

After the set, Fred introduced us. Bob Dylan, spelled D-Y-L-A-N. "As in Thomas?" I asked, innocently. Right. I may have rolled my eyes heavenward. On the other hand, all of us were reinventing ourselves to some extent, and if this guy wanted to carry it a step or two further, who were we to quibble? I made my first acquaintance with his famous dead-fish handshake, and we all trooped back to the Kettle for another drink. The Coffeehouse Mafia had a new recruit.**

The first thing you noticed about Bobby in those days was that he was full of nervous energy. We played quite a bit of chess, and his knees would always be bouncing against the table so much that it was like being at a séance. He was herky-jerky, jiggling, sitting on the edge of his chair. And

---

*The Café Wha? was a tourist trap, but it had some very good acts. For example, Richie Havens got to be a regular there fairly early. It was the best deal a clyde just off the bus from Kansas City was likely to find, because you had to know about the other rooms, but the Wha? had drags out on the street, pulling customers inside.

**Bobby later described that Café Wha? gig in "Talking New York," a song that included a singularly apt description of his harp work: "I blowed inside out and upside down." Bobby's playing always reminded me of an anarchist May Day rally I attended in the 1950s: Holly Cantine, "the Hermit of Woodstock," showed up with a trombone and asked if he could lead the assembled masses in "The International." He proceeded to produce a series of farts and howls that almost emptied the hall. He had just bought the thing, and had never tried to play it before. When I asked him whatever possessed him to do that, he replied, "Hey, I'm an anarchist."

you never could pin him down on anything. He had a lot of stories about who he was and where he came from, and he never seemed to be able to keep them straight. I think that's one reason Bobby never gave good interviews: his thinking is so convoluted that he simply does not know how to level, because he's always thinking of the effect that he's having on whoever he's talking to. But there was also something underlying all of that. For example, there was his genuine love for Woody Guthrie. I have heard him say, in retrospect, that he came to New York to "make it," but that's bullshit. When he came to New York, there was no great folk music scene, no chance of making a career out of the sort of music we were doing. What he said at the time, and what I believe, is that he came because he had to meet Woody. Woody was already in very bad shape with Huntington's chorea, and Bobby went out to the hospital and, by dint of some jiving and tap dancing, managed to get himself into his presence, and he sang for Woody, and he really did manage to develop a rapport with him. For a while, he was going out to the hospital quite often, and he would take his guitar and sit there and play for Woody.

I think that was a big part of what got him into writing songs. He wrote "Song for Woody" specifically to sing in the hospital. He was writing for Woody, to amuse him, to entertain him. Of course it was also a personal thing, he wanted Woody's approval, but it was more than that. We all admired Woody and considered him a legend, but none of us was trucking out to see him and play for him. In that regard, Dylan was as stand-up a cat as I have ever known, and it was a very decent and impressive beginning for anybody's career.

Looking back, what a lot of people don't understand is that it was tough for Bobby at first. He was a new kid in town, and he had an especially abrasive voice, and no one had any way of knowing that he would eventually become BOB DYLAN—he was just a kid with an abrasive voice. Sam Hood, who took over the Gaslight around that time, insists that he would use Bobby only on crowded nights when he wanted to clear the house. So Bobby's experience and his memories of that time would be quite different from mine, because I was at least making a living. Bobby was doing guest sets wherever he could and backing people up on harmonica and suchlike, but there was no real work for him. He was cadging meals and sleeping on couches, pretty frequently mine.

At that point Terri and I were still living over on 15th Street, but very shortly thereafter we moved down to Waverly Place. That was an interesting building, because over the next few years it became kind of a folksingers' commune. The agent who ran the place was a music fan and he got an apartment for Barry Kornfeld, then Barry got an apartment for me on the third floor, and then when I moved to a larger place on the second floor, Patrick Sky was installed in my old apartment. Alix Dobkin was living on the fourth floor, and Billy Faier and John Winn moved in as well at some point. John was a classical tenor, a marvelously good musician who did a lot of John Dowland, and he, Ed McCurdy, Bob Dylan, and I used to do madrigals together, which had to be heard to be believed. There was an endless succession of parties, and a constant stream of people wandering in and out. We eventually had to lay down rules so that we could screw without having to worry about people barging in, which shows how much barging in was going on.

The crowd was a mix of old friends and newcomers, musicians, writers, and acquaintances of all varieties and inclinations: Clayton came around a lot, as did Paul Simon. There were different cliques that developed: Patrick had sort of a swing role, because he was close to the crowd around Eric Andersen, Dave Cohen, and Phil Ochs and also with the crowd of Paxton, Noel Stookey, and me. Then there was the crowd around Fred Neil, which included Tim Hardin, Karen Dalton, and Peter Stampfel, who became the guiding light of the Holy Modal Rounders and later one of the Fugs. We didn't socialize as much with them, except for Peter, who has always been one of my favorite people and is undoubtedly some kind of genius—though so far, no one has ever figured out *what* kind.

If I went through the basement of Waverly Place and checked out the lower strata, I would probably still find memorabilia of that period, including a whole bunch of early drafts of songs by various people, not to mention all the coloring books. We used to get stoned out of our minds and do coloring books, and Dylan never colored anything but what he would sign it. So somewhere I probably have a shitload of awesomely bad coloring jobs signed by Dylan.

At least in the early years, I think Terri and I were the only legally married couple in that particular crowd, and in our way we were a good deal more settled than the other people we knew. That was something that set me apart from the other performers on the scene, though I did not think about it that way at the time: I was married and had sort of made a nest, and I was trying to establish a secure place for myself. Most of the people I knew were trying to get away from a secure place, which was what had brought them to the Village. That was why everybody used to come over and hang out at my house: I was the only one who had a house. I had a bed, a couch, a coffee table. Everybody else was sleeping on floors and proclaiming their holy poverty, and I hated poverty.

In any case, within a very short time after hitting the city, Bobby became a regular visitor and part of the gang. And the more I heard him perform, the more impressed I was with what he was doing. Later, when he became more popular, it was completely different. By 1964 his shows were not even generically similar to what he had been doing at the beginning. Back then, he always seemed to be winging it, free-associating, and he was one of the funniest people I have ever seen onstage—although offstage no one ever thought of him as a great wit. He had a stage persona that I can only compare to Charlie Chaplin's "Little Fellow." He was a very kinetic performer, he never stood still, and he had all these nervous mannerisms and gestures. He was obviously quaking in his boots a lot of the time, but he made that part of the show. There would be a one-liner, a mutter, a mumble, another one-liner, a slam at the guitar. Above all, his sense of timing was uncanny: he would get all of these pseudoclumsy bits of business going, fiddling with his harmonica rack and things like that, and he could put an audience in stitches without saying a word. I saw him one time onstage, with just his guitar and harmonica, and he was playing a harmonica chorus that consisted of one note. He kept strumming the guitar, and every now and again he would blow this one note, and after a few measures you were completely caught up in trying to figure out where the next note was coming. And you were always wrong. By the end of two choruses, he had all of us doubled over laughing, with one note on the harmonica.

He had the same kind of unique timing when he sang, though in that context you would call it phrasing. It was quite different from what anyone else was doing, even before he started to write much of his own material. He was singing Woody Guthrie songs and things like "Pretty Polly," but no one else did those songs that way. And his repertoire changed all the time; he'd find something he loved and sing it to death and drop it and go on to something else. Basically, he was in search of his own musical style, and it was developing very rapidly. So there was a freshness about him that was very exciting, very effective, and he acquired some very devoted fans among the other musicians before he had written his first song, or at least before we were aware that he was writing.

Another thing that worked very much to Bobby's advantage was his populism, the romantic hobo thing. He had that Guthriesque persona, both on and off stage, and we all bought it. Not that we necessarily believed he was really a Sioux Indian from New Mexico or whatever cockamamy variation he was peddling that day, but we believed the gist of his story, and even what we didn't believe was often entertaining. I mean, one night he spent something like an hour showing a bunch of us how to talk in Indian sign language, which I'm pretty sure he was making up as he went along, but he did it marvelously. And when we found out that a lot of his stories were bullshit, that didn't really lower his stock all that much. It was an old showbiz tradition—everybody changed their names and invented stories about themselves. So we kidded him some, but nobody held it against him. I don't think Bobby ever understood that. He never really got the fact that nobody cared who you had been before you hit town. We were all inventing characters for ourselves. Look at Ramblin' Jack Elliott, who had grown up as a Jewish doctor's son in Brooklyn and then gone out west and become a cowboy and Woody's hoboing buddy.

Jack was obviously a very important model for Bobby—both in terms of his music and because he had really lived the life and done all the things Bobby wanted to do—and at first Bobby had no idea that he was anything but a good-coin goyish cowboy. The revelation that Jack was Jewish was vouchsafed unto Bobby one afternoon at the Figaro. We were sitting around shooting the bull with Barry Kornfeld and maybe a couple of other people, and somehow it came out that Jack had grown up in Ocean Parkway and was named Elliott Adnopoz. Bobby literally fell off his chair; he was rolling around on the floor, and it took him a couple of minutes to pull himself together and get up again. Then Barry, who can be diabolical in things like this, leaned over to him and just whispered the word "Adnopoz," and back he went under the table. A lot of us had suspected that Bobby was Jewish, and after that we had no doubts.

That kind of thing was happening all the time, and we tended to just take it in stride. I remember when Jack first blew back into town, which was right around the time Bobby arrived. That was a big deal, so of course I was at Gerde's for his New York debut. Now, Jack's mother and father were very prominent people in Brooklyn; I understand that his father was chief of surgery in a hospital, and the family had been in medicine for several generations. So the fact that Jack had turned into a bum was a great source of grief. However, he had been away for a long time, and now he was home, and they were making some attempt at a reconciliation, so Dr. and Mrs. Adnopoz came down to see the kid. I was sitting at a front table with them and the cowboy artist Harry Jackson, and Jack was onstage, and he was having some trouble tuning his guitar. The audience was utterly hushed—a very rare occurrence in that room—and Mrs. Adnopoz was staring at Jack raptly, and then she lets out with a stage whisper: "Look at those fingers . . . Such a surgeon he could have been!"

All in all, personal reinvention was the order of the day, and I still do not know—I do not think anybody really knows—how much of what Bobby was telling us was bullshit and how much actually had some basis in fact. Once everyone found out that he was a nice middle-class Jewish boy named Zimmerman, it was easy to assume that he had made up all the other stories as well—but then there was the time when Big Joe Williams came to town. Big Joe was one of the legendary Mississippi blues men, and Bobby had been telling stories for months about how the first time he ran away from home, he hopped a boxcar and who did he meet but Big Joe Williams, who began to teach him old blues. Bobby said that he was thirteen or something like that, and that they went all the way down to Mexico together. We listened to this more or less politely, but nobody believed him, and when we heard that Big Joe was coming to New York, a bunch of us arranged to go down with Bobby and see Joe—that was a meeting that nobody wanted to miss. We walked into the club, and Joe spotted us, and he came right over and said, "Hey, Bobby! I haven't seen you since that boxcar down to Mexico!" I will always wonder whether Bobby somehow got to Joe and set the whole thing up, but it certainly blew us away.

For a while there, Terri and I were probably Bobby's biggest boosters, at least when it came to actually getting him jobs. Terri was taking care of my business, such as it was, and also handling some booking and paperwork for people like Paxton, Chandler, Mark Spoelstra, and a couple of others, and she became Bobby's manager, as well—not that there was any competition for that job. No other manager would have touched him with a ten-foot pole. In the professional folk music world, most people were still into Harry Belafonte and the Kingston Trio, and Bobby was too weird, too scruffy, and he sang funny. But there was a sort of Village cabal that had a certain amount of influence within our small world, and among other things, we pushed Mike Porco to book Bobby. Terri had been helping Mike by doing this, that, and the other thing, but she really had to call in every favor to get Bobby that gig. In the end, Mike put him on opening for John Lee Hooker, and it went OK. Then a few months later he opened for the Greenbriar Boys, and Bob Shelton wrote him up in the *Times*, and that was really what got Bobby started.

After that, Bobby's career kind of took off, but it was by no means an overnight thing. In November of 1961, a couple of months after the *Times* piece, Izzy Young booked him into Carnegie Recital Hall for his first solo concert, and only 53 people showed up. Still, there was a definite groundswell of interest, and he soon had a small but fanatical claque of fans who would show up anywhere he was playing; if he dropped by to do a guest set at the Gaslight or one of the other clubs, they would appear by the second song. Then John Hammond signed him to Columbia Records, and that really got people's attention—though many of them thought Columbia was making the biggest mistake in history and I have been told that within the company Dylan was referred to as "Hammond's Folly." Still, that made a big difference, and within a very short time he was doing concerts rather than working on MacDougal. In fact, he boasted to me once that he had played only two club gigs in his life, and although he was wrong about that—he had, to my personal knowledge, played at least five—in essence it was true.*

---

*Bobby shared the common preference for concert halls over clubs, which I have never really understood. Admittedly, there is nothing worse than a bad club, but there is nothing better than a good one. It is just the right mixture of formality and informality. I don't like to see audiences sitting in serried rows in front of me like a Macedonian phalanx. I like to see people relaxing with a drink in their hands and enjoying themselves. But I am aware that, at least among folk performers, I am in the minority.

In a way, what was happening in that period was that the folk music wave that had already hit the rest of the country was beginning to overlap with what had been going on in the Village. Until then, we had managed to ignore the pop folk scene. Of course we knew about the Kingston Trio and Belafonte and their hordes of squeaky-clean imitators, but we felt like that was a different world that had nothing to do with us. For one thing, most of those people were simply bad musicians, and that continued to hold true for a lot of the popular groups right through the 1960s. They couldn't play worth a damn and were indifferent singers, and as far as material was concerned, they were scraping the top of the barrel, singing songs that we had known and dropped ten years earlier. It was a 100 percent rip-off: they were ripping off the material; they were ripping off the authors, composers, collectors, and sources; and they were ripping off the public. Some of them developed a decent stage presence and managed to put on good shows from time to time, but musically the stuff was bad, and we had heard it all before. It was Mitch Miller sing-alongs and the *Fireside Book of Folk Songs* performed by sophomores in paisley shirts who couldn't play their instruments.*

Of course, there were some exceptions, but even those were not really to our taste. For example, when I first saw Bob Gibson, he had this almost Vegas-Tahoe approach and it drove me nuts because I was a folk purist and it was the antithesis of everything I held dear. He was also in a whole different league from me and my friends; he played at the Gate of Horn and places like that, and we thought of him as part of the older generation. But in the early 1960s he was working pretty often in the Village, and after I had seen him a few times, I began to have to admit to myself how good he was. The first thing that tipped me off was when I saw him at the Gaslight, working to this audience of fanatical neo-ethnics, and they loved him. There was obviously something going on that I was not getting, and I really had to listen and to think about it, and what I figured out was that he just had this marvelous touch and a marvelous ease on stage. Bob looked people right in the eye, and he attempted to communicate with them, and he had a way of

---

*Some of the musicians from the commercial groups used to defend their maiming of the music by telling me that they were opening up a new audience and, if it weren't for them, no one would know about people like me. To some extent they were probably right about that, but I suspect that they also drove a lot of people away by making the word "folk" synonymous with the insipid, cutesy crap they were peddling.

dramatizing a song that was very striking. Sometimes he would get carried away and overdramatize, but in general what he did was very effective, and while it was never something I wanted to do myself, I had to appreciate it because it worked. Besides that, he was a good musician. I sometimes think that he and Paxton were my favorite melodists in the folk songwriter field, Paxton for his incredible simplicity and Gibson for his ability to come up with unusual modulations and chord progressions.

I also found that I really liked some of those people personally. Gibson, like Cynthia Gooding, was very polished onstage, but offstage they were both wonderfully cynical and funny. I remember years later seeing Bob at Newport with a group of people singing "Kumbaya," and it was turning into one of those really tacky group-gropes, with everybody joining hands and taking turns leading verses—"Someone's crying, Lord, kumbaya," "Someone's dying, Lord, kumbaya,"—and it gets around to Gibson's turn, and he sings, "Someone's kidding, Lord . . . "

In any case, the scene was changing at a very rapid clip. There was more money around, and that in itself made a difference. There were more clubs and bigger audiences, and it was no longer just our small band of folk devotees. What is more, that small band had never been very unified even before the money hit. People like Len Chandler and Tom Paxton loved traditional folk songs, but they were not hard-core neo-ethnics painstakingly learning licks off 78s. The purist faction had always been balanced by people who were a good deal less orthodox and whose voices were a lot easier on mainstream ears. There was also an interesting split along gender lines, which is obvious if you look at Dylan and then at Joan Baez. Whatever he may have done as a writer, Dylan was solidly in the neo-ethnic camp. He did not have a pretty voice, and he did his best to sing like Woody, or at least like somebody from Oklahoma or the rural South, and was always very rough and authentic sounding, to the best of his ability.

Baez was a completely different kind of artist. With her, it was all about the beauty of her voice. That voice really was astonishing—the first time I heard her she electrified me, just as she electrified everybody else. She was not a great performer, and she was not a great singer, but God she had an instrument. And she had that vibrato, which added a remarkable amount of tone color. I think that I was a technically better singer than she was even then, but she had a couple of tricks that were damn useful, and I learned a few things from her.

The thing about Baez, though, was that like almost all the women on that scene, she was still singing in the style of the generation before us. It was a cultural lag: the boys had discovered Dock Boggs and Mississippi John Hurt, and the girls were still listening to Cynthia and Susan Reed. It was not just Joan. There was Carolyn Hester, Judy Collins, and people like Molly Scott and Ellen Adler, who for a while were also contenders. All of them were essentially singing bel canto—bad bel canto, by classical standards, but still bel canto. So whereas the boys were intentionally roughing up their voices, the girls were trying to sound prettier and prettier and more and more virginal. To a great extent, I think that had to do with wanting to make themselves desirable to the boys, and certainly the boys could not have been more encouraging—we were all entranced by that virginal warble. But the result is that the women were still singing in the styles of the 1940s or 1950s, and that gave them a kind of crossover appeal to the people who were listening to Belafonte and the older singers, and to the clean-cut college groups.

At the time, I was not thinking all of this through in the same way I do now, but in hindsight you can see pretty easily what happened. And there were a few people around even then who seemed to have a sense of where things were going—or who at least were quick to seize the brass ring when it came their way. Chief among these was Albert Grossman, my old nemesis from Chicago. Albert had put together the first Newport Folk Festival in 1959, and in 1960 he moved to New York and began hanging around on MacDougal Street. He was an interesting and amusing man, and I got to know him fairly well, but there was always a distance there. He was very cold and calculating, and you couldn't trust him for a minute. When Dylan met Grossman, it was truly a match made in heaven, because those were two extraordinarily secretive people who loved to mystify and conspire and who played their cards extremely close to their vests. You never knew what scheme Albert was cooking up behind that blank stare, and he actually took a sort of perverse pleasure in being utterly unscrupulous. He could be a wonderful companion, though—it wouldn't be until two days after you saw him that you would realize that your underwear had been stolen.

There you would be: "Shit, man, my shoes are on—what happened to my socks?"

Albert was very smart, with a good eye for talent, and he really knew the business. When he was in the mood—or saw a way to turn it to his advantage—he could be extremely helpful, and I learned a good deal from him. I have mentioned his suggestion that I should stand up when I played, which was not a success, but some of his advice was indispensable. During the brief period when he was managing me, he persuaded me that, along with working on the music, I needed to work at making contact with my audience. For example, he had me sit in front of a three-paneled, wraparound mirror with my guitar and watch myself while I performed, which finally broke me of the habit of looking at my shoes while I was playing. So I owe him at least a few votes of thanks.

Albert had taken a good, long look at all the Weavers clones in their preppy outfits, and he decided that there was an opening for a group that was hipper than that—more musically sophisticated, with a contemporary feel—so he was scouting the local talent with this in mind. One day we ran into each other on MacDougal, and he said that he had a proposition for me: he was putting together a trio, and he had two people already, and he needed a third. I said, "Who are the two people?" and he said Peter Yarrow and Mary Travers.

I thought about it for a day or so and talked it over with Terri, but by this time I was doing pretty well as a solo performer, and I really had no interest in being part of a group. Besides, my immediate reaction was, "Oh, my God, we're gonna have a village-spawned Kingston Trio here," and I wanted no part of it. As it turned out, what Albert had in mind was something quite different, but as usual he was being cagey and short on specifics, and that sounded like exactly what he was proposing. So I turned him down and they got Noel Stookey, and Noel added precisely the ingredient that they needed. Peter, Dave, and Mary would have died the death of a thousand cuts—I would have stood out like a sore thumb, vocally, visually, you name it. And I suppose I would have had to change my name as well. Still, every time I look at my bank balance . . .

In any case, Peter, Paul, and Mary provided me with one of the best paychecks I ever cashed. They had their debut right around the same time Dylan got the *Times* review, at a new club called the Bitter End, which became New York's closest thing to a mainstream folk showcase—it had people like Bob Gibson and Judy Collins, the Chad Mitchell Trio, and even the New Christy Minstrels.*A few months later they released their first record, and it included a song that I had put together and recorded on my second Folkways album. I had called it "River Come Down," but they renamed it "Bamboo." It had originally just been a guitar exercise, but my students demanded that I give them some lyrics to go with it, so I threw together some doggerel based on a song I vaguely remembered hearing Dick Weissman do on the banjo, and used Dick's chorus, "River, oh river, she come down." I recorded it more or less as filler and assumed it would go no further, but that Peter, Paul, and Mary album promptly sold seven trillion copies, and it is probably still my best-known composition. Not only that, but some of the pop music critics homed in on the lyrics, describing them as "surrealist"— one erudite soul even compared them to Garcia Lorca. The end of that story is that I recently read an interview with Noel in which he singles out "Bamboo" for special mention as one of the few pieces in their repertoire that has not stood the test of time. I heartily agree with him. It is the only song I wrote that ever made me any money, and I hate it.

The fact that they did that song, though, was indicative of something that was different about Peter, Paul, and Mary: they were not simply reworking traditional folk songs and doing Weavers covers and that sort of thing. Their material was very carefully chosen, and most of it was quite new, and they had some smart, original arrangements. Of course, we regarded them as "slick," but they were interesting, and in retrospect I think their popularity was deserved. I can't say that I ever spent much time listening to their records, but I was not the sort of listener they were aiming at.

Grossman had his eye on a national audience, but for me the scene was still centered on New York, and I was getting all the work I could handle. In 1962 I signed a two-album contract with Prestige Records, which was not a major label but was considered a definite step up from Folkways. (I was so proud, until I told one of my friends, "I'm recording for Prestige!" He said, "Well, keep it up and sooner or later you might be recording for money.") The guy who ran the label, Bob Weinstock, had excellent taste in jazz, and he was beginning to record a lot of folk and blues as well. After

---

*Also the New Prince Spaghetti Minstrels. I think I owe it to posterity to preserve that name.

we did the first album, he called me up and said, "I'm going to title this album something I really believe is true: I'm going to call it *Dave Van Ronk: New York's Finest.*"

I said, "Bob, for Christ's sake, you're calling me a cop!"

There was a long pause, and he said, "Oh. I hadn't thought of that."

I said, "You can call it anything you want, but for crying out loud, don't call it that." So he released it as *Dave Van Ronk: Folksinger,* whereupon I subsided, muttering, "Better a dork than a narc."

That was the first album of mine that I consider relatively satisfactory in musical terms. I had shaken off a lot of the mannerisms of my earlier records, partly through a natural process of evolution, and partly because I was working so much and getting so much opportunity to test and reshape my material. It also introduced the piece that some people continue to regard as my signature song, "Cocaine Blues." That song became so associated with me that a lot of people assumed I had written it, which caused occasional embarrassment. Sometime in the mid-seventies, I ran into Jackson Browne on the street, and he said, "Hey, Dave, I just recorded one of your songs." At that point things were pretty slow and the royalties from a Jackson Browne record would have made a big difference, so I was very happy, and I said, "Man, that's nice. Which one?" And he said, "Cocaine Blues." I said, "Jackson, that's a Gary Davis song, and here's who you contact to send the royalties to his estate. Now get away from me before you see a grown man cry."

Frankly, that song had some other disappointing aspects as well: When I first learned it from Gary, one of my jazz musician buddies said, "Yeah, that's a good one for you to do, because, you know, when you get finished with your show, there'll be people lined up back in your dressing room to give you toot." That sounded kind of interesting, but as it turned out, he was entirely mistaken. Instead, for a while there I would finish up and go back to my dressing room, and there would be people lined up asking me to give *them* some. It was very disillusioning.

The *Folksinger* album came out just as the folk wave was beginning to crest, and for the next few years I had more work than I have ever had before or since. I was hosting the Tuesday night hoots at the Gaslight, as well as sometimes doing a week as a headliner there or at Folk City, and for variety I was making occasional forays into the hinterlands. I got to Tulsa and

Oklahoma City for a couple of weeks, and I was going to the West Coast, Chicago, Philadelphia, Washington, Canada. Some of those were one-shot deals, but there were also rooms that I could count on working fairly regularly—the Caffé Lena in Saratoga Springs probably paid my rent for 1960. And then, of course, there was Cambridge. That was the other East Coast hub, and it had a scene that was quite different from anywhere else. Baez had come out of there, and I probably went up to check it out for the first time in 1960. I got a kind of strange reception there, because the Cantabrigians had set up this dichotomy between me and Eric Von Schmidt. In their eyes Eric was the greatest white blues singer around, and I was the New York contender. Personally, I had nothing but admiration for Eric's work. He had gotten into the blues thing a year or two ahead of me, and he may have been the first of us to develop his own approach to the music. His singing was excellent, and his guitar playing was powerful and quite unique, but what really made him stand out was that his style was intensely personal. He was never Robert Johnson or Furry Lewis or Leadbelly, or anyone but Eric Von Schmidt, and that made him one of the very few white people around at that time who could sing blues with conviction and make you feel that he was singing about his own life and his own feelings rather than pretending to be someone else.

The Cambridge crowd wanted Eric and me to hate each other, which shocked me and gave me a kind of sour view of the place. The fact is that we hit it off famously, got stinking drunk, got up on stage together, just disported ourselves and had a marvelous time. He had a studio on Brattle Street, and we would go up there and drink and play cards, and when we were thoroughly loaded, we would go downstairs to the Brattle Theatre and watch *Casablanca,* which always seemed to be playing.

I think the Cambridge people in general had a complex about New York. We were Gomorrah, whereas they were the pure guardians of the sacred flame. In a lot of ways the difference was economic. By that time, the scene in New York was relatively professional, made up of all these people who were coming into town and needed to make a living from their music just to pay the rent. We were playing five sets a night in rooms full of drunken tourists, and even if we didn't necessarily think of ourselves that way, we were professional entertainers. Cambridge was a college town, and the scene—not necessarily the performers but the fans and the hangers-on—

was a bunch of middle- and upper-middle-class kids cutting a dash on papa's cash. They did not feel the economic pressures that we did, so their frame of reference was completely different. To be fair, in some ways that made the Cambridge scene much healthier, because without that economic pressure, they could put all their focus on the music. We were constantly being sucked into commercial culture, and they weren't. And sure, they could afford their purity, but that doesn't mean that they weren't pure, and that purist approach produced some very good work. I had great respect for some of the performers up there, and learned a lot from them.

As a scene, though, Cambridge always annoyed me because they were such snobs. It was class snobbery, the whole Harvard mystique, even if they were not actually connected with Harvard. It was like the story about the little Jew from the garment district who makes his pile, goes to England, and wants to get a real English gentleman's suit from a real London tailor. He goes to Saville Row and he's informed that they require four fittings. The guy says, "That's okay, I've got time." So he goes in for the first fitting, the second fitting, the third fitting. Finally, everything is ready except the final touches: getting the shoulders adjusted, dotting the *i*s, crossing the *t*s. He is standing there in this beautiful suit, and he looks like Anthony Eden, but as he is looking at himself in the mirror, he bursts into tears.

One of the tailors says, "Oh sir, is there something wrong?"

He says, "No, everything's perfect . . . but vy did ve hef to lose India?"

That was what that Cambridge scene was like a lot of the time: there were kids from all over the country, and by no means all of them were especially wealthy or cultured, but they all adopted that Harvard attitude. Though I must say that it was the fans who set that tone more than the musicians. People like Von Schmidt, Jim Kweskin, Geoff Muldaur, Joan Baez—if you knew what you were about, they respected you, because we were all working the same side of the street.

Still, for quite a while I was playing more in Boston than I was in Cambridge. The Cambridge people looked down on the Bostonians as well; they didn't have that je ne sais quoi. So I would hang out in Cambridge, but I was not playing there, and it got pretty annoying. I mean, the Club 47 was *the* hip room, but it was Von Schmidt territory and I had the impression that they felt that if they hired me, they would be letting down the side. However, I was very close with Jim Kweskin, and I used to go over to his place and play music with him and Muldaur and whoever else was around. Kweskin in those days was running a hootenanny at the Club 47, so one night I was over there at Jim's place and the reefer was going around—there was always an enormous amount of dope up there—and I said, "Nope, I'll pass. Because if I get stoned, then we'll all go down to the 47, and you'll get up on stage and say, 'Here in the audience we have Dave Van Ronk. Let's give him a big hand and ask him to come up and do a couple of numbers,' and there I'll be, bombed out of my skull. So I'm not going to smoke any of your dope, because I don't trust you, you bastard."

Jim said, "Come on, Dave, I would never do that to you. Have a toke."

So, with some misgivings, I had a toke, and another, and another, and another. Two hours later, I'm sitting in the Club 47, boxed out of my bird, and Jim is onstage, and he says, "Here in the audience we have Dave Van Ronk. Let's give him a big hand and ask him to come up and do a couple of numbers."

What could I do? The audience was applauding wildly. I got up onstage and started into a song, and it was just like that first time back in my jazz days: I was absolutely catatonic, entranced by all the strange and interesting things my fingers were doing. Somehow, though, I managed to get through three songs, and I walked off, and Byron Linardos, the manager, comes over and says, "That was great! When do you want to work here?" Go figure.*

I eventually became a fixture up there—though I still didn't work at the 47 all that often—and I even ran across an old issue of *The Broadside of Boston*, the local folk mag, with their readers' poll for 1964, and I was listed as the Favorite Visiting Performer, followed by Dylan, Jean Redpath, and Phil Ochs, with honorable mention to Jose Feliciano, Jack Elliott, and Doc Watson. It was good company in those days.

Oddly enough, the best friend I met in Boston was Patrick Sky, though neither of us ever lived there. Patrick was from Georgia, but he had crawled

---

*The Cambridge drug scene was actually a lot like the Cambridge folk scene, in that everything was overintellectualized. Timothy Leary and Richard Alpert had created this enormous theoretical structure based on "expanding your mind," and it was all a crock of pseudomystical horseshit and petit bourgeois rationalization to justify getting stoned. The people I hung out with were drinkers who also smoked, and a better bunch of fucked-up boyos you never did meet. The people on the self-awareness trip were silly and boring. They would sit around going, "Boy, am I stoned. Boy! Am I stoned . . ." And the next day it was like the old Jewish joke: "Boy, was I stoned . . ."

out a window to escape a failed marriage, changed his name, and gone to Florida. He was down there hacking away on a guitar and bumped into Buffy St. Marie, and she dragged him up north with her. One weekend I was working at the Café Yana, near Fenway Park, and Buffy, who was working someplace else, came by and said, "I've got somebody you have to meet—this is something I absolutely have to see," and it was Patrick. She knew we would either kill each other or become fast friends, and as it turned out, we hit it off immediately. We settled in with a jug and had a gorgeous gabfest, and after a while I think poor Buffy got bored and wandered away.

Patrick was, and remains, a deeply pessimistic man, and very funny—his mind-set reminds me of W. C. Fields. When it came to songwriting, he had a very direct style, but with the most sardonic point of view, and he also had a love of whimsy that was very rare. For example, he called his second album *A Harvest of Gentle Clang*. I do not think anybody but Patrick could have thought of that title. (There is a wonderful piece of folk ephemera on that album: in a pause between songs, Patrick announces, "And now, the moment you've all been waiting for: Mississippi John Hurt sings Gilbert and Sullivan!" Then the unmistakable tones of John Hurt waft forth: "Gilbert and Sulliva-an!")

My favorite Patrick Sky story happened right around the time he recorded that album. It was 1965, and we had been invited to appear on a Canadian television show called *Let's Sing Out,* which was their version of *Hootenanny*. They were filming at a college in Winnipeg, and Patrick and I happened to be on the same plane out of Buffalo. Patrick had been up for something like seventy-two hours, and so had I, working and drinking and working and drinking, and we had drunk ourselves sober and drunk and sober again—we were seemingly quite coherent, but the only thing that was keeping us going was the steady consumption of bourbon. We arrived at this college auditorium where they were doing the shoot, and they had converted it into a sort of huge dressing room area. All the tech people were running around, setting up lights and patting us down with powder puffs and that sort of thing, and over in a corner, sitting by herself on a folding chair, was this lovely blond lady. She was playing guitar and singing to herself, just warming up, and I don't know how it happened, but after a few minutes everything was completely quiet and everybody had just formed a semicircle around her. It was Joni Mitchell, and she was singing "Urge for

Going," and that was the first time I ever heard it or her. It was simply magical, and by the middle of the second verse, you could hear a pin drop. She finished, and there was just this silence, utter silence.

Then Patrick turns to me, and loudly says, "That *sucks!*"

As it happened, that was the highest compliment Patrick was capable of bestowing, but of course Joni had no way of knowing that. She later told me that she went back to Detroit in tears and told Chuck, her partner and husband, that the great folksingers from New York didn't like her music, and she briefly considered quitting the business. Fortunately, she thought better of it, sensibly concluding that we could go fuck ourselves.

After that first time, Joni and I met up pretty often, and I actually saw her and Chuck perform together a couple times while they were still living in Detroit. They worked as a split bill, with Chuck doing the first part of the show, Chuck and Joni doing some songs together, and then Joni finishing up on her own. It was very interesting to watch, because they had sharply contrasting musical styles: Chuck was of the older, theatrical school and would do marvelous arrangements of Kurt Weill numbers, singing in a fine, trained voice, while Joni was already in the process of developing her completely distinctive approach. Later on, when Joni moved to New York, we got to be very good friends and she taught me an awful lot about songwriting. I thought she was the best writer of the 1960s, a very playful lyricist in the same way that John Donne was a playful lyricist.

There is a lot more to be said about that whole crop of 1960s-era songwriters, but first I suppose I should clear up the famous story about Dylan and "House of the Rising Sun," which has haunted me for the last thirty years. And when I say haunted . . .

Sometime in the early 1990s, I was doing a tour of France and I made a stop at the Hippopotamus Club in Saint-Étienne, which is as *la France profonde* as you can get outside of the Lascaux Caverns. I was standing at the bar between sets when a very drunk customer lurched up to me and said, in barely decipherable English, "Please, to sing 'Rising Sun.'" Bad as her English was, it was better than my French, but I explained as best as I could that I had not sung that song in twenty years and did not even remember my guitar chart for it.

She wasn't having any of that. She opened her mouth and bawled in my face, "There is a house from New Orleans . . . "—to help me get started, I suppose. Apparently that was the only line she knew, but she liked it just fine, so she sang it again, louder and with feeling. And again. And again. Clearly, the woman had found her métier. She kept howling that line at me, her face not ten inches from mine. And her breath—*Quel bouquet!*

I felt a panic attack coming on. There was no escape route—my back was to the bar and she was standing toe to toe with me, howling that line over and over again. Fortunately, before I was forced to kill her in self-defense, a couple of her friends led her away, still bellowing, "There is a house from New Orleans . . . "

But I had not heard the last of her. When I mounted the stage for my second set, there she was, ringside table, stage right. Like the Bourbon kings of old, she had learned nothing and forgotten nothing. Every pause in a song, every comma in an introduction was her cue. I had a microphone and she didn't, but she was matching me decibel for decibel. I have never been driven from a stage in my life, and I have been heckled by experts, but this was beginning to look like a historic first. Finally, her friends came to my rescue once again. They half dragged, half carried her out the door and off into the night. We could still hear her a block away: "There is a house from New Orleans . . ." Did I mention that she was tone-deaf?

When my shattered nerves had mended somewhat, I got to thinking: what I had told our diva of the detox ward was true. I had dropped that tune from my repertory around 1963, although I loved it dearly. I had learned it sometime in the 1950s, from a recording by Hally Wood, the Texas singer and collector, who had got it from an Alan Lomax field recording by a Kentucky woman named Georgia Turner. I put a different spin on it by altering the chords and using a bass line that descended in half steps—a common enough progression in jazz, but unusual among folksingers. By the early 1960s, the song had become one of my signature pieces, and I could hardly get off the stage without doing it.

Then, one evening in 1962, I was sitting at my usual table in the back of the Kettle of Fish, and Dylan came slouching in. He had been up at the Columbia studios with John Hammond, doing his first album. He was being very mysterioso about the whole thing, and nobody I knew had been to any of the sessions except Suze, his lady. I pumped him for information, but he was vague. Everything was going fine and, "Hey, would it be okay for me to record your arrangement of 'House of the Rising Sun?'"

Oh, shit. "Jeez, Bobby, I'm going into the studio to do that myself in a few weeks. Can't it wait until your next album?"

A long pause. "Uh-oh."

I did not like the sound of that. "What exactly do you mean, 'Uh-oh'?"

"Well," he said sheepishly, "I've already recorded it."

"You did what?!" I flew into a Donald Duck rage, and I fear I may have said something unkind that could be heard over in Chelsea. The feud was on, at least as far as I was concerned, and the MacDougal Street gossips were all atwitter with the news. I played the part of the righteously aggrieved artiste with relish, though after a couple of weeks the sheer pettiness of the whole thing began to dawn on me. Terri was no longer Bobby's manager, but the split had been amicable, and she and Suze were still very close. They were lobbying for a reconciliation, but I didn't see how I could back down without admitting that I was being a schmuck.

That was when Dave Cohen—later known as Dave Blue—stepped into the breach. He was the last person I would have thought of as a peacemaker, being by temperament something of a barroom brawler, so when he tore into me for being a nitpicker and taking up time that would be better spent on juicier scandals, I allowed myself to be mollified. Bob and I shook hands, with Cohen looking on like the adult conciliator of a schoolyard punch-up, and that was that. Or so I thought.

Bobby's album came out, but although it presaged a major paradigm shift in American music, its early sales were disappointing. "Rising Sun" was on it, sure enough, and it was essentially my arrangement, but Bobby's reading had all the nuance and subtlety of a Neanderthal with a stone hand ax, and I took comfort thereby. Then events took a turn I would never have predicted. People started asking me to do "that Dylan song—the one about New Orleans." This became more frequent as Bobby's popularity took off, and with a combination of annoyance and chagrin, I decided to drop the song until the whole thing blew over.

Then, sometime in 1964, Eric Burdon and the Animals made a number-one chart hit out of the damn thing. Same arrangement. I would have loved to sue for royalties, but I found that it is impossible to defend the copyright on an arrangement. Wormwood and gall. I also heard that Bobby had dropped the tune from *his* repertoire because he was sick of being asked to do "that Animals song—the one about New Orleans."

That was some slight satisfaction, but the song was not finished with me yet. In 1971 Tony Scaduto's Dylan biography came out, and in it he rehashed the whole sorry nonevent. The book sold very well, and pretty soon everybody was asking me, "Is it true Bob Dylan stole 'House of the Rising Sun' from you?"

That was worse than being asked to sing "that Dylan song." If I said no, they would come back at me with, "But it says in Scaduto's book that blah, blah, blah." If I tried to explain the whole complicated business, they simply didn't get it, or rather, they didn't want to get it. What they wanted was scandal, and while plagiarism was not as good as lechery, they were ready to settle for it in a pinch. And mind you, these were usually Bobby's *fans;* what his detractors were saying I leave to your imagination.

By this time the mere mention of that song would send me into a rant against the copyright laws, Dylan, his stupid fans, and the whole dismal train of events that had landed me in the middle of this tempest in a teapot. It wasn't until the aforementioned *tour de France* that I could bring myself to even consider singing it again. But that's what I did. I even went back and improved the chart, and I have been singing it happily (if a bit uneasily) ever since. Too bad that wino in Saint-Étienne couldn't hear it—and I have carefully avoided re-recording the thing. Who knows what kind of debacle *that* might trigger.

There is one final footnote to that story. Like everybody else, I had always assumed that the "house" was a brothel. But a while ago I was in New Orleans to do the Jazz and Heritage Festival, and my wife Andrea and I were having a few drinks with Odetta in a gin mill in the Vieux Carré, when up comes a guy with a sheaf of old photographs—shots of the city from the turn of the century. There, along with the French Market, Lulu White's Mahogany Hall, the Custom House, and suchlike, was a picture of a forbidding stone doorway with a carving on the lintel of a stylized rising sun.

Intrigued, I asked him, "What's that building?"

It was the Orleans Parish women's prison.

So, as it turned out, I had gotten the whole business wrong from the get-go. Pity I didn't think it was a Sunday school—I might have never sung the damn thing in the first place.

13

The Blues Revival

When the Folk Scare finally hit, it was bigger than even the most optimistic of us had imagined. All of a sudden, they were handing out major-label record contracts like they were coming in Cracker Jack boxes, and there was money all over the place. People who had been sleeping on floors and eating in cafeterias could buy a suit, a car, a house. And the flood of mainstream popularity led to some changes that were very interesting artistically as well, because it attracted a lot of talented people who otherwise would never have been connected with folk music. Jose Feliciano, for example. He played the guitar; he sang; ergo, he was a folksinger. When Jose first hit MacDougal Street, he was just playing in the basket houses, and people were telling me, "You've got to come down and hear this kid. He's fantastic." So I went down and heard him, and he was fantastic—he completely blew me away. He was very young, not even eighteen, and at first I had the impression that he was just a shy kid, a little bit withdrawn. I subsequently discovered that he has one of the most vicious wits of anyone I have ever met. He is hilariously funny, and you do not want to cross swords with that man unless you are at the top of your game. So people like that were showing up, and also Bill Cosby, Woody Allen, Simon and Garfunkel. Of course, the money also attracted a lot of hokey shit, and a lot of people who were simply greedy and couldn't have cared less about art or music or anything else except lining their own pockets. It was a grab bag: if you wanted to make serious music, you could find a berth, and if you wanted to make a killing, you could find a berth, too.

I got to know Paul and Artie pretty well, because for a while Barry Kornfeld was Paul's partner and publisher, so they were coming around the building on Waverly. When they first showed up, they were in a pretty tough situation, because they had already had a Top 40 hit as teenagers, and as far as the music industry was concerned, they were over the hill, but the mouldy fig wing of the folk world despised them as pop singers. I remember hearing them down at the Gaslight, and nobody would listen. I thought they were damn good, but the people who wanted to hear Mississippi John Hurt and Dock Boggs wanted no part of Simon and Garfunkel. Their mainstream connections were still strong enough to get them a contract with Columbia, but the first album went nowhere, and "Sounds of Silence" actually became a running joke: for a while there, it was only necessary to start singing "Hello darkness, my old friend . . ." and everybody would crack up. It was a complete failure, and they had gone their separate ways—Paul had fled to London and Artie was going back to grad school to become a professor of mathematics—but then someone at Columbia did some studio alchemy, overdubbed a few electric guitars and whatnot, and it became one of the seminal folk-rock hits.

I was cheerfully riding the wave, recording at least an album a year straight through the decade. The fact that money was coming in meant that I could experiment a little in the studio, and after my first Prestige album I persuaded Bob Weinstock to let me bring in a full crew of trad players for half the songs on my next one. I used the Red Onion Jazz Band, which included a number of people I had known and worked with over the years, and the album was called *In the Tradition*. We recorded over in Rudy Van Gelder's studio in Fort Lee, New Jersey, where Prestige used to do all its jazz sessions. For a while there, Prestige had just about everybody who was worth having, and the cats used to love to record at Van Gelder's place, because it had natural acoustics you would not believe and he was a terrific engineer. I enjoyed making that record, but the only thing anyone noticed on it was my solo guitar arrangement of "Saint Louis Tickle." The people on the folk scene had no interest in trad jazz. They would stand for someone like me or Judy Roderick doing some of it, but they preferred for us just to play guitar and leave the band home. And frankly, good as that music may have been, there was no question but that its time had passed. It had become archaic, and once that happens, you can do something beautifully, and people can even like it, but it is not going to make any real impression.

With that disc, I had fulfilled my contract with Prestige and was ready to move on. The major labels had come sniffing around, and I had signed with Mercury—but through a fluke, I ended up doing one more Prestige album, which remains an anomaly in my catalog. Basically, I recorded it under duress. I had put together a jug band, and we had worked out a marvelous arrangement of "Saint Louis Tickle," which I wanted to record. However, I had just done that piece as a guitar solo for Prestige, and their contract said I could not re-record any of the songs I had done for them for at least two years. So I called up Bob Weinstock and said, "Bob, I need your permission to record 'Saint Louis Tickle' with my jug band."

Naturally, he said "No way."

Having learned that in all such situations "no" is a temporary, tactical stance, I said, "OK, what do you want?"

He said, "I'll tell you what: you make another album for me on the same terms as your old contract, and I'll give you permission to re-record that tune."

I had to agree to that, but I did not want to do another selection of things I was playing in my regular shows, because I was aware that the market was limited and I did not want to slice that pie too many ways. So I pulled together a bunch of old ballads and a couple of music hall songs I had learned from my grandmother, material that I sang for my own amusement or sitting around with friends but that I rarely performed publicly, and I walked into the studio with an autoharp, a dulcimer, a banjo, a twelve-string guitar—if I'd had marimbas, I would have played marimbas. They called the album *Inside Dave Van Ronk*, and I was actually pretty happy with it, though I was never tempted to take that show on the road— just the idea of carrying all those instruments around to gigs was ridiculous.

As for the jug band, that came about more or less by accident. One weekend Max Gordon, the owner of the Village Vanguard, was in Cambridge for some reason, and he walked by the Club 47 and saw this huge line of people waiting to get in to see the Jim Kweskin Jug Band. In his mind's eye he transposed this queue to 7th Avenue South, where he had his room, and visions of sugarplums started dancing in his head. So when he got back to New York, he called Robert Shelton and said, "Are there any jug bands around town?"

Bob said, "Well, yeah, but what you really ought to do is get hold of Dave Van Ronk and have him put one together." So he did, and I did. I called up a bunch of friends, and we formed the Ragtime Jug Stompers. Sam Charters was back in town, so he was our Pooh-Bah and Lord High Everything Else—he sang, arranged, and played washtub bass, washboard, jug, and occasionally would lend a hand on guitar. Barry Kornfeld played banjo and guitar. Artie Rose was on mandolin, and also played some fine Dobro. Finally, Danny Kalb, who had been a student of mine, played lead guitar and some very nice harmonica. (We also made him sing bass on "K.C. Moan," because he was the youngest and none of us wanted to do it.) It was a very flexible band because the musicians were all good enough to double or triple on various instruments, plus it had all the possibilities offered by kazoos and that sort of thing, so it was capable of more than one kind of sound.

I put that group together for the hell of it, and because I thought it would be fun and I wanted to try my hand at doing some larger arrangements, but from a professional angle I knew that Gordon's fantasies of cashing in on the jug band craze were a crock of shit. Along with the Kweskin band, there was also a New York outfit called the Even Dozen Jug Band, and I thought they made some good music—though they also did some things that made me want to play PLO to their Mossad—but I did not believe that any of us had a hope in hell of making serious money. In our case, at least, I was exactly right. We played for a while at the Vanguard, and I really enjoyed working with those guys, but we did not even get paid what we had originally been promised, much less go on to greater things. (The fine points of this financial fiasco are an object lesson in the inner workings of the music world: it turned out that one of the guys in the band did not have a union card, and that provided Gordon with an excuse to stiff us.)

I was very happy with the record we made, though, and still think it is one of the best things I ever did. We did not play much of the typical jug band repertoire; we were more of a string ragtime outfit with trad jazz overtones, and actually we could sound even better than we did in the studio, because we were at our best when we were goofing around. We rehearsed a lot, we took it damn seriously, and we put together some intricate arrangements of classic rags, which we played very carefully and note for note; but the rest of our repertoire was blues and jazz, and except for Artie, who was a bluegrasser, everybody in that band knew all those tunes inside out and we were an improvising band. We would work out a rough chart, but when it was a performing situation, we tried to have fun. In the end, that whole thing lasted about six months. We made the record, we had our run at the Vanguard, and then Danny got sick with mononucleosis, and since he was a key player in all our arrangements, we had to cancel whatever other jobs were outstanding. There was only one exception: we had been invited to Newport, and I wanted to cancel that one too, but various people in the group said, "That's all well and good for you; you have your Newport credit"—I had been there the previous year—"but what about us?" My natural inclination was to say, "Yes, I've been thinking about that, and I've come to the conclusion: 'Fuck you.'" But I did not follow it. I accepted the invitation, and we showed up and played at Newport with Bob Brill sitting in for Danny and died the death of a thousand cuts.

Newport, as it happened, was always the kiss of death for me. I have never much liked festivals, because they are like three-ring circuses, with too much going on—and in any case who wants to sing for fifteen thousand people with Frisbees? I did OK on the workshops, but what really counted at Newport were the evening concerts. The first time I got on one of those, I went out and gave what I think was one of the best shows of my life, and people went wild. I was all jazzed up, figuring that I had finally broken through to the big time and would be met backstage by a bunch of guys with big cigars and briefcases full of cash, all fighting to make me the hottest thing since Sinatra. So I walked off, and on came Jose Feliciano, playing "The Flight of the Bumblebee" followed by a flamenco version of "La Bamba." By five minutes into his set, nobody even remembered that I had been onstage.

As for the jug band's appearance, it was a complete mess. Finally, we got to our last song, which was our version of "Mack the Knife." We had worked out an arrangement that was very stark, a classic Brechtian reading set off by Artie's Dobro, and it was going over perfectly. The audience was dead quiet, and I figured I had just managed to pull our chestnuts out of the fire—and then people began to laugh. I was completely baffled; it was one of the most horribly uncomfortable moments I have ever experienced onstage. What had happened, as it turned out, was that Jack Elliott, who had been on before us, had finished his set by throwing his hat in the air, and he chose that moment to come out and retrieve it. He was goofing around behind us, waving at the crowd, and I had no idea what was going on, and was simply dying. I later learned that as Jack walked off, Terri met him at the side of the stage and coldcocked him, knocked him flat on his ass. Small consolation.

I have come to believe that, for most musicians, the pleasure of working at those huge festivals is not so much what happens onstage as the fact that they function as a sort of folksingers' convention. You meet people you haven't seen for a while or that you have only heard on record or know about by word of mouth, and of course after each day's performances there is a party. At Newport we all ran around schmoozing, and a great deal of bed-hopping went on—it was essentially Shriners with guitars.

There was a special kind of magic, though, about those first two or three years after Newport got going again in 1963 (there had been a two-year hiatus after the 1960 festival), because that was when all the old bluesmen were making their reappearances. John Hurt was the first, in 1963, and in 1964 they had Skip James, Sleepy John Estes, Robert Wilkins, and Fred McDowell, and the next year Son House showed up. It was incredible, because we knew these guys from hearing them on old 78s, but it had never occurred to us that they would still be alive and playing, and now they were turning up all over the place. It got to be like the Old Blues Singer of the Month Club: "This week, from sunny Tennessee, we bring you Furry Lewis!" And next week it would be Booker White, and a week after that Yank Rachell. It was like an enormous, unbelievable party that just kept going.

I got to know some of the old-timers pretty well, because I was working in the same clubs, so we had a chance to hang around between shows. They were some remarkable men and women, to say the least. Gary Davis was the first that I spent a serious amount of time with, and then when I began working more, I would run into people like Josh White, and Brownie McGhee and Sonny Terry, who had been on the folk scene since the forties but had also made 78s back in the "race records" period. When I started to spend more time on the road, I saw a lot of Brownie and Sonny, and it was always a pleasure.

Brownie had been one of my favorites back to when I was first getting into blues: there was a period when I could probably have fought my way through a couple dozen of his songs. My favorite was "Sporting Life Blues," which I had picked up on a 78 when I was about fifteen years old. When I first came across that song, it just knocked me out. "That night life, that sporting life is killing me"—no one has *nostalgie de la boue* like a fifteen-year-old, and it was the most wonderfully morbid thing I had ever heard. I had to learn it, so I buckled down and worked and worked, and I put together a pretty decent version. But somewhere along the way, I had a rare attack of common sense. It hit me: "What's it going to look like, a fifteen-year-old kid singing a song like this? There's no way I've paid enough dues yet." So I decided to table that song until such time as I had enough experience to back it up, and there matters rested for many a long year. The song would come to my attention, and I would potchke around with it for a while, and then I would say, "Nah, not yet."

Finally, sometime in the late 1960s, I said to myself, "That's it. Fuck the dues, I'm going to sing that song." I put together an arrangement of it and I tried it out onstage, but the weirdest thing happened: every time I would play it, something would go wrong—I would forget a verse, blow a lick. It was like there was a hex on that song for me, and I had almost decided to forget about doing it. Then I happened to be doing a show in Atlanta, and in those days the city had two acoustic clubs, and Brownie and Sonny were working at the other. I had a brainstorm: if I can sing this song for Brownie, I can sing it anywhere. So after my first set, I packed up my guitar, trundled over to the other room, went backstage, and said hello to Brownie. We chatted and swapped some gossip and whatnot, until finally I screwed up my courage. I said, "Brownie, you know your song, 'Sporting Life Blues'? I've worked up a version and I'd like to play it for you."

What could he say? I had him trapped like a rat, cornered in his own dressing room. So I broke out the guitar, and I went through the song perfectly. Not a single mistake. All I could think was, "I got it. I got it." I was ecstatic, and to top it off, when I finished Brownie said he liked it, and I think he actually did. So I packed up my guitar and was heading out the door, when a thought crossed my mind. I turned around and said, "Hey Brownie, how old were you when you wrote that song?"

He said, "Oh, about fifteen."

Brownie was a very funny cat. He and Sonny knew each other better than most husbands and wives do, and when they were getting along, they were getting along, but a lot of the time they were kind of at odds with one another, and they really knew where all the buttons were. Around 1962 I was working a club in Philadelphia and they were working right down the block. In those dear dim days, you would get booked into a room for a week at a time, or even two weeks, and we were all three staying at the same hotel, the old Rottenhouse. So every night after I finished my last show, I would go over to where they were working, and the three of us would take off to South Street, where there was this marvelous soul food restaurant.

Sonny had some trouble with his weight, and right then he was on the most heartbreaking diet I have ever seen. Brownie and me would be piling on the viands, scarfing down chitlins and collard greens and pecan pie, and Sonny would be sitting there with a salad and a glass of water, practically crying. Every now and again, he would say, "Brownie, could you give me just a taste of that?" And Brownie would say, "Come on, man, you're getting fat as a pig. You look like hell up there on that stage. You got to lose some weight." So Sonny endured, and every morning, around ten or eleven o'clock, the three of us would meet and go down for breakfast at this luncheonette across the street. There was a scale there, and Sonny was blind, so he would have Brownie lead him over to the scale, put in a penny, and read off his weight. And every day, Brownie would tell Sonny that he had gained another pound.

One afternoon during that Philadelphia sojourn, there came a knock on my door and it was Brownie, and he had a guy with him who was wearing a sleek, impeccably cut, rust-colored zoot suit. I hadn't seen a zoot suit since I was seven, and I was dazzled enough just by that. Brownie gave me a big smile and said, "Hey, look who I found." I must have looked very blank and stupid, because he says, "You don't know who this is?" I said no. He said, "This is Lonnie Johnson."

Now, Lonnie Johnson was the man who invented jazz guitar. He made a lot of blues records and was a very influential singer from the 1920s right up through the late 1940s, but what I knew him for was his duets with Eddie Lang and his work with Louis Armstrong's Hot Five and Duke Ellington—I mean, this was the guy who played behind Baby Cox on "The Mooche"! Brownie had just happened to run into him, and it turned out that he was working in the kitchen at the Ben Franklin hotel as a saucier. As far as I know, he had not performed since the early 1950s, but shortly the blues fans got wind of his existence and Lonnie had a new career. Unfortunately, it never really worked out the way either they or he would have hoped. Part of the problem was that Lonnie had not done any fingerpicking since the 1930s, and he simply did not remember how to do that stuff. Instead, he would get onstage with a flat-pick and play jazz standards, improvising lovely, long choruses on things like "Red Sails in the Sunset." All the hard-core folkies and blues buffs would be sitting in the audience, going "Arghhhh! Sing 'Mean Old Bed Bug Blues!' What's the matter with you?" They were really disappointed and upset—and they were a bunch of tone-deaf snobs. If they had just listened with an open mind to what the guy was putting down, they would have loved it, but they could not bring themselves to do that.

Naturally, Lonnie was unhappy about this state of affairs. I talked with him about it one time when we were playing at a benefit for the Hazard miners' strike. We were backstage, and he said, "Man, they want me to play all this stuff I recorded in 1925 . . . That was a long time ago!" I felt very bad for him, because as far as I was concerned, he was playing as well as he ever had. But, like any scene, the revival had its own aesthetic, and he did not fit it.

Of all the old blues players, the one who fitted best into the folk scene, and the one I got to know best aside from Gary Davis, was Mississippi John Hurt. I had been a fan of John's work ever since hearing him on the Harry Smith *Anthology*, but he had recorded those sides in 1928 and already sounded like an old man back then, so we all assumed that he was long dead. Then, in 1963, a blues fan named Tom Hoskins was listening to John's record of "Avalon Blues," which starts out, "Avalon, that's my home town, always on my mind," and it occurred to Tom to wonder whether there was an Avalon, Mississippi. He checked, and indeed there was, and he went down there—it was just a wide place in the road, a general store and a post office—and he went up to some guys who were lounging around, and he says, "Look, I'm trying to find some guy here, he used to make records in the 1920s, his name's Mississippi John Hurt."

They say, "Oh, you mean Ol' John . . . Yeah, he's right down the block."

I met John later that year, at the Café Yana. I was working in Cambridge and I had the night off, so I went over and caught his show, and then we went to a party that was being thrown by some relatives of his who lived in Roxbury. It seems it was his birthday, and the family was anxious to make sure Uncle John was shown a good time. I had a good time myself, and much of the evening is a blur, but the last thing I remember was a snowball fight in a graveyard. John was seventy that year, but he had a high, hard pitch that you would not believe—I think I still have a lump on my head.

John had never been a professional musician prior to his rediscovery. He used to play at picnics and play-parties and that sort of thing, but he was essentially a farmer, and he was the sweetest, gentlest man that ever came down the pike. To get an idea of his personality, you just have to listen to his records, because that is exactly the kind of man he was. In life as in music, he was an understater and a minimalist. Most blues artists deal in intensity, but he dealt in subtlety and nuance. The beat was always there, rock solid, but there was also a lyricism and deftness, and he was very, very easy on the nerves.

John spent a lot of time around the Village and seemed to genuinely enjoy hanging out with us. I remember one time somebody was passing around a joint, and it came to John. He looked at it for a moment, and said, "Oh yeah, I remember this. We used to call it 'poor man's whiskey.'" And he just passed it on. He was a delight. One of the odd things about him was that he did not like beds; he preferred a good, comfortable armchair. He was the easiest man to put up overnight: "Here John, we have a couch."

"Oh, I don't need a couch. Say, that looks like a great chair . . ."

John never had a bad word to say about anyone, not even people who really did deserve a few bad words. We were sitting around one night, and someone brought up the subject of Tom Hoskins, the guy who had rediscovered him. That relationship had ended badly: Hoskins had signed John to a contract where he earned a ridiculous percentage of John's wages, owned his publishing, and controlled all his business, and John actually had to go to court to get out from under his thumb. Naturally, we were filled with righteous indignation, and I was cursing Hoskins up hill and down dale, and John was just sitting there and listening, not saying a word. Finally, I paused and looked at John, waiting to hear him chime in. And John said: "Well, you know . . . if it weren't for Tom, I'd still be chopping cotton in Mississippi." No way to argue with that.

I had been playing John's "Spike Driver's Blues" ever since the mid-1950s, and it wasn't until I met him that I realized I had got the basses backward. John and I were sitting around with a guitar one evening down at the Gaslight, and I was playing my version for him, and this puzzled look came over his face. He started watching my right hand, and he said, "You've got those basses backward." And he played me a few measures of it the way he did it. It was just like on the record, and by God, he was right. I said, "Oh, shit, back to the old drawing board." And he says, "No, no, no. You really ought to keep it that way. I like that." That's the folk process for you: some people call it creativity, but them as knows calls it mistakes.

"Spike Driver's Blues" was one of two songs by John that had been included on the *Anthology*. The other was this gorgeous piece of fingerpicking called "Frankie's Blues." It was a beautiful arrangement, and when those albums came out in the early 1950s, we all immediately set ourselves to learn that thing. It was incredibly fast, though, and after a week or two I dropped by the wayside. A few persisted, and my friend Barry Kornfeld, for one, disappeared into his chambers and emerged six weeks later, blinking like a mole, and he had it. Note for note, just as clean and fast as on the record.

When I first saw John at the Café Yana, there he was playing "Frankie's Blues." However, I noticed that it was a lot slower than on the record. Of course, he was a good deal older, but it also struck me that it sounded better at that tempo. I wanted to ask him about it, but I wanted to be as diplomatic as possible—I didn't want to just say, "So, Pops, can't cut it anymore, eh?" Very tentatively, I said, "You know that 'Frankie' thing you played . . . "

Apparently I was not the first person to have asked, because John intervened and saved me any further embarrassment. He just smiled and said, "Oh, you want to know why it's so much slower than on the record."

I said, "Yeah . . . "

He said, "Well, you know, that song was so long that they had to speed it up to get it all on one side of a 78."

All I could think of was Barry, sidelined with acute carpal tunnel syndrome.

John played the Gaslight pretty regularly, and he would also hang out there whenever he was in town. Clarence Hood, the owner, was from the same part of Mississippi, and they would sit around for hours, talking over old times. It was the strangest thing, because they obviously had lived very different lives down there, but they really seemed to enjoy each other's company. John would also join us upstairs at the Kettle of Fish, and one night we were sitting around, and it was just John, me, Jack Elliott, and Sam Hood. At that time, we had an understanding with the owners of the Kettle, only I never understood it: whenever a group of us was at a table, they would bring over a bottle, make a line with a wax pencil to show how much whiskey was in it, and then when it was finished, charge us for three bottles. But what the hell, those were flush times.

John's favorite drink was Old Grandad, so there we were with a bottle of Old Grandad. We had gotten down to where there was about two inches left in the bottle, and we were feeling no pain, and boys will be boys, even if one of these boys was seventy-some years old. So I don't know whose idea it was, but we started to arm-wrestle. Jack was just back from out west, where he had been bulldogging steers, Sam was an all-state Mississippi high school football champion—he had been given the Order of No Neck by the governor, personally—and I was a big, strong guy, as well. So we're arm-wrestling, and John is sitting there, kind of bemused by our antics. Finally, somebody says, "Come on, John, give us a shot." Now, John was a little guy, and damn near as old as the three of us put together, but he plants his elbow on the table, and blam! blam! blam! He throws all three of us.

This did not sit well with me. I do not have a sporting drop of blood in my body, and I was damned if this superannuated sharecropper was going to make us look like idiots. But I figured, look, he just threw these three bohrans; his arm must be tired by now. So I said, "John, that was just a fluke. We weren't ready. Let's try it again." And, blam! blam! blam! He threw us again. As I remember, he even did it a third time, just to put us in our places. By now that man has been dead for almost forty years, and he's probably still in better shape than I am.

All in all, the number of colorful characters and the amount of talent that was around in those days was incredible. Skip James showed up a year or so after John, and did a week at the Gaslight on a double bill with Doc Watson. Lightnin' Hopkins was around pretty regularly, as was John Lee

Hooker. Those guys were an integral part of the scene, as much as people like me and Dylan and Ochs, and that is one reason that I tend to cock a jaundiced eye at the recurring rumors of another folk revival. There will undoubtedly be times when there is a heightened interest in folk music, but we simply do not have the deep sources of talent that we had in the 1960s. Unless we can hatch another generation like Gary, Skip, and John, or John Lee and Muddy Waters, the quality will be sadly second-rate—and the world that produced those people is long gone.

Even at that time, the older musicians often seemed like emissaries from a vanished, mythic age—though of course that was our perception and not theirs. I have often been asked whether it wasn't awfully strange for them, especially the ones like John who had spent their lives working on farms in Mississippi, to suddenly find themselves in this completely foreign situation, carried off to the big city and being carted around clubs full of young white fans. Obviously, there is no single answer to that: some of them loved it, some didn't; some of them really did not like to be in the cities, and some thought it was very interesting; some were amused, some were bemused, and some were annoyed. But overall there was a lot less culture shock than one might think. These people were mature men and women who knew who they were. That was one of the most important things about their music, and why they had become famous in the first place: because they played and sang like people who knew who they were. So they were not people who could be overawed all that easily. It doesn't much matter if you are a sharecropper from Texas or a Harvard grad; if you don't know who you are, you are lost wherever the hell you find yourself, and if you do, you do not have much of a problem. A lot of them actually found the whole thing kind of funny: "Gee, look at this. What am I doing here?" But in a way it was not all that different for the rest of us. While we weren't coming from rural Mississippi, none of us was prepared to suddenly be onstage in front of twenty thousand people. Anybody who did not from time to time think, "Gee, what am I doing here?" had to have something wrong with him. Because what is anybody doing in a situation like that? But then again, it's like when somebody asks me, "What the hell are you doing in Sandusky?" The flag follows trade! It was a good payday, and most of them were glad to get it. Different people took it different ways, but I dare say you can say the same about any group of traveling musicians.

What some people have trouble understanding is that these were remarkable men and women, not exotic exhibits in the blues museum. They were friends of ours, and they were working musicians. When we would sit around and shoot the shit, it was not just us youngsters asking, "Tell me about Charlie Patton in 1927." A lot of the time, the conversation would be, "That sonofabitch at the so-and-so club stiffed me last time through. Did he do that to you?" There was a lot of shop talk. And that was a good way to get to know them.

There is one last story that perfectly illustrates this point. I did not get this firsthand, and it probably has improved some in the telling, but it gives an idea of what I mean. Champion Jack Dupree was one of my favorite blues singers and piano players. He was originally from New Orleans, but in the late 1950s he moved to Europe and ended up settling in Germany. In the 1980s I started to tour over there a lot, and for a while it seemed as if we were playing tag across the continent. I would hit town, and there would be posters plastered all over the place: "One night only! Champion Jack Dupree! You just missed him, schmuck!" or "One night only! Champion Jack Dupree! But you'll be playing in Dusseldorf that night!" So I never got a chance to meet him, but you could not be a blues musician in Europe and not hear Jack Dupree stories. The man really carved himself out a legend, and this story is a good example.

Sometime in the early 1960s Jack was living in Hamburg, and he got a call from an agent there. The guy said, "Jack, I'm going to put you on the tour of your life. We're going to start you in Stockholm, and we're going to send you from Lisbon to Leningrad." It sounded all right, so Jack signed on. He was traveling with a small band, and they trundled from country to country, town to town, and eventually they got to Kiev, I think it was. That was still the Soviet Union, and this was the height of the Cold War—how they arranged to get in there at that time is anybody's guess. In any case, there they were, and all of a sudden, the tour just evaporated. There Jack was, stranded in Russia, with no money, three or four musicians, and no way to get home.

God knows how he wiggled out of that one, but musicians get to be very good at that sort of thing—our improvisational skills are by no means limited to music. In any case, somehow or other he limped back to Germany, licking his wounds.

The years go by, and then one fine day he gets a call from the same guy, with the same offer: "Jack, I'm gonna put you on the tour of a lifetime. We'll start you in Stockholm, and you're gonna be in Lisbon, in Marrakech, in Kiev . . . "

Dupree said, "Now, wait a minute. I remember you. First of all, I am going absolutely nowhere unless I have airline tickets covering every single stop on the tour, in my pocket before I leave my house." There was an audible gulp at the other end of the line. And Jack added, "I fly first class."

There were more gulps, but eventually the guy said, "Well, OK, Jack."

Jack said, "All right, I'll be at your office tomorrow morning, and you just have those tickets ready. Then we can talk through the rest of the terms."

The next morning, Jack showed up at the agent's office, and the agent handed over a sheaf of tickets for him and his band that looked like a Gutenberg Bible. Jack went through them carefully, checked that they covered the whole tour from beginning to end, and said, "Yes, this looks all right." Then he left, went over to the Lufthansa office, cashed them all in, and went home.

Man! To an over-the-road musician, that is sheer poetry.

14

The New Song Revolution

Blues and traditional material were integral to the Folk Scare, but what defined the period in most people's minds were protest songs and the appearance of what has since become known as "singer-songwriter" music. This was in many ways a quite new style, but it tended to be generically lumped in the folk category and praised or damned as such, at least until Dylan plugged in his guitar in 1965. I can't blame the average consumer for failing to note the change—crowds are never long on analytical thought— but excusing the music critics is quite another matter, and even today many of them continue to refer to this music as "folk." This is both silly and an abdication of responsibility. Although some of the new songwriters— Dylan and Paxton, for example—had a deep grounding in traditional styles, even in those cases calling their music "folk" is like calling the music of Duke Ellington or Lester Young "ragtime." As for Joni Mitchell or Leonard Cohen, they have as much to do with folk music as Schubert or Baudelaire.

In an attempt to avoid the migraines brought on by serious thought, most of the critics and music marketers have relied on a simple formula: if the accompaniment to this music is acoustic, it's folk music. With amplified backup, it's rock 'n' roll, except in those instances where a pedal steel guitar is added, in which case it's country. To be fair to the critics—which is no fun at all—the performers themselves have rarely been more perceptive when it comes to labeling their work. I have heard everyone from Paxton to Suzanne Vega refer to themselves as folksingers, though the last time Tom sang a folk song was roughly 1962, and I doubt that Suzanne has ever sung one in her life. The problem is that, in order to eat, people have to sell records, and to sell records, there has to be a way of marketing them. I once heard a record producer remark about Janis Ian, "Her music isn't folk, it isn't rock, it isn't country—who the hell am I supposed to sell it to?" Janis got lucky, but a lot of talented writers have died on the vine simply because there was no convenient pigeonhole for them. Calling such people "singer-songwriters" avoids that particular pitfall, but I have never liked the label because it defines the performer rather than the music. Also, if followed to its logical conclusion, it puts Joni Mitchell and Hoagy Carmichael in the same closet (interesting thought, that), which leaves something to be desired, to say the least. The best idea would be to classify all of this music as "new song," which is what Latin American musicians call their own version of the style, and while I have little hope of anyone following my advice on this point, that is how I think of it.*

In any case, that period spawned a new style of songwriting that was quite different from what had come before it. Any music is the music of its time, of course—you can't avoid that—but a great deal of the music written in the 1960s was also *about* its time. It dealt directly, almost on a one-to-one basis, with the experiences that people were going through at that moment. Pop lyrics have tended to be of the most vague and general nature: "I love my baby," "Get down and boogie." Generally it's pretty mindless, and mindlessness has a certain eternal quality. But the songwriting in the sixties was often very specific, whether it was about politics or about what people were going through in their personal lives. Of course, a lot of

---

*Incidentally, the new song movement has so completely taken over the remains of the folk scene that I recently heard a friend say of someone who, like myself, is best known for interpreting material written by others, "Oh, she only does 'covers'!" I had a sudden vision of a CD titled *Pavarotti Covers Puccini*. Suffice it to say, Louis Armstrong did not do "covers" nor did Billie Holiday, Bing Crosby, Frank Sinatra, Edith Piaf, or Aretha Franklin. While none of these people were primarily songwriters, their interpretations were a hell of a lot more original than a lot of the "original" songs being written on the current scene. Any music worth its salt depends as much on great interpreters as on great composers. What is more, in the absence of interpreters, songs will never be sung by anyone other than their composers, and I cannot imagine why anyone would wish that kind of planned obsolescence on their work.

that material suffered from its specificity—if you weren't the person who had written it, you couldn't get next to it. I am reminded of an anecdote about Lenin: The Soviet state publishing house had brought out a book of love poems written by a poet to his wife. When it was presented to Lenin, he said, "Don't you know there's a paper shortage on? We should have printed two copies: one for him and one for his wife."

Dylan is usually cited as the founder of the new song movement, and he certainly became its most visible standard-bearer, but the person who started the whole thing was Tom Paxton. When Tom came to New York, around 1961, he had precisely one song of his own in his repertory, "The Marvelous Toy," but over the next six or eight months he wrote some more, and as he tested his songs in the crucible of live performance, he found that his own stuff was getting more attention than when he was singing traditional songs or stuff by other people. It gradually dawned on him that his vocation in life was to be a songwriter, and at that point he decided, "OK, if I'm gonna be a songwriter, I'd better be serious about it." So he set himself a training regimen of deliberately writing one song every day, and he kept that up for about a year. The songs could be good, bad, or indifferent; the important thing was that it forced him to get into the discipline of sitting down and writing. In the course of that year he wrote some of the most dreadful things I have heard in my life—I still treasure "The New York Mets Victory and Commiseration Song"—but he also wrote "Ramblin' Boy" and "The Last Thing on My Mind." Dylan had not yet showed up when this was happening, and by the time Bobby came on the set, with at most two or three songs he had written, Tom was already singing at least 50 percent his own material.

That said, it was Bobby's success that really got the ball rolling. Prior to that, the folk community was very much tied to traditional songs, so much so that songwriters would sometimes palm their own stuff off as traditional. So in some ways the most important thing that Bobby did was not to write the songs but to show that the songs could be written. I think people like Joni Mitchell and Leonard Cohen felt toward Dylan sort of the way Ezra Pound felt toward Walt Whitman: "You cut the wood; now it's time for carving." From a stylistic perspective, I was always rather dubious of Bobby's contrived primitivism, and his later obscurantism reached a point where he wasn't even trying to make sense anymore. But if Bobby had not succeeded in breaking out with what he was writing, almost all of the original material to come out of the folk boom would have been protest songs, because up to that point those were the only things you were allowed by consensus to write.

As in the days of the Almanac and People's Songs, the Folk Scare of the 1960s rode in on a wave of social protest, and neo-ethnics like myself were simply carried along on its coattails. The Civil Rights Movement and the Vietnam War profoundly changed the political atmosphere, and pulled a lot of people to the left. The hipsters of the 1950s had tried to divorce themselves from all things political, but in the sixties that was no longer an acceptable option. With the Civil Rights Movement, any kind of identification with black culture took on a whole new meaning, and a lot of people who a decade earlier would have been apolitical beatniks no longer felt comfortable simply standing on the sidelines. Meanwhile the war was affecting the folk audience even more directly, because most of us were of draft age and the government was threatening to ship us overseas to get killed.*

This was the height of the culture wars, and while the McCarthy era was dying, it had a hydralike ability to keep regenerating heads as fast as you chopped one off. The blacklist, for example, resurfaced with some regularity throughout the early 1960s. By 1963 Joan Baez had been on the cover of *Time* magazine; Peter, Paul, and Mary were in the Top 10; and ABC television jumped on the bandwagon with a show called *Hootenanny*. About a month before *Hootenanny* was supposed to go on the air, *Broadside* magazine broke the story that Pete Seeger was not going to be allowed to appear. This was particularly outrageous because Pete had been the person responsible for giving the word "hootenanny" any currency, and ABC made its position even worse by saying it was not blacklisting Pete, but had simply decided he was not up to their artistic standards. At that the entire entertainment business, left, right, and center, broke into howls of laughter—I mean, you should have seen some of the crap they had on that show. A bunch of us promptly got together and formed an organization called

---

*Personally, I did not have to worry about this. I showed my draft card to a guy I knew over at the War Resisters League, to find out what my classification meant in terms of getting hauled off by the Feds, and he glanced at it and drawled: "Well, what it means is that when the Red Army is marching down 5th Avenue, you'll be told, 'Don't call us, we'll call you.'"

Artists against the Blacklist, and a lot of the top names on the scene, including Baez, Dylan, and Peter, Paul, and Mary, announced that they would not appear on *Hootenanny* or any other show that did not let Pete appear.

Pete himself was kind of embarrassed by the whole business. He had always felt that the music was the important thing—the man is nothing; the work is everything—and he thought that a lot of performers who deserved a national hearing were depriving themselves of an opportunity. His basic attitude was "For God's sake boys, leave me behind; just leave me one bullet." Of course, we paid absolutely no attention to him. Our position was, "Sorry, Pete, old man, but you're a symbol." And although that organization did not stay together, and in any case *Hootenanny* was so laughably awful that it barely lasted a season, that flap really did help put an end to the blacklist.*

My politics had never been a secret, and I continued to show up and play for benefits whenever asked and to work with various radical organizations. As in the past, I rarely sang political songs, but there were exceptions even to that rule. The night of the Cuban Missile Crisis, I was working down at the Gaslight, and I opened my set with "This Land Is Your Land" and closed it with "The International," including the verse that goes, "We want no condescending saviors." I cannot remember any incident in history that made me feel more lefty than that business. I thought Khrushchev was being an opportunist and an asshole, but he had every right to make a deal with another country to put missiles on their turf—the United States had made a deal with Turkey to do exactly the same thing and nobody made any big issue of it. So at that point, to all intents and purposes, I was a better Stalinist than most of the Stalinists. They were all running around trying to find some kind of a deal, while we Trotskyists went down to the UN to demonstrate in support of Cuba and their damn missiles. Truth to tell, I did not want the missiles there; they made me nervous. Nonetheless, fair is fair.

I was encouraged by a lot of the changes that were happening in the 1960s, but as an orthodox leftist I was also a very strong critic of the student movement and the New Left. Of course, I agreed with a lot of their

---

*This victory was by no means instant or complete. Pete did not get on a major network program until 1967, when he appeared on the Smothers Brothers variety show, and even then, the CBS brass censored his performance of an anti–Vietnam War song, "Waist Deep in the Big Muddy."

stances—I was strongly pro–civil rights and strongly antiwar—but most of those people were not really radicals, just a bunch of very pissed-off liberals. They had no grounding, and indeed no interest, in theory, and their disdain for studying history and learning economics infuriated me. The core problem with the New Left was that it wasn't an ideology, it was a mood—and if you are susceptible to one mood, you are susceptible to another. They wanted the world to change, but essentially it was a petty bourgeois movement that had no connection with what was really going on. The working class at least has some power—if the working class folds its arms, the machinery stops—and as for the ruling class, its power is obvious. But what power does the middle class have? They have the power to talk: yak, yak, yak. To interpret, reinterpret, and re-re-reinterpret. And that is the history of the New Left in a nutshell.

When it came to political music, I looked on most of what was being written around me with a similarly jaundiced eye. My feeling was that nobody has ever been convinced that they were wrong about anything by listening to a song, so when you are writing a political song, you are preaching to the choir. Of course, the choir needs songs, and when a group sings together, that builds solidarity. When the cops were coming down on them with the dogs, the clubs, and the cattle prods, the civil rights workers would be standing there singing "We are not afraid"—and you better believe they were afraid, but the singing helped. It had a real function, and in that situation it was very important. But when it came to singing these things in a coffeehouse or at a concert, I always felt that politics is politics and music is music. Brecht was a Stalinist, but his best songs are not Stalinist songs. Brecht's work expressed a *weltanschauung*, a worldview, and that view was often consonant with radical politics, but as a poet and a songwriter, Brecht was more of a philosopher than a politician. And when it came to Paxton, or Ochs, or Dylan, I liked their songs when they were well written, regardless of what they were about, and when they were not well written, I had no interest.

My attitude is essentially that of a craftsman, and I thought a lot of times the politics got in the way of the craft. Also, there is a built-in flaw to topical songs, which is that if you live by the newspaper, you die by the newspaper. You may expend your greatest efforts and do some of your best writing about an incident that will be forgotten in six weeks. I mean, Phil

Ochs was one of my best friends and I love a good many of his songs, but it always struck me as a tragedy that so much of Phil's material became dated so quickly. I remember when I heard him sing his song about William Worthy, I thought, "That's not one of Phil's best, but it doesn't matter, because two years down the line he won't be able to sing it anymore." And sure enough, he couldn't, because nobody remembered who William Worthy was. But unfortunately that was also true of some of his other material that I liked a lot more. Paxton dealt with that kind of planned obsolescence by disciplining himself to the point that if you give him a topic, he can give you a song, just like that. Len Chandler did the same thing; for a while he had a radio show in LA where he would improvise songs over the air from the daily newspaper. And if you have that kind of skill, I suppose you can keep going indefinitely as a topical songwriter. But nothing less than that will do, and very few people can do that or would want to, year in and year out. I think that was one of the things that destroyed Phil, in the end: he had painted himself into a corner, and he tried to work his way out of it by doing things like "Pleasures of the Harbor," but they never had the immediacy of his topical material, and he knew it.

When I first met Phil, he was working at a place on 3rd Street called the Third Side. It was the same story as with Dylan: Somebody was making the rounds of the clubs, happened to hear him, and came barging into the Kettle of Fish and said, "There's a guy over at the Third Side who's really fantastic. You've gotta check him out." I don't think he had been in town for more than a week or so, and as I remember, the owner of the club was letting him crash there as well, sleeping on the pool table.

Phil was very much his own man, right from the beginning. For one thing, although he was never going to be nominated to any best-dressed lists, he was one of the last of the jacket-and-tie holdouts. He used to wear this thing that had once been a blue suit, but he had worn it so long that, if you had got him to stand still, you could have shaved in your reflection in the back of the jacket. He had a way with neckties, though. I remember one that looked like it was made out of crepe paper, which he carried around in his back pocket to use for formal occasions.*

---

*I never understood how anyone could sing while wearing a tie. I wore a suit for concerts a few times in the 1950s because that was considered the appropriate attire, but I always felt as if my tie was strangling me. Save the noose till after the show . . .

Musically, what struck me first about Phil's work was that he was a very interesting extension of Bob Gibson. He had Bob's approach to chords and melodic lines, and also a lot of Bob's guitar style, but he had harnessed all of this for political commentary, which Bob was not all that interested in doing. Later on, when he and Bob were collaborating on some songs, it was perfect, because it was like Bob collaborating with his political self and Phil collaborating with his nonpolitical self.

Phil's chord sense was quite advanced, and he was the only person around aside from Gibson who used the relative minor and secondary keys. He was also one of the few songwriters on that scene who knew how to write a bridge. He was no Jerome Kern, but considering the limitations almost everybody else was struggling with, his work stood out. That may in part explain why he was not a very influential songwriter. There were a few Ochs clones, but not many, and that was probably because most of the people who wanted to sound like him couldn't do it. He was also a surprisingly effective guitarist—not a virtuoso by any means, but he filled in all the spaces and never lost the impetus. And man, he pounded the shit out of his instruments. He borrowed a guitar from me once at a festival, and you can still see where his flat-pick gouged into the top.

As a lyricist, there was nobody like Phil before and there has not been anybody since. That is not to say that I liked everything he wrote, but he had a touch that was so distinctive that it just could not be anybody else. He had been a journalism student before he became a singer, and he would never sacrifice what he felt to be the truth for a good line. In a way that was a shame, because he would have come up with more good lines if he had been willing to compromise now and then. But at its best, there was a deftness to his writing that went beyond straight journalism. He wrote a song about the conservatism of big labor in that period called "Links on the Chain," and its last line was, "It's only fair to ask you boys, now which side are you on?" That is goddamn good. There is a dialectic to that line; it has a history, and all of that is right there. A lot of people I knew on the working-class left were upset by that song—they felt he was using "Which Side Are You On?" to attack the people it was written for—but as far as I was concerned, he was laying it on the line to those guys, and that was just what the situation called for. And he not only called 'em the way he saw 'em but made the call a work of art. Phil was very prolific for a while, and he committed as much hackwork as almost any other songwriter of the period, but when that boy cooked, he really cooked.

Phil and I fought like cats and dogs, about politics and everything else. I was a socialist; he was a left liberal. I was a materialist and he was a mystic. So we could argue about everything from the meaning of life to yesterday's headlines. I thought a lot of his stances were too simplistic, which was typical of that whole crowd. His positions would make sense in a limited way, but he had not really thought them through. Like when he wrote "Here's to the State of Mississippi," I understood that he had just been down there and had been horrified by what he was seeing, but I thought that singling out Mississippi as a racist hellhole was unfair to the other forty-nine states. As Malcolm X used to say, "There's down south, and there's up south." Without all the activists who were from there, none of that movement would have happened, and having some northerner come down and shit all over Mississippi was unfair to the people who were living there and trying to fix up their state. And it was also too damn easy.

Like a lot of people on that scene, Phil was essentially a Jeffersonian democrat who had been pushed to the left by what was happening around him. Two consecutive Democratic presidents had turned out to be such disappointments that it forced a lot of liberals into a sort of artificial left-wing stance, and Phil was of that stripe. That may seem a surprising thing to say about the man who wrote "Love Me, I'm a Liberal," but I think it is accurate. He had believed in the liberal tradition, and it had betrayed him, and naturally he had a special contempt for the people who espoused lukewarm liberal views but were supporting the Cold War, the war in Vietnam, the crackdown on the student movement. Someone like John Wayne—an out-and-out conservative, prowar patriot—could earn Phil's admiration in a way. As a matter of fact, Wayne was one of his heroes, and he always believed that if he had somehow gotten a chance to talk with him, he could have won Wayne over to the revolution.

I must add that, along with our honest disagreements, Phil and I also had a lot of very good *dis*honest disagreements. We both loved to argue, and quite often he would take a position just to be ornery and annoy me. (Me, I was utterly sincere all the time, of course ...) In an argument, Phil's weapon of choice was the rapier. He would lead you down a primrose path to the place where he had an ambush set, and then he would skewer you with a one-liner. If Bob Hope had been a lefty, he would have been very much like Phil.

Dylan was never as devoted to politics as Phil was, but I think that if you could have managed to pin him down, his views were roughly similar. He was a populist and was very tuned in to what was going on—and, much more than most of the Village crowd, he was tuned in not just to what was going on around the campuses but also to what was going on around the roadhouses. But it was a case of sharing the same mood, not of having an organized political point of view. Bobby was very sensitive to mood, and he probably expressed that better than anyone else. Certainly, that was Phil's opinion. Phil felt that Bobby was the true zeitgeist, the voice of their generation.

One of the great myths of that period is that Bobby was only using the political songs as a stepping stone, a way to attract attention before moving on to other things. I have often heard that charge leveled against him, and at times he has foolishly encouraged it. The fact is, no one—and certainly not Bobby—would have been stupid enough to try to use political music as a stepping stone, because it was a stepping stone to oblivion. Bobby's model was Woody Guthrie, and Woody had written a lot of political songs but also songs about all sorts of other subjects, and Bobby was doing the same thing.

Woody was an inspiration not only to Bobby but to almost all the songwriters on that scene, and in some ways he had a very baleful influence on their work. Woody was a genius, but he was often sloppy. He had created this wonderful, Will Rogers–style persona, and as part of that he fostered the myth that his songs just appeared out of the air—that he did not have to sweat over them, and rewrite, and polish. Bobby bought the myth lock, stock, and barrel, and that was always a problem with his work. He would write an incredible line, then follow it with a line that was utterly meaningless, and he never felt the need to go back and work that through. He always seemed to think that it was easier to write a new song than to fix an old one. That was probably true for him, at least at that time, but you can see the result in his work. Phil was a much more careful craftsman, and that is one of the reasons I liked him so much: he really took care of his craft.

One thing that was striking about both Bobby and Phil in those days was their sheer output. Bobby had a much stronger background in traditional material, and when he first came to town he had a large repertoire of older songs, but once he started writing his own stuff he took off at a great clip. As for Phil, he was a phenomenon. He wrote so fast that all you could do was stand back and say, "Wow!" Of course, both of them wrote a lot of turkeys, but the proportion of good stuff was very high. And I think that was really a product of the milieu—they were the tip of a large and growing iceberg. Everybody was showing off for their friends. You wrote for yourself, of course, and for the public, but you were also writing for the community, and that was a very well-informed and critical audience. The approval of your peers meant more than a three-column write-up in the *Times*, because after all, that's what Shelton did for a living—he had to write somebody up, and it was your turn—but the approval of Joni Mitchell really counted for something.

As for what was being written, there was a lot of agitprop stuff, but that was by no means all that people were putting down. Fred Neil was writing personal, subjective stuff from the very beginning, and Bobby picked up on that very early on. In a way, the whole question of who influenced whom is bullshit. Theft is the first law of art, and like any group of intelligent musicians, we all lived with our hands in each other's pockets. Bobby picked up material from a lot of people, myself included, but we all picked up things from him as well.

In fact, I think I was the first person other than Bobby to record one of his songs. The way that came about was that one night we were hanging around in the Kettle, and by that time Bobby had already acquired quite a reputation as a songwriter, though only among the local crowd. A bunch of us were sitting at a table, and this guy came in and walked up to us, and he looks down at Bob and snarls, "So you're the hot-shot songwriter, huh? All right . . ." And he reaches into his pocket and slaps a twenty dollar bill on the table, and says, "I'll bet you can't write me a song called 'If I Had to Do It All Over Again, I'd Do It All Over You.'" That was an old joke title, one of those things like "When the Bed Breaks Down, I'll Meet You in the Spring" or "Take Back Your Heart, I Ordered Liver."

Bobby stared down at that twenty, and at that point in his career it must have looked as big as a window shade. So he looks the guy in the eye, and says, "Oh, yes I can."

We agreed that the money would be deposited with Babe the bartender and that the guy would come back around the same time the following night. Sure enough, the next evening the guy comes in again, and Bobby reaches into his pocket and pulls out a sheaf of paper, and he has not only written a song to the title, it has six long verses. So what could I do? I had to record it.

I did that song with the Red Onion Jazz Band, and they all thought I was crazy. They would look at the lead sheet and say, "Jesus, that's a strange chord change there," and I would say, "I know. Just play it." And I could not memorize all those lyrics—they were too insane—so I read them off a sheet of paper. If you listen closely to that album, you can probably hear the paper rustling, and I also mess up at one point and start to laugh—I think Bobby was in the studio, making faces at me.

Within a couple of years, Bobby changed the whole direction of the folk movement. The big breakthrough was when he wrote "A Hard Rain's A-Gonna Fall," because in that song he fused folk music with modernist poetry. The tune was borrowed from an old English ballad called "Lord Randall," and it was in the same question-and-response form, but the imagery was right out of the symbolist school. It was not a flawless work—the "clown who cried in the alley" always sounded to me like the verbal equivalent of a painting on velvet—but the overall effect was incredible. I heard him sing that for the first time during one of the hoot nights at the Gaslight, and I could not even talk about it; I just had to leave the club and walk around for a while. It was unlike anything that had come before it, and it was clearly the beginning of a revolution.

Incidentally, Bobby would never admit to having read any poetry. He always pulled his "I'm just a country boy" act, which irritated the hell out of me—and incidentally had a very negative effect on a lot of the people who came after him. They fell for that pose and thought that masterpieces should just drop on their heads out of the sky while they were walking down 4th Street. Of course, Dylan didn't invent that myth; romantic naturalism had been a strain in poetic circles since at least the eighteenth century, along with a strong element of *nostalgie de la boue*, this fascination with misery and despair. And that skein runs from Robert Burns, through Baudelaire and the Beats, to the singer-songwriter scene: "Oh, I am such a sinner! Oh, I am so depressed!" Snore . . . The parallels between Dylan and people like Rimbaud and Mallarmé were being talked about almost as soon as he started writing, and I don't know if he was aware of them before that, but he checked them out pretty early on. Somewhere in my bookcases I probably still have a paperback collection of modern French poetry with Bobby's underlinings in it. I have never traced any of the underlinings to anything he actually used in a song, but he was reading that stuff very carefully.

When Bobby went in that direction, it opened the floodgates. A lot of other people followed his lead, but he had a jump start, and for a few years he was clearly out in front of the pack. I mean, Paxton was a pretty experienced songwriter by that time, but he deferred to Bobby. Ochs worshipped the ground Bobby walked on—it actually became a sort of fixation, and did him a lot of harm. And that's not to mention Eric Andersen, David Blue, Patrick Sky . . . The list goes on and on.

I had been writing songs all along, but rarely for public consumption, and I figured out pretty early that I did not want to be in that particular race. Of course, I had always been a cheerful participant in the folk process, and if I felt like a song could do with some chopping and changing, I would rewrite some lines or add a verse or two. I even put together a few blues of my own, but blues is different. Blues is like a kielbasa, those long Polish sausages: you don't sing a whole blues, you just cut off a section.

Bobby's example spurred me to broaden my range and increase my output a little, but not by much. First of all, I was in the middle of a songwriting explosion, and there was no shortage of material for me to choose from. There were unknown songwriters like Joni Mitchell out in the hinterlands, and there was a grapevine that reached all around the country, so as far as new songs went, I was surrounded by an *embarrassment de richesse*. Second of all, by the time I started writing I already had a large repertoire of songs that I had chosen very carefully, and very little of my own stuff came up to my standards. Over the years I have written enough songs to fill several albums if I included all my culls, but if I write a song that does not stand up to the rest of my repertoire, I ditch it. As the Bible says, "If thy right eye offend thee, pluck it out." I am absolutely ruthless about this, because I have no incentive to pad my repertoire with second-rate material of my own when I could just as easily add some first-rate material by someone else.

Furthermore, the more self-consciously "artistic" the writing became, the less interest I had in taking part. As someone once said, "When I hear the word 'art' I release the safety catch on my Browning." That whole artistic mystique is one of the great traps of this business, because down that road lies unintelligibility. Dylan has a lot to answer for there, because after a while he discovered that he could get away with anything—he was Bob Dylan and people would take whatever he wrote on faith. So he could do something like "All Along the Watchtower," which is simply a mistake from the title on down: a watchtower is not a road or a wall, and you can't go along it.

Of course, that sort of sloppiness did not begin with Dylan. There was already a long tradition of poets writing things that sounded wonderful but made no sense. Poetry is automatically suspect to me, because if you are a good enough poet, you can make bullshit sound so beautiful that people don't notice that it's bullshit. I used to hear Dylan Thomas over at the old White Horse Tavern back in the 1950s, and when he had had enough to drink—which was frequently—he would recite his poetry, and my jaw would drop. It was beautiful, gorgeous stuff, and he recited it marvelously. But when I would go back and look at it on the page, a lot of it was bull-shit. Not all of it, by any means, but I would challenge anyone to explain what some of those things were about.

I eventually came to the conclusion that you should never say anything in poetry that you would not say in prose. Poetry has the same obligation to make sense as any other statement made by the human mouth. That was something that was driven home to me by reading Ezra Pound, of all people. Pound's poetic oeuvre includes some of the most piss-poor obscurantism ever to sully a page, but he also wrote *The ABC of Reading*, and that book taught me that poetry is first of all obliged to make sense, because if it doesn't, no one will read it, and if no one reads it, it might as well not be written. As for songwriting, if something has a pretty enough melody or a strong enough arrangement, people will listen to it even if the lyric makes no sense—but that does not make it a well-written song. When songs get pretentious, overflowery and obscure, the songwriter is proclaiming that he or she is an artist, and the whole concept of "art" as we understand it today is an early-nineteenth-century intellectual construct based on a set of what I consider to be false romantic notions. I think it was a good thing that, back in the Renaissance, people like Michelangelo were treated like interior decorators. A well-written song is a craft item. Take care of the craft, and the art will take care of itself.

All of that being said, Leonard Cohen used to point out that the greatest problem for a writer is that your critical faculties develop faster than your creative faculties, and it is very easy to get so wrapped up in what is wrong with your songs that you quit writing entirely. I developed some very so- phisticated theories about what made a good song, and while I think that on the whole they were sound, they also served as cover for an absolutely immutable, self-imposed writer's block. What got me out of that was spending more time with both Leonard and Joni Mitchell. They had no pa- tience with my excuses and rationalizations. They just said, "That's non- sense. Any damn fool can write. So write, and stop complaining."

There was no arguing with that, and though my output was never pro- lific, over the ensuing years I composed about two dozen songs that I like well enough to consider "keepers." The first one that I recorded was about MacDougal Street, since I have always believed the old maxim that you have to write about something you know, and God knows I knew that. I had a lot of good times on that street, but by the mid-1960s the hard drug epidemic had hit, and it was getting pretty ugly. The song I wrote about it was called "Zen Koans Gonna Rise Again"—a terrible pun that has noth- ing to do with the lyric—and it was heavily influenced by the work of one of my favorite poets, François Villon. Villon's approach seemed particularly appropriate because what he did back in fifteenth-century France was very similar to what we were trying to do in the 1960s. His poems were not folk- songs in any sense, but he wrote in the vernacular of his place and time. In fact, many of his poems are written in Parisian thieves' argot, and the slang gets so thick that they are practically unintelligible to modern readers—but even though you cannot understand every word, this gives his work a live- liness that very few writers of that period can match. On MacDougal Street, when we were talking among ourselves, we used a kind of hipster- carny slang that most of the people in our audience would not have under- stood—which was one of the reasons we did it—and I tried to use this language to capture the feel of what was going down at that point:

In the alleys and doorways of old Greenwich Village,
You can see the lanes walking the streets up and down.
From your tenement top you can drop down your garbage,
And a clyde or a cop may fall dead to the ground.

You'll see bodies burning, faces on fire,
Wear death on their back like a john wears his coat,
For this is satori, the end of desire,
To O.D. in the gutter with a curse in your throat.

Some are in slam and some are still scuffling,
With nothing to keep but a twenty-cent jones.
Jiving and boosting, while their chicks are out hustling,
While the A in their veins whispers death to their bones.

In the alleys and doorways of old Greenwich Village,
You can see the lanes walking the streets up and down.
From your tenement top you can drop down your garbage,
And a clyde or a cop may fall dead to the ground.

That was around 1967, and it already felt like the end of an era.

15

The Waning Days of Babylon

"I once thought the biggest I could ever hope to get was like Van Ronk. But it's bigger than that, now, ain't it? Yeah, man, it's bigger than that. Scary as all shit."
—*Bob Dylan, c.1964*

By the mid-1960s the Village scene was going stronger than ever, but something had been lost as well. More and more people were moving away, buying houses in Woodstock or wherever, and there was less feeling of camaraderie.* You could tell where things were headed when Andy Warhol and his "beautiful people" showed up at the Gaslight. That towhead was like a vulture—when he appeared, you knew the fun was over.

All things considered, we hung on longer than we had any right to expect. Once the big money came in, the changes were inevitable. Rents went up, costs went through the ceiling, and how much can you charge for a cup of coffee? It used to be that people would just hop on the subway, go down to the Village, wander into a club and see who was playing, and if they didn't

---

*I never understood why everybody wanted to move out to Woodstock. I liked the Village, and I still like it, and I would not like to live anywhere else. The country is a city for birds.

like what they heard, they'd walk out and catch somebody else. When the clubs started having to charge admission, you couldn't do that anymore.

In the meantime, the music itself was changing very rapidly. The folk revival had largely been a reaction to the pop scene of the 1950s, which was so insipid that we were driven to seek out alternatives. It was either that or "How Much Is That Doggie in the Window." (Of course, there was also Little Richard and Chuck Berry, but by the late fifties they were out of the picture, replaced by Fabian and *Blue Hawaii*. In any case, to someone weaned on jazz, even the good rock 'n' roll seemed pretty simplistic, and once the corporate machine took over, we dismissed the whole genre as pinhead music.) In the 1960s we got a new wave of pop, with people like the Beatles doing genuinely interesting and creative work, and that was a very different situation. So basically we had our moment and then the scene moved elsewhere. Some of us made a lot of money, and a lot of us made some money, and a few became stars, and a few got hurt. In retrospect, I think it was a very good, productive period, though not as important as some of the participants would like to believe. I remember one time Phil came back from a recording session, and when I asked him how it had gone, he said, "How did it go? I'll tell you how it went. We have just changed the entire course of Western music!" And he was serious. That is an extreme example, but it gives an idea of the feeling that was going around.

In fact, looking back on that period, very little of what got put down had much permanent value. There was a genuine artistic impulse, but the paradigms were flawed, and if you compare it to what was happening on Broadway in the 1930s, that scene was infinitely more creative and important than ours. The forms that were accepted as part of the folk matrix were too limited, both technically and in terms of staying power, and the ideology of the scene allowed for a great degree of sloppiness, which meant that nobody had to push themselves. Most of the songwriters were writing well below their abilities, and people who were capable of learning and employing more complicated harmonies and chord structures confined themselves to 1-4-5 changes. Some of them were enormously talented, but they were like an enormously talented boxer who insists on fighting with one hand behind his back.

The result was that we produced a Bob Dylan, a Tom Paxton, a Phil Ochs, a bit later a Joni Mitchell—but we did not produce a Johann Sebastian Bach or a Duke Ellington. Some very good songs came out of that period and some very good entertainers, but there has been no period in human history when there have not been good songs and good entertainers.

I do not believe that there is such a thing as progress in the arts. They peak, they decline, they hit a plateau, and it is often impossible to say why a certain period produces great work and another does not. I am a Marxist and a materialist, but I have never been able to convince myself that there is an economic interpretation that would explain Shakespeare, Marlowe, and Jonson all being on the set at the same time. In retrospect, one can formulate theories about that, or the confluence of American writers in Paris in the 1910s, or the period in Chicago in the twenties when you could go into one club and hear Jimmy Noone, another and hear Benny Goodman, or King Oliver, or Louis Armstrong, or Jelly Roll Morton. The Village in the early 1960s was like that, and I could argue that at the same time the economic situation in this country was probably the best it has ever been in history, but I cannot show a connection. Maybe it was just sunspots. In any case, we were lucky, and we knew it.

Most of the books that have been written about this period do not really capture the feel of it, at least in part because so many of the people who were involved are not able to talk about it honestly. A lot of them are bitter because they have not done as well as they hoped to do, for one reason or another, and they look back at the people who did better and think: "That should have been my success. I was robbed, I was cheated." So they talk about how much was stolen from them, how they were screwed, how all their friends fucked them and turned their backs on them. But all of that is after the fact. Nobody except a handful of real paranoids felt that way at the time.

Back then, we weren't all clawing over each other's bodies, trying to fight our way to the top. Mostly we were having the time of our lives. We were hanging out with our friends, playing music, and sitting around at all-night poker sessions in the room upstairs from the Gaslight. Win, lose, or draw, there was always something absolutely ridiculous happening, and we were laughing all the time—when we weren't fighting or brooding drunkenly. It was very mercurial.

For me, one of the great things about that period was that I could make a living without leaving the Village. I was working weeks and weeks on end in clubs that I could walk to, so my living room was my dressing room, and I could even go home between sets. I was listening to music that interested me, and making music that interested my friends, and I felt that I belonged to a community of singers, songwriters, performers who were really cooking. It was very exciting, and yeah, we had our jealousies—when somebody got too big a piece of the action, all of us felt, "How dare that son of a bitch . . . "—but that was not the dominant mood of the period. There was a lot of money around, and we all wanted a taste, but for a few years the trickle-down theory was actually working—the only time that has ever happened, in my experience—and it did not get particularly mean or petty except in the case of people who had not liked each other to begin with.

Personally, I was doing very well, thank you. I wasn't making Dylan's kind of money—that's corporate wealth, the gross national product of El Salvador, and very few of us made anything like that. But I must have spent three or four years without ever being in a subway, which for a New Yorker pretty much sums it up. It was the kind of situation where if there was something I wanted and I didn't have the money, I could just make another record or do an extra gig. That was when I acquired my collection of primitive art, as well as books, records, not to mention enjoying a lot of fabulous meals and parties. We were all living *wie Gott in Frankreich*, indulging our various whims. Some people bought houses in the country, some built recording studios, some developed expensive drug habits. Almost none of us bothered to hoard any money; it was all too unreal. Every time you went out for a couple of drinks, you would hear that someone had just signed a contract with Columbia or Warner Brothers for mucho buckos, and suddenly another town house was being renovated on Commerce Street. It was like a rolling bonanza.

Dylan's success sparked the real explosion, but he was part of a broader phenomenon. In terms of the mass audience, Peter, Paul, and Mary had two hits with Bobby's songs before he even got on the charts. Dylan made it as a popular music figure on the coattails of Peter, Paul, and Mary, the Byrds, and other people who were doing covers of his songs, and as late as 1964 it was still pretty hard to sell him to anyone but the cognoscenti. He was a difficult artist, from the mainstream point of view, so when he took off, it was really a case of overdue recognition.

As for the charge that Bobby was "selling out" when he stopped writing protest music, or when he went electric, it makes no sense in the context of that moment, because there was no reason to think that there would be any buyers. It never occurred to me that he was scuttling his artistic vision in a cynical grab at fame and fortune, and if he had been, I would have been very dubious about it working. I was at Newport in 1965, when he plugged in for the first time onstage, although I missed the famous incident and did not hear about it until the next morning, by which time there were already 212 different versions of what had happened. It was certainly the big news of the moment, but I had no sense that the musicians felt that Dylan was betraying us or betraying folk music. Some of us liked what he was doing and some of us didn't, but our judgment was a musical judgment, not a political or a sociological judgment. The question was, Does it work musically?*

Myself, I thought that going electric was a logical direction for Bobby to take. I did not care for all of his new stuff, by any means, but some of it was excellent, and it was a reasonable extension of what he had done up to that point. And I knew perfectly well that none of us was a true "folk" artist. We were professional performers, and while we liked a lot of folk music, we all liked a lot of other things as well. Working musicians are very rarely purists. The purists are out in the audience kibitzing, not onstage trying to make a living. And Bobby was absolutely right to ignore them. It is like the old socialist I knew who was an editor of a newspaper in the early 1960s: A bunch of New Leftists marched into his office and presented him with a set of nonnegotiable demands, insisting that he change this, that, and the other thing about what he was printing. He listened to them as long as he could stand it and then just said, "I've been a socialist for fifty years. Do you know what you're going to be ten years from now? You're going to be dentists." It was the same with the fans who got bent out of shape about Bobby's

---

*There's a story that Pete Seeger got all bent out of shape and actually tried to cut the cables with an ax, but as I understand it, what was bothering him wasn't the fact of Dylan going electric; it was the sound system. The mix was dreadful, and you couldn't hear Dylan's voice, all you could hear was the band. Paul Butterfield's outfit had problems with that, too, during their set.

going electric. They were all very pure and self-righteous, but forty years later Bobby is still out there making music, and they're all dentists.

The point is that categories such as "folk" and "blues" are inherently limiting, and any serious musician tries to steer clear of them as much as possible. Listeners and record companies want to fit you into these neat little boxes, but as a performer you need to be open to all the possibilities around you and to use whatever tools are appropriate for the job at hand. In my own case, I was typed as a blues singer back in the 1950s and have had to come to terms with the fact that no matter what I sing, most people will continue to think of me in those terms. But I concluded quite early on that I was essentially a saloon or cabaret performer. A lot of my material comes out of the blues tradition, but overall I have more in common with someone like Peggy Lee or Blossom Dearie than I do with Mississippi John Hurt or the Reverend Gary Davis. So when Dylan became a rock star, it was not really a shock to me—or more precisely, the shock was not musical. The shock was how it changed the scene.

We had all been hanging out on MacDougal Street, singing for one another and for a small group of devoted fans, and suddenly one of us had hit the mass market. The result was that a lot of people who had never been greedy in their lives began having visions of El Dorado. Dylan was one of ours and he had struck gold, and everybody thought that they could get rich, too. There were essentially two reactions. The first was jealousy, variations on "Why him?" and "He copped this from me; he stole that from so-and-so." Of course, we had all been stealing from each other all along, but it had never mattered, because we were all in the same situation. We had been playing for tips and sleeping on floors, and when one of us suddenly could get a suite at the top of the Plaza, naturally that hurt.

The other reaction, which was even more damaging, was "I'm gonna be next. All I have to do is find the right agent, the right record company, the right connections, and I can be another Bob Dylan!" Yeah, sure you could. All you had to do was write "A Hard Rain's A-Gonna Fall"—for the first time. That was what Bobby had done, and none of the rest of us did that. Bobby is not the greatest songwriter in history, but he was far and away the best on our scene, and whether we admitted it or not, we all knew that. Still, there were a lot of poor slobs who were working very hard and in some cases producing very good music, and who were getting nowhere at all. So it is not surprising that some of them got awfully bitter—I cannot deny that at times I felt a pang myself.

Meanwhile, the sycophants appeared, crowding around and telling us how wonderful we were. I don't think that even the most vain among us really liked them, but when someone comes up and says, "Boy, you're so great," it is certainly better than the alternative and has an obvious seductive quality. Dylan drew more than his share of this attention, and after a while a sort of hierarchy was established of knights of the round table, princes of the blood, all paying court to the emperor with the long, bushy hair. And because of who he was, that became a pretty nasty scene. Bobby had always been kind of paranoid, and now he felt that he had to surround himself with people he could trust. But it was not reciprocal; he never felt that he had to be trustworthy himself. He was always testing the loyalty of the people who were near him, and it could really get vicious at times. There was this group around him—David Blue, Victor Maimudes, Bobby Neuwirth, and various others—and they would back up whatever he said, including when he chose to turn on one or another of them.

For myself, I consider it fortunate that Bobby and I reached our parting of the ways fairly early. Shortly after his third or fourth record had come out and gone diamond or whatever, he was holding court in the Kettle of Fish, and he got on my case and started giving me all of this advice about how to manage my career, how to go about becoming a star. It was complete garbage, but by that point he had gotten used to everybody hanging on his every word and applauding any idea that came into his head. So I sat and listened for a while, and I was polite and even asked him a couple of questions, but it became obvious that he was simply prodding and testing me. He was saying things like "Why don't you give up blues? You do that, and I'll produce an album on you; you can make a fortune." He wasn't making a lick of sense, and I finally pushed back my chair and said, "Dylan, if you're so rich, how come you ain't smart?" And I walked out.

That was that, thank God, and while I have seen Bobby off and on over the years, and we are always perfectly cordial, we were never close again. I decided just to go about my business, and to let him and his spear-carriers do whatever they wanted to do. Because I could see what was happening to people who let themselves get caught up in that scene.

As for the star-making rap, I had already heard versions of that from Albert Grossman, but Albert was a good deal funnier about it and he had the track record to back it up. Still, in essence it was the same routine, and the point was to prove that everybody has a price. Albert was a great fan of *The Magic Christian*, Terry Southern's novel about a man who does things like filling a swimming pool full of sewage and offal with some $100 bills mixed in, just to prove that people will dive in. So he came up to me one night and said, "Look, I have a proposal for you: I'll arrange all your bookings, and I'll guarantee you $100,000 a year. You can pick your own material, sing anything you want. You just have to make one change in your act: I want you to wear a helmet with horns on it, and change your name to Olaf the Blues Singer." He was completely serious, and I think if I had gone along, he would very likely have done it—not because he believed it was a good idea, but just to prove that I had my price. He died without ever knowing that it was $120,000 . . .

The truth is that I was by no means immune to the lure of money, and I say that without any shame. I deeply mistrust the notion that musicians or other artists are "selling out" when they make a sound commercial choice. A lot of people who have grown up to be stockbrokers or dentists feel that they have abandoned their youthful ideals, and it is very important to them that their idols remain pure, as proof that there is purity somewhere out there in the world. Apparently, musicians don't have to make a living; only dentists and stockbrokers have to do that. So when someone comes up to me and says, "I admire you because you stuck to your guns, you never sold out," my temptation is to say, "Listen: I've been standing on 42nd Street, bent over with my pants around my ankles for thirty years." Obviously, there are things I am willing to do and things I am not willing to do, but the bottom line is that I have a certain set of skills and I have done the best I can with them, and if the cards had come up differently and I had had more mainstream success, that would have been very nice.

For a while there, it seemed quite likely. The people who run the music business are always on the lookout for a trend. When the Beatles came along, there was a momentary panic: "What's going on? Here we've been selling Pat Boone all these years, and all of a sudden this happens! How can we retool the assembly line?" They had scouts combing England from the Shetland Islands to Cornwall for any Englishman with an electric guitar, and then there was an audible sigh of relief when they managed to manufacture the Monkees: "Whew, we got it licked. Now we can manufacture groups, package them with a good, reliable system of interchangeable parts, market it, and we're all gonna get rich, baby." That's the way their logic works, and when Dylan hit, they all descended on the Village. They didn't know exactly what they were looking for, and since Dylan was kind of weird looking and had that scratchy voice, they were open to the idea that there might be other stars out there who did not fit the standard pattern. So for a moment it seemed genuinely possible that just by doing more or less what we were doing already, any one of us might suddenly wind up a millionaire. Naturally, all kinds of people got their heads twisted out of shape and began making desperate grabs for the brass ring, and I was no exception.

I had nothing against rock 'n' roll—it was a perfectly reasonable extension of some of my favorite music. I had always loved Fats Domino, whom I considered the master of understatement, and Little Richard, who was the master of overstatement. I thought the Beatles were sweet and amusing and had some very interesting ideas, especially when George Martin got involved. And I loved Frank Zappa and the Mothers, who were working for a while at the Garrick on Bleecker while I was playing upstairs at the Café Au Go-Go. Frank was the best amphetamine guitar player I ever heard, and he was also such a marvelous lunatic, one of my favorite people. So I was open to a lot of the new sounds that were coming through, and for a while I actually became kind of fascinated by the possibilities inherent in electronic music—though in the end I came to the conclusion that the most efficient and advanced instruments are still the ancient ones. I enjoyed fooling around with tape loops and weird electronic gizmos the same way I enjoyed fooling around with jugs and kazoos, but neither can keep my interest like a good guitarist or trumpet player.

I resisted the temptation to form a band for several years, because I have always preferred to work as a soloist. I really enjoy going *mano a mano* with my audience, and after doing it for so long, that is the way my mind works. Still, by about 1967 I was beginning to feel like the only kid on the block who didn't have an Erector Set. Everybody I knew was going electric and getting rich and famous, and they all had thousands of dollars in their pockets and were eating at La Grenouille and smoking Larañagas, and it

The Waning Days of Babylon   219

was embarrassing. And there were the record execs, with pens in their hands, saying, "Put together a rock band and you too will have Cuban cigars, eat Caspian caviar, and smoke ganja from Afghanistan." Who was I to shovel shit against the tide of history? I have always believed that nothing is too good for the working class, and here was a chance to put my beliefs into practice. So I called up my old buddy Dave Woods, and we formed the Hudson Dusters.

Dave is one of the finest musicians I have ever known, a versatile jazz and blues guitarist and a deft and cunning arranger. (I have been playing what is essentially his guitar chart for "Come Back Baby" since the late 1950s.) With the Hudson Dusters, our idea was to make a pile of money while exploring some of the untapped musical possibilities inherent in the standard rock band lineup. On the second point, I think we succeeded surprisingly well. Dave is one of the hardest-working men I ever met, and with me cheering him on, we indulged our love of Charles Ives and made a polytonal rock 'n' roll record. We were doing things like arranging songs simultaneously in two keys, with the chorus in both keys, resolving into key A, then returning to the chorus and this time resolving into key B. In retrospect, I can see why that didn't sell, but at the time it seemed like a stroke of genius.

The band was excellent, with Dave and me on guitar, Pot (Phil Namanworth) on keyboards, a guy named Rick Henderson on drums, and Ed Gregory, a sometime associate of Jimi Hendrix who is the best goddamn bass player that ever walked the face of the earth. I felt like a kid with a new locomotive and a basement full of track, and that remains one of the few albums of mine that I enjoy listening to. Among other things, I managed to cut a couple of vocals that I am particularly proud of—though that was a matter of luck more than planning: We were recording between tours, so although I had come down with a hideous case of flu, we couldn't cancel the session. As a result, I went into the studio sick as a dog, and somehow the flu had an effect on my voice that was as if someone had been messing with the octave valve. All of a sudden, I had an entire falsetto register that normally was not there. I started to sing, and I was going up and up and up, and I was still getting the notes, so I thought, "Whoopie!" and cut "Dink's Song"—technically the best piece of singing I have ever done on record—and a couple of other numbers. We finished up the session, and when I got into the cab to go home, I had to write out my address, because I could not say a word.

My record label at that point was Verve/Forecast, and for once I had a guy at the company who was really behind me. I also had a song that was an absolute, no-question, sure-fire hit. Joni Mitchell was living in New York by that time, and we were spending quite a lot of time together, and I had concluded that she was the finest songwriter on the set. Both as a person and an artist, she presented the unusual combination of a very determined personality working in tandem with a kind of ethereal quality. Her songs were always carefully crafted, but the artistry was often very subtle. I would have missed some of their finest points if I had not actually read the lyrics, because when you heard her sing them, these marvelous effects would just drift past you, and it was only when you saw them in print that you realized how much work went into them. But there were also songs that were obvious masterpieces from the first time you heard them. One day we were sitting around, and she played me "Both Sides Now," and I immediately knew I had to record it. Our only disagreement was about the title. It was clear to me that the feeling of the clouds was a sort of motif, running all through the song, and I thought she should call the song "Clouds." Naturally, she refused; she liked her title, and she stuck to her guns, and I stuck to mine. So when I recorded the song, I called it "Clouds (from Both Sides Now)." The next year, she recorded it with her original title—but she called the album *Clouds*.

With a song like that, I knew I simply couldn't miss. Woodsy and I put together a nice, subtle arrangement (based on a riff we copped from the Rolling Stones' "Ruby Tuesday"), and I sang it very plainly, so people could really hear the lyric. My man at Verve smelled a hit, and he got on the phone to all the disc jockeys around the country, prepared a big ad campaign and the whole nine yards. The idea was to break it slowly, one market at a time, get it on the radio and let it build, then jump on the wave as it began to crest. Everything went perfectly for a month or so—it was moving up the charts in Cleveland, in this town, in that town—and then Judy Collins came out with her version and promptly sold eight billion copies, and that was that.

Basically, it was the luck of the draw: I had a high pair, drew three cards, and came up with nothing. It did not help that MGM, which was the parent company of Verve/Forecast, was already well on its way into bankruptcy, though I did not have any idea of that at the time. They were MGM, goddammit—who knew that a year and a half later they would be auctioning off Dorothy's ruby slippers?

In any case, that was my shot at the rock world, and I found it an uncomfortable match. I remember one gig in particular, an early-morning TV show in Philadelphia called something like *Aqua-rama*. It was one of those teenage dance shows like *American Bandstand*, only their gimmick was that they shot it in an aquarium, with huge tanks of fish all over the place. They did not have the facilities to do live music, so I had to lip-synch, which I had never done before and swore never to do again. I try not to phrase my songs the same way twice, so if I were going to lip-synch properly, I would have to listen to my record over and over and memorize the way I had happened to sing it on that day, and I can imagine nothing more boring. So there I was, moving my mouth out of sync with the music, and all these kids were gyrating around—we didn't really play dance music, but they were there to boogie and would have danced to an amplified cricket. And as each couple went past the camera, they would flip it the finger. Then we had a bit of banter with the host—I remember saying, "Actually, I only came here to see the piranha, but you'll do"—and trucked off to the next lousy club date.

Maybe if we had kept plugging away, or if we had had better representation, or this, that, or the other thing, we would eventually have gotten somewhere, but I shortly concluded that it wasn't worth the effort. For one thing, I was going broke because the clubs weren't paying any more for the band than they did for me as a single, but the expenses were five times as high. Meanwhile, I was feeling more and more constricted by having to fit myself into an ensemble. I was used to being able to chop and change my sets as I went along, and having to do the same goddamn songs every night was excruciating. So what with one thing and another, the Dusters disbanded and I went back to doing what I did best.

The record companies did not give up on me for another few years. I bounced from Verve to Polydor and from there to Cadet, and they gave me impressive recording budgets, and we worked out some pretty interesting arrangements, with strings and horns and what all. I enjoyed that, at times, and it gave me a chance to do some material that I would not have otherwise done—everything from Jacques Brel's "Port of Amsterdam" to "I Want to Go Back to My Little Grass Shack in Kealakakua, Hawaii"— though I also was coaxed into doing some arrangements that even at the time seemed overblown and buried the material. In any case, in another few years the Folk Scare was well and truly over, and the major labels had figured out that I was never going to sell a million records, and they stopped coming around.

That was not a particularly pleasant feeling, and I felt frustrated for a while, but then I adjusted to the situation. In a way I was lucky, because the people who arrived between 1963 and 1968 thought they had found Fat City, and when the money dried up, it was a terrible shock—some of them haven't adjusted to this day. Since I had gotten into the business before there was any money to speak of, it was relatively easy for me to come to terms with the thought that what goes up must come down. What is more, I have always been something of a doom crier and had been predicting grass growing on MacDougal Street for years, so when the scene shut down, I felt the satisfaction of a Seventh Day Adventist on the day the world really does come to an end. And as a Village resident, I enjoyed being able to walk down the street without having to fight my way through the hordes of tourists.

I had to tour a little more than I liked, but between the concerts and some teaching I was making a reasonable living playing the music I loved, and that was a hell of a lot more than I had expected when I started out in this business, or than my education or my family background would have led anyone to predict. So for the last thirty years I have been fighting a reasonably successful holding action, and as the Irishman who fell off the Empire State Building said as he passed the forty-first floor, "So far, so good." I am still making my own musical choices, and people have kept coming to the shows and buying the records. There are perhaps two hundred people in the country whose musical opinions I really care about, and most of them like my work, and that was the object of the exercise from the get-go. Being a musician—even a good musician—is not a ticket to ride. It's a job, and at times it can be very hard work. But then someone will come up and say, "Hey, Dave, I heard you in 1962 in Samarkand," and that's nice. I never made a fortune—as a matter of fact, I have often been deeply in debt—but dammit, this is what I wanted to do, and I have been able to do it for almost fifty years, and I haven't had to do anything else, and what more can I ask? I wanted to be a musician, and I am a musician, and that's what it's all about.

16

Last Call

And so we've had another night
Of poetry and poses,
And each man knows he'll be alone
When the sacred gin mill closes.

And so we'll drink the final glass,
Each to his joy or sorrow,
And hope the numbing drunk will last
Till opening tomorrow.

And when we stumble back again
Like paralytic dancers,
Each knows the questions he will ask,
And each man knows the answers.

And so we'll drink the final drink
That cuts the brain in sections,
Where answers never signify
And there aren't any questions.

I broke my heart the other day,
It will mend again tomorrow.
If I'd been drunk when I was born
I'd be ignorant of sorrow.

And so we'll drink the final toast
That never can be spoken:
Here's to the heart that's wise enough
To know when it's better off broken.

And the tin pan bended, and the story ended.

Afterword

By Elijah Wald

This book was born over the course of many nights, sitting around in Dave's apartment on Sheridan Square, talking, eating the amazing meals he would spend hours preparing, and listening to his library of recordings. The original plan was for us to work together, with me doing historical research and a good deal of the writing, and Dave providing the flavor and the first-person slant. He did not plan it as an autobiography, and had a long list of people he wanted to interview—he taped conversations with about a dozen of them—with an eye to producing the definitive history of the Greenwich Village folk years.

The stumbling block was that Dave was acutely conscious of how much time and energy would be required to do the project right, and we never found a publisher who would pay the kind of advance that would have allowed him to take a year off from performing and devote himself to writing. Then, in 2002, he discovered that he had cancer. He canceled all future gigs and went into the hospital for an operation, and we agreed that as soon as he got out, we would devote the next months to finishing the book. The best-laid plans, as oft-times, ganged aglee . . . He taped a few reminiscences in the hospital, and I made one unsuccessful trip to tape some more after he came home, but then he snuck out on me.

So I had to finish the book myself, combining the few sections he had already written with what I could glean from years of interviews, stage patter, and random jottings. I am happy with the result, but it is a quite different book than what Dave and I envisioned. His model was H. L. Mencken, specifically the "Days" books, and he wanted to capture the full flavor of the Village in the late 1950s and early 1960s. He planned to focus on the folk scene, but also to give a sense of everything else that was going on around it: the writers, comedians, painters, crooks, and all the uncategorizable denizens of the streets, bars, and cafés. Brendan Behan should be here, for example. Dave enjoyed remembering the big dinners Behan would host when he had a play opening on Broadway, at which he would treat the guests to food, booze, and self-penned ditties like "Don't Muck About with the Moon." But few interviewers bothered to ask Dave about anything but the folk and blues scenes, so few of those memories were preserved. There are tantalizing hints of what is missing, like a mention of teenage visits to the Cedar Bar, where painters like Franz Kline and Willem de Kooning were regulars; but they are only brief mentions, rarely pursued.

Even on the subject of music, Dave would have wanted to range farther afield. He always thought of himself as a jazz musician manqué, and while he was proud to have been part of an exciting, productive movement, he kept his sense of perspective. At the peak of the folk boom, a single evening's entertainment in the Village could also include Ben Webster, Coleman Hawkins, Charles Mingus, Thelonious Monk, and Lennie Tristano. Bob Dylan opening for the Greenbriar Boys at Folk City was historic in cultural terms, but musically Dave would not have considered it in the same league with the week at the Village Gate when Aretha Franklin opened for the John Coltrane Quintet, and he would have wanted more of that in here.*

---

*There are also some minor inaccuracies that Dave might have cleared up if we had finished this together. For example, he recalled learning "St. James Infirmary" from *The Fireside Book of Folksongs*, but the song is not in that book. Or when he says Mitch Mitchell helped him get his seaman's papers; I found another interview in which he credits another friend with the same favor. Had he stuck around, we would have done our best to sort those things out, but in his absence I decided that it was better to preserve some of Dave's mistakes than for me to introduce new ones. When an error was minor and easily corrected, I did so, but when I had any doubt about how he would have resolved the problem, I let it be.

Still, this is a fair representation of Dave's memories of and opinions about the "Great Folk Scare"—a favorite phrase, coined by his old friend Utah Phillips—and that was always our primary intention. Some readers may find it odd that a man who continued to be very productive for another thirty-plus years should end his story in the late 1960s, but Dave never considered this an autobiography. He wanted to write a personal history of an exciting scene that changed the course of American music, with plenty of first-person anecdotes and opinions, and he had no interest in detailing his own comings and goings beyond that period.

I think that was a smart choice, but not because he ceased to be a vital and interesting artist and thinker. As a musician, Dave kept growing until the end of his life, and much of his greatest work was done long after the peak of his sixties-era fame (including an album of Bertolt Brecht, two of swing jazz, and a jug band version of Prokofiev's *Peter and the Wolf*). As a raconteur, philosopher, and all-around Johnsonian presence, he came into his own only in the 1980s, and it is a pity that there was not a Boswell handy to jot down his conversation—for anyone who spent an evening sitting across from him as he reclined on his immense couch, sipping wine and smoking innumerable cigarettes, those performances were as great as anything he ever put onstage.

Dave and I became friends in the mid-1970s, after I showed up at his door to take guitar lessons. By the second or third week, he had moved my lesson to the end of the day, and when my hour was up, he would cook dinner, then regale me with stories, opinions, and recordings he thought I should hear, until I staggered home sometime after daylight. Though I was not aware of it at the time, this was probably the low point of Dave's life, both professionally and personally. The folk scene had all but disappeared, and he had attempted to beat a tactical retreat by setting up once again as a guitar teacher, but bills were piling up, and as he turned forty, he balefully pictured a dull future of schlepping his guitar from club to club, shouting over noisy drunks, or providing a moment of recaptured youth for graying fans in Unitarian church basements. He was drinking heavily, and often by the second fifth of Jameson he would be grumbling, "If I had just stayed in the goddamn merchant marine, I could be a first mate by now."

To me, he was a genius, and despite the grumbling, I learned more from him in those evenings than I have from anyone else, before or since. Dave was the most voracious reader I have known, and he would send me home with thick volumes of history or slim paperbacks of his favorite science fiction—"It's mind rot, but good mind rot," he would say. (He loved those intermediate categories: "That's first-rate second-rate jazz," he would say of something like the Joe Venuti–Eddie Lang duets, and he took it as the ultimate compliment when I said the same of his final jazz album, *Sweet and Lowdown*. It was a way of maintaining perspective, being able to love and acclaim something while remembering that there are people like Shakespeare and Louis Armstrong.) When I became a writer, he loaded me up with Mencken, Calvin Trillin, and A. J. Liebling, hoping they would teach me the craft. And his musical tastes were equally broad. He rarely played me any folk or blues records, but I heard Bing Crosby, Jo Stafford, Groucho Marx, the Bulgarian Folk Ensemble of Phillipe Koutev (Dave would sing bass along with the women's choir), and endless Duke Ellington and Jelly Roll Morton.

He was himself making astonishing music at that time. I was with him when *Sunday Street* came out, the first solo album he had done in years. It was on a small New England label, Philo Records, and in purely economic terms it represented a drastic step down from his previous few releases, which had been richly produced sets on major labels. Musically, though, it was at least as good as anything he had done in the 1960s—a lot of people still consider it his finest album. The return to teaching had led him to a new fascination with the guitar, and his arrangements were understated marvels that ranged from Morton and Scott Joplin to Joni Mitchell and old acoustic blues pieces. It was his singing, though, that was the revelation. He was phrasing with a taste and intricacy that was beyond anything on his previous records. He knew it, too, and on bad nights that would help to fuel his frustration: the audiences were caught up in their memories of a phase he had outgrown, still yelling for "Cocaine Blues" and failing to note the improvements. He tried to be philosophical about it: "The poor we have always with us," he'd growl. "So, the folk fans don't really listen—that just means they're like everybody else." But it annoyed him. He had no particular affection for his past work and was proud to still be refining his craftsmanship.

Luckily, Dave was not a man to dwell on the frustrations. By the 1980s he was creating a new life for himself. In part, this was sparked by an odd stroke of luck: After a lifetime of refusing to fly, in 1981 he received the irresistable offer to come over to England and appear on the BBC's *This Is Your Life* TV show as a surprise for Jim Watt, the world lightweight boxing champion, who happened to be a devoted fan. That led to a series of European tours, as well as trips to Australia and Japan, which substantially altered his financial situation as well as finally providing him with an opportunity to see all sorts of places he knew only from books. He also hooked up with Andrea Vuocolo, who eventually became his second wife, and with her support adopted a new lifestyle. He lost over a hundred pounds, wine replaced whiskey, and the nights became somewhat shorter. He still entertained visitors into the wee hours, and few of us left sober, but there was none of the bitterness of those middle years.

The visitors also got younger and more varied. The eighties brought a new wave of singer-songwriters to MacDougal Street, based in a club called the Speakeasy, and many of them took Dave as their adviser, inspiration, and éminence grise. Christine Lavin, Tom Intondi, David Massengill, Frank Christian, Bill Morrissey, Rod MacDonald, Jack Hardy—there are literally dozens of names that could be added to that list. Some came for guitar lessons, but most just met Dave at the club or were brought over to his place by friends and quickly learned that he was a man worth listening to, as well as the main link to the glory days whose legend had lured them to New York.

Dave occasionally talked about those days, but his real interest was what was happening around him. He constantly reminded his young friends that the singers of the past had been no more naturally talented than any other crop; they had just been lucky enough to arrive at the right moment. He enjoyed recounting anecdotes of the fifties and sixties, but refused to get caught up in the romance: "There was a lot that was great about that period," he would say, "but if I start bloviating about how wonderful it was, what I say and what you hear will not be the same thing. It has been my observation that when you ask some *alter kocker* about the old days, his answer—however he may phrase it—will always be, 'Of course, everything was much better then, because I could take a flight of stairs three at a time.' The truth of the matter is that some things have gotten worse and some things have improved. For example, the quality of Chinese food in New York is a hell of a lot better than it was in the 1950s . . . "

That attitude was what made me so eager to have him put his thoughts down on paper. Because Dave was not only a supremely engaging story-teller but a wise and insightful one. I wish he had written about the dozens of other subjects he knew so well, but I am happy and proud that at least we have this book. His story of the Great Folk Scare was an obvious place to start, and I doubt anyone will give us a more measured, fair, and entertaining picture of that time.

Index

Gambling, 52, 111–112, 115, 118, 154

Gardyloo (fanzine), 67, 125

Garfunkel, Artie, 179–180

Gaslight Café, 126, 127–128, 132, 141, 143, 144, 145–146, 147–148, 149, 150, 151, 153–154, 159, 165, 170, 190, 199, 206, 211

poetry readings at, 148

"Gaslight Rag," 151–152

Gate of Horn, 55–56, 57–58, 84, 166

Gavin, Jimmy, 122, 129, 132

Geer, Will, 108

George Lefty, 80

Gerda's Folk City, 141, 142–143, 163, 170

Geremia, George, 81–82

Gerlach, Fred, 23, 134

Germany, 35, 192

Ghettos, 28

"Ghost Riders in the Sky," 61

Gibbon, Johnny, 134

Gibson, Bob, 126, 165–166, 169, 202

Gigs, 8, 16, 50, 62, 81, 96, 115, 119, 120, 121, 128, 164, 222

Gillespie, Dizzy, 14

Gilpin, Dick, 35

Ginsberg, Allen, 126

Glaser, Gina, 42, 71, 72, 88

Glaser, Lenny, 32, 51, 94

Glazer, Joe, 69

Godfrey, Arthur, 6, 7

Golden Gate Bridge, 52, 52(n), 113

Goldkette, Jean, 9

Goldman, Emma, 36, 113

Goldsmith, Pete, 49

Goldstein, Kenny, 87, 90, 91

"Goodbye, Old Paint, I'm Leaving Cheyenne," 106

Gooding, Cynthia, 46, 74, 85, 126, 166

Goodman, Benny, 2, 14, 213

Gordon, Max, 181–182

Gorky, Arshile, 45

Gospel music, 29

Graham, Al, 115, 118–119

Grant, Coot, 44

Green, Freddie, 10

Greenbriar Boys, 164

Greenhaus, Dick and Kiki, 71

Greenhill, David, 74

Greenwich Village, 12, 13, 33, 53, 54(n), 73, 83, 122, 127, 149, 213, 223

block between Bleecker and 3rd Street, 155–156

Spring Street parties in, 50

See also Washington Square Park

Gregory, Ed, 220

Grossman, Albert, 55, 57–58, 146, 167–168, 218

Grossman, Stefan, 134

Guitar playing, 5, 8, 9, 13, 14, 15, 33, 82, 85, 91, 96, 115, 116, 133, 180, 186, 202, 219

classical, 10

fingerpicking, 24, 25, 41, 42, 87, 136, 187, 188

flamenco, 44, 149, 183

of Reverend Gary Davis, 133–134, 135–137, 139–140

Gumping, 16

Guthrie, Woody, 31, 42, 91, 108, 123, 204. *See also under* Dylan, Bob

"Gypsy's Warning, The," 4

Haiti, 64

Hammond, John, 164, 176

Handbill magazine, 83

Handy, W. C., 19

"Hanging Around a Skin Game," 116

"Hangman, Slack Your Rope," 46(n)

Hardin, Tim, 160

"Hard Rain's A Gonna Fall, A," 206, 216

Haring, Lee, 71

Harmonotes, 7–8

Harms-Whitmark publisher, 139

Harney, Ben, 3

Harrigan and Hart, 3

CPSIA information can be obtained at www.ICGtesting.com
Printed in the USA
BVOW04s2259100314

347233BV00001B/55/P